The Synoptic Vision

The
Synoptic Vision
essays on the philosophy
of Wilfrid Sellars

by
C. F. Delaney
Michael J. Loux
Gary Gutting
W. David Solomon

UNIVERSITY OF NOTRE DAME PRESS
NOTRE DAME
LONDON

Library of Congress Cataloging in Publication Data

Main entry under title:

The Synoptic vision.

    Bibliography: p.
    1. Sellars, Wilfrid—Addresses, essays, lectures.
I. Delaney, Cornelius F.
B945.S444S95   191   76-22406
ISBN 0-268-01596-1

Manufactured in the United States of America

To

ERNAN MCMULLIN

*whose own vision has meant so much
to philosophy at Notre Dame*

Contents

Preface

While much of recent philosophy has been of the piecemeal variety, one contemporary philosopher who has carried on the tradition of philosophy in the "grand manner" is Wilfrid Sellars. His work not only ranges over the various systematic areas of philosophy but unifies the various areas in terms of a distinctive perspective. As a result, while the corpus of most contemporary philosophers is simply the sum of self-intelligible atoms of inquiry, in Sellars' case the result is a systematic unity. Moreover, his *synoptic vision* involves not simply a theoretical unification of scientific understanding with our ordinary conception of the world but also embraces the practical dimensions of human existence. Philosophy as he sees and practices it bears on a systematic understanding of man-in-the-world both as a knower and as a doer.

In addition to this distinctiveness of content, Sellars' philosophical style also has its distinctive features. His method of exposition is characterized by an attempt to carry on a continual dialectic with both the historical tradition and what he sees as the contemporary alternatives. His work exhibits his dual conviction that philosophy must be carried on in the context of its own history and in contact with contemporary perspectives. Man's historico-social character should manifest itself in his attempt at philosophical understanding.

One unwelcome by-product of the combination of the systematic structure of Sellars' philosophy and the dialectical character of its exposition is a definite difficulty of access. It is this fact, i.e., that his work puts such heavy initial demands on its readers, that is our justification for this volume. It is designed primarily as an *exposition* of Sellars' philosophy, and criticism has been kept to a minimum so that an initial understanding of his overall view might be achieved. While each essay focuses on a specific area of his philosophy, there is not only considerable cross-referencing but also an overlapping of discussions where such seemed in the interest of intelligible exposition. It is hoped that this attempt to articulate Sellars' synoptic vision will make access to his thought easier for others.

This volume grew out of informal discussions over many years at Notre Dame, discussions occasioned by Sellars' many visits to campus.

ix

Given the genesis of the volume, special acknowledgment must be made of the contributions of Dr. Vaughn McKim, who was not only the moving force in these informal discussions but also an invaluable critic of the work as it progressed. The authors—and the readers—of this book owe him a special debt of gratitude. Special gratitude is also owed to Wilfrid Sellars himself for his careful reading of all the essays in progress and his helpful suggestions with regard to them. Professor Sellars' approval and endorsement was a great encouragement to the authors. Acknowledgment is also in order of Dr. Cale Crowley, who compiled the bibliography included in the volume, and of Ryan Welsh, who with her customary reliability transformed the scratching of the authors into an intelligible manuscript. Finally, the authors are particularly grateful to James Langford, director of the University of Notre Dame Press, for his continual encouragement and patience.

Abbreviations

Since many of the principal articles are collected in *Science, Perception, and Reality, Philosophical Perspectives* or *Essays in Philosophy and Its History,* the page references will be given to their appearance in these collections rather than to the original. Full bibliographical information on these entries is to be found in the bibliography at the end of the book.

AAE	"Actions and Events," chap. 10 of *Essays in Philosophy and Its History (EPH).*
AE	"Abstract Entities," chap. 9 of *Philosophical Perspectives (PP).*
APM	"Aristotelian Philosophies of Mind."
ATOS	"The Adverbial Theory of the Objects of Sensation."
BBK	"Being and Being Known," Chap. 2 of *Science, Perception and Reality* (SPR).
CC	"Conceptual Change," chap. 9 of *EPH.*
CDCM	"Counterfactuals, Dispositions, and the Causal Modalities."
CE	"The Concept of Emergence."
CHT	"Comments on Mr. Hempel's Theses."
CIL	"Concepts as Involving Laws and Inconceivable Without Them."
DAM	"The Double-knowledge Approach to the Mind-body Problem."
ENW	"Epistemology and the New Way of Words."
EPH	*Essays in Philosophy and its History.*
EPM	"Empiricism and the Philosophy of Mind," chap. 5 of *SPR.*
FD	"Fatalism and Determinism."
GE	"Grammar and Existence: A Preface to Ontology," chap. 8 of *SPR.*
GEC	"Givenness and Explanatory Coherence."
IAM	"The Identity Approach to the Mind-body Problem," chap. 15 of *PP.*
IIO	"Imperatives, Intentions, and the Logic of 'Ought'."

IM	"Intentionality and the Mental."
IREH	"The Intentional Realism of Evertt Hall," chap. 8 of *PP*.
IV	"Induction as Vindication," chap. 16 of *EPH*.
LT	"The Language of Theories," chap. 4 of *SPR*.
LTC	"Language as Thought and as Communication," chap. 5 of *EPH*.
LRB	"Languages, Rules, and Behavior."
MCP	"Metaphysics and the Concept of a Person," chap. 11 of *EPH*.
MFC	"Meaning as Functional Classification."
MMB	"Mind, Meaning, and *Behavior*."
NDL	"Are There Non-deductive Logics?" chap. 17 of *EPH*
NI	"Notes on Intentionality," chap. 12 of *PP*.
NS	"Naming and Saying," chap. 7 of *SPR*.
OPM	"Ontology and the Philosophy of Mind in Russell."
P	"Phenomenalism," chap. 3 of *SPR*.
PP	*Philosophical Perspectives.*
PR	"Physical Realism," chap. 7 of *PP*.
PSIM	"Philosophy and the Scientific Image of Man," chap. 1 of *SPR*.
RA	"Reply to Aune."
RD	"Reply to Alan Donagan."
RM	"Reply to Marras," chap. 6 of *EPH*.
RNW	"Realism and the New Way of Words."
SE	"Science and Ethics," chap. 16 of *PP*.
SK	"The Structure of Knowledge: (1) Perception, (2) Minds, (3) Epistemic Principles."
SM	*Science and Metaphysics: Variations on Kantian Thomas.*
SPR	*Science, Perception and Reality.*
SRI	"Scientific Realism or Irenic Instrumentalism: A Critique of Nagel and Feyerabend on Theoretical Explanation," chap. 14 of *PP*.
SRLG	"Some Reflections on Language Games," chap. 11 of *SPR*.
SSI	"Seeing, Sense Impressions and Sensa: A Reply to Cornman."
SSMP	"A Semantic Solution of the Mind-body Problem."
SSS	"Seeing, Seeming, and Sensing."
TA	"Thought and Action."
TIHI	". . . this I or he or it (the thing) which thinks . . . ," chap. 4 of *EPH*.
TC	"Truth and Correspondence," chap. 6 of *SPR*.

TE   "Theoretical Explanation," chap. 13 of *PP* and chap. 18 of
          EPH.
TTC   "Towards a Theory of the Categories," chap. 14 of *EPH*.
TWO   "Time and the World Order: A Metaphysical and Epis-
          temological Analysis of Becoming."

The Synoptic Vision

Theory of Knowledge

C. F. Delaney

The theory of knowledge has been construed in many ways, but on most construals it includes at least the three interrelated issues of *meaning, justification,* and *truth.* How is it that our statements about the world acquire meaning? How is it that our beliefs about the world are justified? And in what precisely consists the truth or falsity of the propositional content of our beliefs? Both historically and on the contemporary scene the various answers to these and related questions form natural groupings that then begin to gravitate toward the ideal types that have been characterized as the *foundationalist* and the *coherentist* pictures of knowledge. While nonsectarian in principle, these types do have classic instantiations: the foundationalist account is characteristically identified with Descartes and the empiricists, while the coherentist view has taken its classic form with the idealists.[1]

Foundationalism is typically rooted in an account of meaning. The principal argument is to the effect that although the meaning of a term is most often given by means of another more familiar term, not all terms can be introduced in this way because the technique presupposes a previous understanding of terms. There must be some terms that are introduced into discourse not by correlation with other terms but by direct correlation with the language-independent world. These are observation terms, and they are introduced by ostensive definition. These observation terms, whether the observed be public physical objects or private mental states, would be the first principles of meaning in the sense that the meanings of other terms somehow derived from or reduced to the meanings of these. In short, there must be some terms that are independently intelligible and that function as the source of the intelligibility of all other terms.

The argument that justification requires foundations has the same form. While most beliefs are warranted inferentially and thus justified in terms of their relations to other beliefs, it seems clear that if any beliefs are going to be ultimately justified there must be some beliefs that are noninferentially warranted and either self-justifying or at least justified independently of their relations to other beliefs. The argument is that if there are no epistemologically basic beliefs in this sense then one is faced with an infinite regress or a closed circle of justification. And if one allows an infinite regress or a closed circle of reasons alone to count as justificatory, then, since one can always find something that if believed would support his present belief, all beliefs would be equally justifiable. But this would be tantamount to the rejection of the concept of justified belief. Hence, there must be some basic beliefs that are independently credible and that function as the source of credibility of other beliefs. Again, these can take either physicalist or phenomenalist forms. The "givens" that are to function as the epistemic foundations can be either self-justifying, noninferential perceptual beliefs or self-justifying, noninferential introspective reports. The epistemological account would take a quite different form in each case, but in both cases justification would have its firm starting point.

The third dimension of this picture of knowledge is the notion of truth, and some form of correspondence is suggested if not implied by the foregoing accounts of meaning and justification. Beyond this sugges-tion, moreover, there are conceptual arguments against coherence and in favor of correspondence. Since there can be a plurality of internally consistent systems of statements that are mutually incompatible, it would seem that the very concept of truth would demand that the true account be built up from some statements that are independently true, i.e., true not simply in terms of their coherence with other statements but in terms of their direct correspondence with an independent world. The obvious candidates for such foundational truths would be the basic units of meaning and justification introduced above. Thus, in charac-terizing meaning, justification, and truth as intricate superstructures resting on strong foundations, this overall account of knowledge is appropriately characterized as foundationalist.

At the opposite pole is the coherentist account of knowledge, and this too begins with a theory of meaning. This account stems from a basic critique of the observational "givens" that are so central to the foundationalist picture. The general claim is that no term acquires meaning in virtue of direct empirical associations alone because mean-ing is a matter of "role in a system of concepts" rather than "correlation with the world." Any description of the world insofar as it is significant must go beyond what is given in experience because it must contain general classificatory terms that are instruments of interpretation. For the coherentist, just as the terms in the observation statements of science are seen to derive their very meanings from the theories of which they form a part, so also the observational component of ordinary language is a theory-laden interpretation of an ineffable given. Far from being neutral sources of meaning, even these basic descriptions have their own meaning in virtue of their relations to other parts of our world picture. There seems to be no neutral point for meaning to enter with the result that a holistic account of meaning seems to be dictated.

The notion of justification receives similar treatment. If the meaning of a statement is a matter of its relation to other statements, so also is its evidential force. All beliefs have an inferential structure, and there is no in-principle priority among them. Justification is seen to be not a matter of basic statements being independently credible and then communicating that credibility to others but rather a matter of any statement's fitting in as an integral part of a coherent and otherwise satisfactory account. No statement is immune to revision, and, conversely, any statement can be maintained if we are willing to make drastic enough adjustments elsewhere in the system. Justification is ultimately a matter of the various elements of a consistent set mutually supporting one another, the warrant of each being a function of the incoherence or incongruity introduced by the inclusion of its complement in its stead.

Given this direction of thought, the correspondence theory of truth begins to lose hold, and the coherence theory moves back onto the scene. If meaning and justification are seen to be matters not of simple dyadic relations but of integral systems, it is natural to think of truth along the same lines. Coherence has always been recognized as a mark of the truth, and there now seems to be little reason to stop short of seeing it as constitutive of its nature. With this final move, the coherentist picture of knowledge takes on its final form.

Wilfrid Sellars' theory of knowledge falls somewhere between these two ideal types and is consciously articulated with these two extremes in mind.

> One seems forced to choose between the picture of an elephant which rests on a tortoise (what supports the tortoise?) and the picture of a great Hegelian serpent of knowledge with its tail in its mouth (where does it begin?). Neither will do. (EPM, 170.)

Sellars' account can be viewed as a systematic attempt to integrate the positive insights of these two traditions while avoiding their obvious deficiencies. But this is easier said than done and certainly involves more than the simple juxtaposition of their attractive theses. Within the context of a fully elaborated philosophy of mind, Sellars develops a theory of knowledge that embodies a holistic theory of meaning, a correspondence theory of truth, and an account of justification that could be described either as a mitigated foundationalism or a mitigated coherentist position depending on one's categorial proclivities. In this essay I will attempt to exhibit the essential structure of Sellars' theory of knowledge. In the first section I will focus on his general theory of cognition as providing the necessary background for the more specific discussion of his epistemological views in the second section.

I. Theory of Cognition

With regard to the structure of empirical knowledge, the issue between the foundationalists and the coherentists was seen to revolve around the status of *perceptual beliefs* and *introspective reports*. The foundationalists insist that there must be a well-defined subset of these beliefs that are noninferential and self-justifying and that function as the foundations of empirical knowledge, while the coherentists claim that all beliefs are inferentially warranted and hence that knowledge has no such foundation. I have suggested that Sellars' position is a mediation between the two. Before the question of his position in these epistemological polemics can be broached, however, his positive views on cognition in general and on impressions and thoughts in particular have to be explored.

The Kantian dictum, "thoughts without content are empty, intuitions without concepts are blind," can serve as an appropriate guide to any exploration of Sellars' theory of cognition. In its attempt to avoid both the excesses of rationalism and the shortcomings of empiricism, Sellars' theory of cognition is clearly situated in the Kantian tradition. Of equal importance, however, are his efforts to overcome the transcendental features of Kantianism in the attempt to put the philosophy of man on a truly scientific basis. Both these positive dimensions of his relations to Kant will become clear as we explore his theory of cognition. The first section of this paper is divided into two parts: the first concerns itself with our knowledge of the external world and involves a discussion of sensing, perceiving and thinking; the second part focuses on our knowledge of our own mental states and involves a more specific discussion of the way in which the language of thoughts and impressions is introduced. This exposition of his theory of cognition will reveal positive accounts of *perception* and *introspection,* which go far toward determining Sellars' epistemological views.

(a)   Our knowledge of the external world.

It is almost a truism to claim that knowledge begins with sensation, but Sellars maintains that much can go wrong with our construal of this beginning. Seeing both a phenomenalistic or even a representational theory of perception and an abstractive theory of concept formation as philosophical deadends, he fashions an account of sensation that will enable us to avoid temptations in these directions by construing sensations both instrumentally and nonepistemically. Sensations are neither the direct objects of knowledge, nor are they primordial knowings. In themselves they belong to the causal rather than the cognitive sphere.

On the first point, Sellars wants to maintain that while our sensations do mediate and guide our perceptual knowledge of the world (i.e., our knowledge of objects is causally *mediated*), this knowledge is not a second-class knowing either constructed out of or inferred from a first-class knowledge of items like colors and sounds (i.e., our knowledge of objects is *direct*). Whereas the naive realist wants to construe our knowledge of the physical world as direct and unmediated, and the representationalist construes it as mediated and indirect, Sellars is trying to fashion a middle course that sees our knowledge of the physical world as direct but mediated. Perceptual knowledge properly so called will be mediated by sensations but will not be directly about sensations (cf. PR, 194-95).[2]

This dovetails with the second point, namely, that sensations are not in themselves knowings. They are states of perceivers that are nonepistemic in character and normally brought about by external causes.

> My thesis will be that sense is a cognitive faculty only in the sense that it makes knowledge possible and is an essential element in knowledge, and that of itself it knows nothing. It is a necessary condition of the intentional order, but does not of itself belong to that order. (BBK, 46.)

Considered simply in itself, there is nothing at all epistemic about undergoing a sensation. This is no way implies, however, that these nonepistemic states of sentient organisms are unrelated to the cognitive order. They are not only causally necessary conditions for knowledge but are also important ingredients in other more complex states that are truly epistemic.

It is important to be clear about the nonepistemic status of sensations because Sellars thinks that many of the difficulties of both Humean and Aristotelian empiricisms stem from their assimilation of sensation to the intentional order. It is also important to appreciate the temptations to so assimilate sensations. Aside from the epistemological mileage an empiricist might envision getting from sensations so construed, there are several independent facts that can tempt us to view sensations as epistemic. Firstly, there is a grammatical similarity between the language we use to characterize sensations ('a sensation of a red triangular thing') and the language by which we refer to and characterize items in the cognitive order ('a thought of a red triangular thing'). Secondly, there is the logical point that 'there is a sensation of a red triangle' fails to entail 'there is a red triangle' just as 'there is a thought of a pink elephant' fails to entail 'there is a pink elephant'. Thirdly, there is the psychological point that undergoing a sensation can be easily confused with the unreflective judgment that is built on it. Sellars urges us to overcome these temptations. The grammatical similarity in our ways of characterizing sensations and thoughts may not be due to a first-order similarity between the former and the latter but to a second-order methodological similarity between the ways in which talk of both are introduced. Moreover, the fact that 'sensation of' shares the logical property of nonextensionality with 'thought of' is not a sufficient reason to assimilate it to that particular nonextensional context (for there are many others) or to any other nonextensional context (for it may be distinctive). Finally, an elaborated theory of perception may be able to give us a handle on the precise role of sensations in cognition (cf. BBK, 46; EPM, 155.)

The basic epistemic units for Sellars are instances of perceptual experience, and the objects of such basic knowings are ordinary physical objects. He directs us to avoid all the impasses of phenomenalism and representationalism by "affirming that physical objects are really and directly perceived, and that there is no more basic form of (visual) knowledge than seeing physical objects and seeing that they are, for example, red and triangular on this side." (P, 87.) Granted that perceiving is a higher order activity than sensing and that it is about physical objects, it remains for us now to become clear about the structure of perceptual experience.

Perceptual experience, according to Sellars, is a very complex state of affairs. In the first place, while it is true that we often contrast perception and thinking, there is a proper sense in which perceiving essentially is or involves a thinking. Roughly, seeing this to be a red triangle involves thinking this to be a red triangle (cf. SK, 303). Furthermore, while apparently a matter simply of singular truths about material things, perceiving presupposes a knowledge of general truths about material things and our perception of them. Perceptual experience involves both knowledge of singular matters of fact and knowledge of general truths. Neither is possible without the other. But nevertheless it is clear that perceiving is not merely thinking. There is a descriptive core to the perceptual experience of seeing a red triangle that distinguishes it from merely thinking about a red triangle. These various dimensions of perceptual experience must be sorted out, specifically, the *propositional component* must be separated from the *descriptive core* (cf. SK, 297).

A characteristic presupposition of most empiricisms is the view that we are aware of things of determinate kinds simply by virtue of having sensations and images. Sellars' account of sensation goes far toward undermining this thesis. He agrees, however, that our basic perceptual experience is of determinate sorts of things, and from this concludes that perception is more than merely sensing and involves the conceptual realm. Perception is a matter of coming to be aware of something as characterized in a certain way, i.e., it is an awareness of a *this-such*. This is a matter of subsuming sensory cues under general concepts.

> The coming to see something as red is the culmination of a conceptual process which is the slow building up of a multi-dimensional pattern of linguistic responses (by verbal expressions to things, by verbal expressions to verbal expressions, by meta-linguistic expressions to object language expressions, etc.) the fruition of which as conceptual occurs when all these dimensions come into play in such direct perceptions as that this physical object (not that one) over here (not over there) is (rather than was) red (not orange, yellow, etc.). (P, 90.)

Experience, then, to the degree to which it is epistemic, essentially involves the conceptual order. It is a matter of identifying individuals as instances of kinds and predicating of them certain characteristics as opposed to others. Moreover, it is not enough to say that it merely involves the conceptual order. It is literally a thinking and involves the occurrence of the judgment 'that, over there, is a red triangle'. We can think of this as the propositional component of our perception of a red triangle (cf. SK, 303).

Even more than this has to be said, however, about the conceptual component of perceptual experience. It is not simply the case that a limited number of kind concepts are involved in our basic perceivings of individuals. To be in possession of any concept presupposes a whole battery of concepts so that perception presupposes a whole conceptual framework:

> One is not in a position to be perceptually aware of any fact, however minimal, unless one has a whole system of concepts. (SK, 314.)

In a sense, to have one concept is to have them all. To have the ability to perceive is to have the ability to think, and thinking is not something that one does in bits and pieces.

These points can be made concrete by exploring in some detail the apparently simple act of perceiving a green triangle. This obviously involves identifying an object as a triangle and recognizing it to be green, but much more than these two concepts and the resulting proposition is involved in the perceptual situation. What exactly is involved in seeing (or hearing, etc.) that something is thus and so? Sellars' first point is that 'see' is an achievement word and thus to characterize an experience as a seeing is in some broad sense to apply the semantical concept of truth to that experience; and this is an extremely complicated matter conceptually. To make this point, Sellars distinguishes between what we might call the perceptual modalities—'looks G', 'merely looks G; and 'is seen to be G'.

> Now the suggestion I wish to make is in its simplest terms that the statement 'X looks green to Jones' differs from 'Jones sees that X is green' in that whereas the latter both ascribes a propositional claim to Jones' experience *and endorses it*, the former ascribes a claim but does not endorse it. . . . Of course, if I say 'X merely looks green to S' I am not only failing to endorse the claim, I am rejecting it. (EPM, 145.)[3]

To say that 'x looks green to Jones' or to say that 'x merely looks green to Jones' is to say that Jones has that kind of experience that if one were prepared to endorse the propositional claim it involves one would characterize as 'Jones' seeing x to be green'. And, of course, this is true even in those cases where I am Jones. The point is that these three perceptual modalities are on the same conceptual level and are evoked only when certain circumstantial considerations have conspired to occasion the question whether or not to endorse the report that 'x is G'.

The concepts 'merely looking green', 'looking green,' and 'seem to be green' are parasitic on the concept of 'being green'. One cannot get below 'being green' because, for example, 'looking green' is to be ultimately parsed as 'how green objects look'. But what about the concept of 'being green' itself, which is presupposed by these others and is the normal characterization of such objects in unproblematic situations? It is with regard to such apparently simple concepts as this that Sellars most clearly illustrates his claim that to have one concept is to have a whole battery of concepts. Really to have the concept of 'being green' involves the ability to tell what colors objects are by looking at them, and this involves knowing in what circumstances to place an object if one wishes to ascertain its color by looking at it. To know the latter is to know what are the *standard conditions* for certain kinds of perception, and to know what kind of short term propensities (e.g., to utter "this is green") are *reliable symptoms* of the presence of certain properties under standard conditions. Hence, not only is it the case that a whole battery of concepts is involved in perception, but the perceptual facts so conceptually classified presuppose a knowledge of facts about the world in general and about perceivers in particular. One could not perceive any single fact unless one knew many other things as well (cf. EPM, 168).

But all this having been said about perceiving involving thinking, it is obvious that perceiving is not merely thinking. We must move from an acknowledgment of a propositional component of perception to a discussion of its descriptive core. We can begin to focus in on this descriptive core by a process of elimination. Take the three following situations:

> Seeing that x over there is green
> Its looking to one that x, over there, is green
> Its looking to one as though there were a green object over there

The idea 'that x, over there, is green' is the common propositional content of these situations. There is also the matter of the extent to which this content is endorsed, which is conveyed by 'seeing', 'looking', and 'looking as though' respectively. The residue in these situations is what Sellars refers to as the descriptive content (what others have referred to as sensuous content). In characterizing these experiences in the above manner we do not specify this common descriptive content save indirectly by implying that if the common propositional content were true, then these three situations would be cases of seeing that x over there is green. But, more directly, what is the intrinsic character of the common descriptive content of these three experiences? (Cf. EPM, 151.)

Granted that a seeing involves a thinking, surely there is all the difference in the world between seeing something to be a green triangle and merely thinking it to be such. And even if we take into account the fact that perception involves a causal dimension in that a green triangle is usually the cause of our perception thereof, we have not yet captured the distinctive intrinsic descriptive content of the seeing involved. Sellars maintains that, phenomenologically speaking, it is clear that there is a common nonpropositional component to these three experiences. Visual perception, to remain with these examples, is not just a conceptualizing of colored objects within visual range but is "in a sense most difficult to analyze, a *thinking in color* about colored objects." (SK, 310.) We must be very careful in our attempts to characterize this sensory component. In particular, we must guard against the temptation to think of the descriptive core as itself an experiencing; it is but one component of a total experience which is an ostensible seeing. Sellars begins modestly:

> So far we would be little better off than if we simply said that *ostensibly seeing* that there is in front of one an object which is red and triangular on the facing side differs from *merely thinking* that there is an object in front of one which is red and triangular on the facing side, by virtue of being a thinking which is *also* an ostensible seeing. But we can say more. For, phenomenologically speaking, the descriptive core consists in the fact that *something* in *some* way red and triangular is in some way present to the perceiver *other than as thought of*. (SK, 310.)

It remains for us to remove to some degree the multiple indefiniteness in this description.

The impressions of the classical empiricists or the sense data of their more contemporary counterparts reenter the story at this point. We have already seen that Sellars rejected the empiricist program as an analysis of knowledge on two counts: it is physical objects rather than impressions that are directly known, and the impressions in themselves are in no way instances of knowing. But an appeal to sense impressions considered not as an analysis or description of knowledge but as a postulational account of the descriptive core of perceptual experience holds out more promise. Again we must remind ourselves that we are interested in an *intrinsic* characterization of the descriptive core of perceptual experience. If we can only characterize impressions by what is logically a definite description, i.e., as the kind of entity that is common to perceptual situations, then we would be no better off than if we simply viewed talk about impressions or sense data as a notational convenience for speaking of how things look and what there seems to be.

But how are we to characterize intrinsically this sensory constituent of perceiving? The standard use of sensory predicates would seem to be inappropriate because, if Sellars' realistic account of perceiving is correct, both the proper and common sensibles are to be construed as qualities of public physical objects, and experiences are not physical in that ordinary sense of the term. But the fact that talk about sense impressions is being introduced in the theoretical rather than the analytic mode opens up the possibility of analogical predication based on a model, a familiar strategy in theory construction.

In our reintroduction of talk of sensations we must take care not to compromise the realistic character of perception that is dictated by ordinary language. We must avoid the temptation to construe sensations as inner particulars which are the direct objects of our awareness.

Sellars' first step is to construe sensing as a state of a perceiver: 'x has the sensation of a red triangle' has the form 'x is in a state of kind ϕ'. This adjectival construal of impressions (impressions-of-the-red-triangle-kind) gives way to an adverbial form so that we can now construe the object of sensing as a *manner* of sensing: 'sensing a red triangle' has the form 'sensing-a-red-triangle-ly'. In summary, 'x has an impression' has the form ϕx rather than xRy just as 'x wore a smile' has the form ϕx rather than xRy. That is, granted that there is a sense in which both statements have a relational form, this form is derivative from and dependent on that of the nonrelational statements 'x is impressed thus' and 'x smiled'. (Cf. RA, 286-87.)

The second step consists in conceiving of these visual impressions of red triangles so construed as items which are analogous *in certain respects* to physical objects that are red and triangular on the facing side. Of course, it would be incoherent straightforwardly to attribute to impressions the familiar perceptible qualities of physical objects: only physical objects can have these. Here we must attend to the fact that in any instance of theory construction the model has both positive and negative analogies vis-à-vis the entities for which it is the model. In our case the essential feature of the analogy is that visual impressions stand to one another in a system of ways of resembling and differing that is structurally similar to the ways in which the colors and shapes of physical objects resemble and differ. Specifically, impressions of red triangles resemble and differ in a way that is formally analogous to that in which physical objects that are triangular and red on their facing side resemble and differ; and it is similarly the case for other colors and shapes. These analogies have the force of postulates implicitly defining two families of predicates, $\phi_1 \ldots \phi_n$ and $\psi_1 \ldots \psi_n$, applicable to impressions, one of which has a logical space analogous to colors and the other a logical space analogous to that of the spatial properties of physical things (cf. P, 94).

Given the first step (construing sensing as a state of a perceiver), we must now note that the analogies involved are transcategorial analogies for they are analogies between states and physical things (cf. P, 93). While this does complicate the picture, Sellars maintains that the second-level analogy between the characteristics of admittedly different kinds of states of affairs is sufficient to give some content to such an intrinsic characterization of sensory states (cf. P, 93; RA, 191ff).[4]

While acknowledging that his account of sensation bears a family resemblance to what has been called "the adverbial theory of sensing," Sellars maintains that it is different in a very important respect. The usual adverbial theory would analyze our example in terms of *sensing redly*. Red, as a feature of the descriptive core of an ostensible seeing of a red triangle, would be interpreted as a manner of sensing. But what is to be explained is the fact that the ostensible seeing makes present to us not just redness but a red triangle. The point of the analysis is to render intelligible our ordinary perceptual framework. To do this, the adverbial theory must construe not 'red' but 'red item' as the relevant adverb. Hence, Sellars' account, given the job such an account is called on to do, construes as a manner of sensing, *sensing-a-red-triangle-ly*. This accounts for the seamlessness of primary and secondary qualities in our perceptual experience, i.e., the fact that color and extension are experienced to be equally properties of objects. On Sellars' account sensing a-red-triangle-ly is sensing in a way that is normally brought about by the physical presence to the senses of a red and triangular physical object but that can also be brought about in abnormal circumstances by objects that are neither red nor triangular. Moreover, these manners of sensing are analogous to the common and proper sensibles in that they have a common conceptual structure. Thus, the color-manners-of-sensing form a family of incompatibles where the incompatibilities involved are to be understood in terms of the incompatibilities involved in the family of ordinary physical color characteristics. Correspondingly, the shape-manners-of-sensing would exhibit, like physical shapes, the abstract structure of a geometrical system (cf. SK, 312-13).

So far we have been following Sellars' account of the existing conceptual framework of perception and the role of impressions in it, and the spirit of the Sellarsian account has been that of direct realism as opposed to the many forms of phenomenalism or representationalism that are characteristic of the empiricist tradition. The descriptive core of our perceptual experience is not itself a prior experience from which physical objects and their properties are either constructed or inferred. It is independent physical objects that are directly characterized by the proper and common sensibles with the descriptive core of our experiencing being similarily characterized only indirectly and by analogy. This, however, is not all that can or must be said about perceptible qualities. There is a final chapter to the story, but it involves a shift from philosophical analysis to scientific explanation. When all is said and done from an explanatory point of view, there is a sense in which the perceptible qualities of physical objects do have their ontological locus in perceivers. This dimension of the story is much more complicated than is ordinarily recognized.

The first stage in the ontological account of perceptible qualities is the recognition that the whole framework of physical objects is phenomenal in a quasi-Kantian sense such that *nothing* literally has these characteristics. This is because the logic of color predicates, for example, is such that only physical objects can have such predicates, and there really are no physical objects. But if appearings are not to be *mere* appearings, there must be explanatory units to account for there even seeming to be colored objects. This brings us to the second stage, which consists in the recognition that, to the degree that the argument up until now has been sound, the sensory cores of our acts of perceiving have intrinsic properties that have a logical space formally similar to the logical space of the colors of physical things. This suggests that in the ultimate scientific account of the world the counterparts of the colors of the physical object framework will turn out to be aspects of percipient organisms. But the road here is not smooth. In the scientific account of the world, it would seem that the perceiver as a single logical subject would have to give way to a view of him as really a plurality of logical subjects, and this would undermine the logic of impressions. If we really have a logical plurality, that would preclude them from serving either jointly or separately as the subjects of the verb 'to-sense-red-triangle-ly'. Hence, as a third stage in our account, we seem driven to turn each individual instance of sensing into a logical subject in its own right by introducing a new category of entity, i.e., *sensa,* with predicates the logical space of which is modeled on that of visual impressions as the latter is modeled on that of colored and shaped physical objects. Perceptible qualities can then be said to exist ultimately in the brain in the sense that when a person is perceiving an object with certain characteristics, part of what is really going on is that a sensum having these characteristics (in our doubly analogous sense) exists where certain microtheoretical cortical processes are going on. It is to such particulars that the organism responds when, for example, it looks to a person as if there is a red and triangular object over there (cf. P, 99-103).

Sellars cautions us with regard to our characterization of these sensa.

> It would, of course, be incorrect to say that, in the ordinary sense, such a particular is red and triangular. What *could* be said, however, is that whereas in the common sense picture physical objects are red and triangular but the impression 'of' a red triangle is neither red nor triangular, in the framework of this micro-theory, the theoretical counterparts of sentient organisms are Space-Time worms characterized by two kinds of variables: (a) variables which also characterize the theoretical counterparts of *merely* material objects; (b) variables peculiar to sentient things; and that these latter variables are the counterparts in this new framework of the perceptible qualities of the physical objects of the common sense framework. (EPM, 194.)

It is possible that, given an ideally completed neurophysiology, what we ordinarily call perceptible qualities will be seen to be qualitative dimensions of natural processes that occur only in connection with those complex physical processes that in the current scientific accounts are the central nervous system. The dualistic or epiphenomenalistic cast of this description ("in connection with") is simply a function of the impoverished state of the present scientific accounts and will be dissipated when the ultimate account is enriched so as to accommodate these qualitative dimensions (cf. PSIM, 37).

In the account of cognition so far, we have been invoking the notion of *thinking* as an ingredient in perceptual experience. Perceiving a red triangle involved thinking of a red triangle as its propositional component. It remains for us now to give a more systematic and critical account of this thinking component of our cognitive processes.

Sellars explicates thinking in terms of what he calls a *verbal behaviorist model*: "According to this model, 'thinking-that-p', where this means having the thought occur to one 'that-p', has as its *primary* sense *saying-p* and a derivative sense in which it stands for a short term propensity to say 'p.' '' (SK, 319.) For example, on this model, 'the thought that the triangle is red occurred to Jones' becomes 'Jones said (or had a short term proximate propensity to say) "the triangle is red" '. Hence, in their primary mode of being, thoughts are public episodes—people saying things—and in their secondary mode are short term propensities to say things. At this point it remains open whether or not there is a tertiary mode in which thoughts can be said to be pure occurrents underlying these saying and propensities to say. The priority involved here, of course, is in the order of knowing rather than in the order of being.

When Sellars claims that "thinking-that-p is, in its primary episodic sense, to be equated with candidly and spontaneously uttering 'p' '' (LTC, 104), he intends to exclude a number of construals of saying-p that would render the account implausible from the very beginning. On the one hand, he is excluding the mere utterance of noises that sound like the words or sentences involved (as in the primitive stages of language learning) and, on the other, those more complicated linguistic activities that are verbal performances in the stronger Austinian sense. He wants to focus on those spontaneous and candid utterances of the form 'there is a red triangle' (by one who knows the language to which this sentence belongs) that are simply occasioned by the environment rather than being directed to an audience. Learning to think is in its primary sense learning to respond verbally to one's environment. We can know that we are thinking in this primary sense by literally hearing ourselves think: "when we hear ourselves say (in a candid frame of mind) 'I've just missed my bus' we are literally hearing the thought occur to us that we have just missed the bus." (SK, 323.)

The obvious objection to this model of thinking is that surely we are often thinking when we are not saying anything. At this point Sellars shifts to the second component of the model—the secondary sense of thinking-p—the short term propensity to say that-p. Anyone who has learned a language has built up innumerable short-term propensities to respond linguistically to his environment, and these can shift with tremendous rapidity. Exploiting this feature of the model, we can account both for thinking-in-silence and the lightning rapidity with which our thoughts succeed each other. Furthermore, we could come to learn to respond not only to the propensities of others but to our own propensities and thus come to know what we are thinking even when we are not candidly thinking-out-loud (cf. SK, 322, 326).

There is another chapter to this account. Dispositions and propensities cannot be the last word. It is a generally accepted strategy with regard to accounts of material objects to distinguish between, on the one hand, the propensities and dispositions themselves (which are iffy states

definable in terms of empirical conditions) and, on the other hand, the
ultimate explanation of these in terms of occurrent or structural properties. Accordingly, it would seem that the concept of thought episodes
that are pure occurrents rather than propensities to think-out-loud is
called for to give a full account of what thinking really is. This is the
methodological background for Sellars' claim that at bottom we need a
theory of mental acts construed as pure occurrents to explain our
propensities to think-out-loud (cf. SK, 328).

Remaining true to his methodological behaviorism, he construes
these postulated thought episodes as items that have a strong positive
analogy to thinking in the primary sense:

> In my view the fundamental concept pertaining to thinking is thinking-out-
> loud as conceived by our logical behaviorists. This is not to say that I agree
> with him in rejecting the classical conception of thoughts as inner episodes in a
> non-dispositional sense. Rather, I accept mental acts in something like the
> classical sense, but argue that the concept of such acts is, in a sense I have
> attempted to clarify, a derivative concept. (LTC, 108.)

In short, he construes thoughts (in the sense in which thoughts occur to
one) "as the occurrence in the mind of sentences in the language of
'inner speech', or as I shall call it, 'Mentalese'." (SK, 303.)

There is one final dimension to the theory. We must distinguish
between the functional conception of thoughts as items in inner speech
and the further conception of the vehicles of these functions. At first
approximation, what this theory postulates by way of vehicles are
processes and acts rather than individuals. In addition to sayings and
short-term propensities to say, we now conceive of persons as characterized by pure occurrent episodes of thinking in our analogous sense.
These are in persons as states of the person and are "inner" only in that
sense. But in the ultimate scientific account "inner" may come to have a
richer and more specific meaning when we come to construe the
neurophysiological processes of the central nervous system as the proper ontological locus of these activities (cf. SK, 329).

(b)   Our knowledge of our mental states.

In this account of cognition, while thoughts and impressions are
certainly central, our awareness of our thoughts and impressions has
played a secondary role. For epistemological reasons it is most important to take a more detailed look at the way in which talk about mental
states gets introduced and functions so that we can become clearer
about the whole notion of "inner experience."

Sellars proposes to approach this issue through a myth, *the Jonesian
myth*, and he is clear about the precise point of this myth.

> I am beginning my myth *in medias res* with humans who have already mastered a Rylean language, because the philosophical situation it is designed to clarify is one in which we are not puzzled by how people acquire a language for referring to public properties of public objects but are very puzzled indeed about how we learn to speak of inner episodes and immediate experiences. . . .
>
> The questions I am in effect raising are, "what resources would have to be added to the Rylean language of these talking animals in order that they may come to recognize each other and themselves as animals that *think, observe,* and have *feelings* and *sensations,* as we use these terms?" and, "How could the addition of these resources be construed as reasonable." (EPM, 179.)[5]

Starting, then, with a mythical stage in prehistory in which humans are limited to a Rylean language (a language the fundamental descriptive vocabulary of which speaks only of public properties of public objects), Sellars is going to attempt to reconstruct the gradual enrichment of that language until it has all the essential features of the rich natural language in terms of which we come to recognize others and ourselves as beings which think, observe, and feel.

The first enrichment Sellars envisions bears on the development of the fundamental resources of semantical discourse. These mythical ancestors of ours gradually come to be able to characterize each other's verbal behavior in semantical terms, i.e., to develop the resources to say of each other's verbal productions that they *mean* thus and so ('rot' means red) and that they are *true or false*. The important point to note here is that the semantical notions bear directly on *verbal performances*; it is these that mean such and such and are either true or false. Given the resources of semantical discourse, the primitive language has now acquired a dimension that is an essential part of the stage setting for the introduction of 'thoughts'. For characteristic of thoughts is their meaning, intentionality, or aboutness, and on reflection it is clear that "semantical talk about the meaning or reference of verbal expressions has the same structure as mentalistic discourse concerning what thoughts are about." (EPM, 180.) If, then, we have a good reason to introduce the notion of 'thoughts', the categories of intentionality are available because they are, at bottom, semantical categories pertaining to overt verbal performances.

The second stage enrichment of our Rylean language bears on the enlargement of the logical space so as to accommodate the distinction between the language of postulational *theory* and the language of *observation*. Although this distinction is most clearly drawn in modern science where a postulated domain of unobservable entities is invoked to explain matters of observed fact, Sellars maintains that these later sophisticated developments are but "refinements of the ways in which plain men, however crudely and schematically, have attempted to understand their environment and their fellow men since the dawn of intelligence." (EPM, 183.) Thus, he supposes that these primitive ancestors gradually elaborate, without any methodological sophistication, sketchy and vague theories to explain why things that are similar in their observable properties differ in their causal properties and why things that are similar in their causal properties differ in their observable ones.

Given this double enrichment of our primitive Rylean language by its expansion so as to include the logical space of both semantical and theoretical discourse, the stage is set for Jones. Jones notices that his fellow men behave intelligently not only when their conduct seems to be guided by overt verbal episodes—by "thinking"—but also when no detectable verbal output is present. He conjectures that these latter intelligent activities must also be guided by thinkings, but not thinkings of the former overt sort. Jones gets theoretical.

> Jones develops a theory according to which overt utterances are but the culmination of a process which begins with certain inner episodes. And let us suppose that his model for these episodes which initiate the events which culminate in overt verbal behavior *is that of overt verbal behavior itself. In other words, using the language of the model, the theory is to the effect that overt verbal behavior is the culmination of a process that begins with 'inner speech'. (EPM, 186.)*

So, even in his theoretical moments Jones does not relinquish his native behaviorism but introduces his theoretical entities in terms of a basic vocabulary pertaining to overt behavior. He calls these theoretical entities 'thoughts', and it is most important to note that, inasmuch as the theory is built on a model of speech episodes, it carries over to these inner episodes the applicability of semantical categories. Thus, just as Jones has all along been speaking of overt utterances as *meaning* or *being about* this or that, he now speaks of these 'thoughts' in a like manner. (Cf. EPM, 187.)

It is most important to be clear about the relations between overt speech and these inner episodes. Although it is the overt speech episodes characterized in semantical terms that are explained in terms of thoughts that are also characterized in semantical terms, this does not mean that the notion of the meaning of overt speech is to be analyzed in terms of the intentionality of thoughts. It is overt-verbal episodes that are primarily and independently the subjects of semantic characterization and it is these linguistic events as semantically characterized that are the model for the 'thoughts' introduced by the theory. Moreover, it is most important to note that these thoughts are introduced as theoretical episodes, not as immediate experiences. In fact, Jones does not yet have the concept of immediate experience; and even if he did have this further concept, it is not obvious that inner episodes introduced for one theoretical purpose—thoughts—comprise a subset of immediate experiences, inner episodes introduced for another theoretical purpose (cf. EPM, 188).

Now once Jones has developed this theory to explain the behavior of others, it is but a short step to the use of this theoretical language in self-description. When A is observing B and has behavioral evidence that warrants 'B is thinking "p" ', B using the same behavioral evidence can also say 'I am thinking "p" '. Given this, cannot B be trained to give reasonably reliable accounts of his own thinking *without having to observe his own behavior.*

> Can we not as children be trained by those who know us intimately (our parents), and who therefore know (ceteris paribus) what our short-term verbal propensities are (i.e., what we are thinking), *to respond* reliably to our own short-term propensities to say that-p, as well as to respond to our actual sayings of 'p'?
>
> And cannot this ability be generalized in such a way that we can reliably respond to new propensities, i.e., to thoughts other than those in terms of which we have been trained? And would not the fact that such responses are *reliable* constitute the core of the explanation of non-inferential knowledge of what one is thinking (in the proximate propensity sense)? (SK, 326-27.)

As a result of such conditioning, then, our ancestors begin to speak of the privileged access each of us has to his own thoughts. We have made a giant step forward: "What began as a language with a purely theoretical use has gained a reporting role." (EPM, 189.)[6]

It is important to note, however, that the privileged access involved is not a *logically* privileged access because those concepts that come to have a reporting use when one is not drawing inferences from behavioral evidence are still logically tied to such behavioral evidence and are unintelligible without this tie. The concepts pertaining to such inner episodes are as intersubjective as the concepts of a molecule, and the reporting use of these concepts is built on and presupposes this intersubjective base. Hence, the privacy of these episodes is not a logical privacy for the fact that overt behavior is evidence for these episodes is built into the very logic of the concepts, just as the fact that the observable behavior of gases is evidence for molecular episodes is built into the very logic of molecule talk (cf. EPM, 189).

The next chapter in our Jonesian myth grows out of the realization that a subset of the inner-thought episodes just introduced are perceptual thinkings, e.g., seeing that the triangle is red. Prior to Jones' theory, the only concept our fictitious ancestors had of perceptual episodes was as overt verbal reports made in the presence of sensible objects. Now, *seeing that the triangle is red* is construed as an inner episode which has as its model *reporting, having looked, that the triangle is red*. But these perceptual thinkings seem to be more than propensities to say or even the theoretical causes of our propensities-to-say. "Inner experiences" (impressions, sensations, feelings) seem to be involved but as yet our ancestors have no such concept.

Jones, satisfied with the success of his theory to this point, expands it so as to include a theory of sense perception. He postulates a class of inner, theoretical episodes called 'impressions' that are the end results of the impingement of physical objects and processes on parts of the body. These are states of the perceiving subject, not particulars, and they explain the qualitative content of and the communality between perceptual experiences. For example, the presence of an "impression of a red triangle" accounts for the difference between seeing a red triangle and merely thinking of a red triangle and also accounts for the communality between those situations in which (1) one sees that an object over there is red and triangular, (2) the object over there looks to one to be red and triangular, and (3) there looks to one to be a red and triangular physical object over there. Because of these features, the postulation of such entities provides the logical space to handle illusion and error. In virtue of the explanatory tasks they perform, these inner episodes are understood to be intrinsically characterized by, for example, 'red' and 'triangular' in analogous senses of these terms.

Jones now teaches his theory of impressions to his fellow men. As in the case of thoughts, people begin by using the language of impressions to draw theoretical conclusions from behavioral premises, e.g., "you have a red triangular impression because you are presently identifying that object as a red triangle" or "I have a red triangular impression because it looks to me as if there is a red triangle over there." Then, again through conditioning, Jones brings it about that this talk of impressions takes on a *reporting role*: "he trains them, that is, to say 'I have the impression of a red triangle' when and only when, according to the theory, they are indeed having the impression of a red triangle." (EPM, 194-95.) As a result of this conditioning, our ancestors begin to speak of the "privacy" of these inner experiences and of the "privileged access" each of us has to his own. Again, the important point to note is that concepts pertaining to certain inner episodes—in this case impressions—can be primarily and essentially intersubjective without being resolvable into overt behavioral symptoms and that the reporting role of these concepts, their role in introspection (the fact that each of us has a privileged access to his impressions), constitutes a dimension of these concepts that is *built on* and *presupposes* their role in intersubjective discourse (cf. EPM, 195).

The final chapter in Sellars' myth records both the crowning glory and the ultimate failure of our primitive genius, Jones. Jones goes on to imagine the way in which future science will develop such that certain particulars in an adequate neurophysiological account of man will *really be* the inner episodes we are invoking to explain thinking and perceiving, and he can even imagine teaching himself and others to use this new scientific language in a reporting capacity. But then he makes his fatal mistake. *He confuses his own creative enrichment of the framework of empirical knowledge with an analysis of knowledge as it is*: "he construes as *data* the particulars and arrays of particulars which he has come to be able to observe, and believes them to be the antecedent objects of knowledge which have somehow been in the framework from the beginning." (EPM, 195.) Jones ends up confusing his scientific *theory* of knowledge with an *analysis* thereof and thus bequeaths to his successors the snares of modern epistemology.

In his general theory of cognition, Sellars has attempted to juxtapose a realistic analysis of knowledge with a scientific explanation thereof in such a way as to do justice to both.

> Direct Realism gives an excellent reconstruction of the ways in which physical things, perceivers, sense impressions, perceptions *of* physical objects, perceptions *that* they are thus and so, privileged access to one's own thoughts, feelings, and sense impressions, etc. etc., fit together to make one framework of entities and knowledge about these entities. To say that the framework is phenomenal in a quasi-Kantian sense, as I am doing, is to say that science is making available a more adequate framework of entities which *in principle, at least,* could serve all the functions, and, in particular, the perceptual functions of the framework we actually employ in everyday life. It is not, of course, to say that there is a good reason to put it to this use. (P, 97.)

The important point is to keep distinct the analysis and the explanation. Phenomenalism and representationalism give way to direct realism on the level of analysis, but the ontological purport of this direct realism is seen to be a function of its incorporation into the scientific framework.

II. Epistemology

Having explained Sellars' positive views on cognition in general and on our knowledge of our own mental states in particular, I am now in a position to situate his views in the epistemological context sketched in the introduction to this essay. It will be recalled that the rift between the foundationalist tradition and the coherentist tradition principally focused on the former's insistence that there must be a well-defined subset of our beliefs that, because they are noninferential and self-justifying, function as the foundations of empirical knowledge, and the latter's counterclaim that all beliefs are inferential so that knowledge neither needs nor could have such a foundation. Sellars' position was characterized as a mean. We will now return to these epistemological issues and to the polemic between foundationalism and coherentism to discuss Sellars' specific views on meaning, justification, and truth.

(a)   Meaning.

Sellars' views on meaning are clearly in the coherentist tradition. On the level of a general theory of meaning, he espouses what might be called a classificatory as opposed to a relational account, and on the specific issue of concept formation, his views are holistic as opposed to atomistic. Moreover, there is a connection between the general and the specific in this case.

The empiricist tradition has taken it for granted that linguistic meaning expresses a relation between a word and a nonverbal entity. For example, 'red' is understood to signify the quality *red* by virtue of its syntax as a predicate and, most importantly, in virtue of the fact that it is a learned response to red items. The relation in question has the simple form xRy, where the R is that of association between a given word and an independent nonverbal state of affairs. This general theory of meaning naturally suggests, if it does not imply, that concept formation is ultimately a matter of ostensive definition. Learning to use the word 'red' is a matter of associating it with an antecedent awareness of red. A system of empirical meanings can be built up piecemeal in this fashion, and other meanings can be later introduced on this foundation. It is no small matter that this relational theory of meaning makes readily available a simple account of concept formation and of the ties our language has with the world.

Sellars rejects this picture of concept formation and the general theory of meaning in which it is embedded. In the first place, this view of concept formation "takes it for granted that the process of teaching a child to use a language is that of teaching it to discriminate elements within a logical space of particulars, universals, facts, etc., of which it is already indiscriminately aware, and to associate these discriminated elements with verbal symbols." (EPM, 161-62.) But on Sellars' general account of cognition, since the fundamental epistemic unit is perceptual thinking, there cannot be any awareness of logical space prior to or independent of the acquisition of general classificatory concepts. Cognitive awareness at its most basic level is a matter of, for example, 'taking x to be red' rather than an awareness of redness. Secondly, and on the general level, statements of the form ' " . . ." means . . .' are not for

Sellars relational statements at all. While it is indeed the case that the word 'rot' could not mean the quality *red* unless it were associated with red things, he maintains that it would be misleading to say that the semantical statement ' "rot" means red' says of 'rot' that it is associated with red things, for this would suggest that the semantical statement is but a definitional shorthand for a longer statement about the associational connections of 'rot' which is clearly not the case. Thus, having rejected the empiricist's accounts both of concept formation in particular and of meaning in general, Sellars owes us a positive account (cf. EPM, 163).

Rather than begin with potentially misleading examples such as ' "red" stands for redness', Sellars suggests that we attend instead to examples such as ' "und" means *and*' and ' "rot" means *red*'. With regard to the first example at least, we are not even tempted to construe it relationally unless we are prepared to posit conjunctions in the world, and both examples lend themselves to a much more plausible account of what is involved. In these and other translational cases of 'means', it seems reasonably clear that what is going on is a functional classification of an unfamiliar linguistic item by reference to a familiar one.

> The rubric ' ". . ." means . . .' is a linguistic devise for conveying the information that a *mentioned* word, in this case "rot", plays the same role in a certain linguistic economy of German-speaking peoples, as does the word "red", which is not *mentioned* but *used*—used in a unique way; *exhibited,* so to speak—and which occurs on the right-hand side of the semantical statement. (EPM, 163.)

What we are saying with ' "rot" means *red*' is that ' "rot"'s are our "red"'s. In these cases meaning is clearly an intralinguistic matter and does not directly involve a word-world relationship. But, of course, these translational cases of meaning are not the instances of meaning the empiricist's took as paradigmatic.

Sellars, however, sees this account of the translational cases as but a fragment of a general intralinguistic classificatory theory of meaning that can also give us a handle on such apparently different semantical locutions as those of the form ' "not" stands for negation' and ' "red" stands for redness'. Focusing on the former, there seems to be a perfectly good sense in which 'not' stands for negation, although it neither names, denotes, nor has (in the technical sense) an extension. Sellars feels that if we can get clear about this particular example, "we will have the key to the status of senses generally, both of those senses which are intensions and those which are extensions." (*SM,* 79.)[7]

In this example, what exactly is the force of the abstract singular term 'negation'? Sellars calls our attention to distributive singular terms (*the bishop* moves along diagonals) and conjectures that since statements with distributive singular terms in the subject position are equivalent to general statements, there could well be a convention whereby statements with a distributive singular term in the predicate position would be equivalent to statements involving the corresponding common noun. On this construal ' "Not" stands for negation' would be equivalent to ' "not" stands for the •neg•', which would be a way of saying ' "not"'s are •neg•s' where the dot-quoted expression would invoke the notion of a *linguistic type*, in this case one designating a certain syntactical function across languages. This reconstruction is then subject to the following generalization:

Statements of the *surface* form
    (the) '. . .' (in L) stands for (abstract singular term)
are classificatory in nature and have, from a more searching point of view, the form
    '. . .'s (in L) are •. . .•s (*SM*, 82.)[8]

Thus, ' "not" stands for negation' reduces to ' "not"'s are •neg•s' just as ' "rot" means *red*' reduced to ' "rot"'s are our "red"'s.

The same analysis holds for ' "red" means the quality *red*' or ' "red" stands for redness'. Just as we would be most reluctant to say that "not" 's meaning negation was a matter of "not" 's standing in a certain meaning relation to negation, so we should resist the temptation to construe the present case as a matter of "red" 's standing in a certain meaning relation to redness. Rather, what is involved here is a somewhat less perspicuous instance of an English term being classified by reference to a linguistic type, in this case •red•.

In all these cases, to state the meaning of a word is to classify it functionally. This is most perspicuous in the translational cases where we are telling someone how a term in another language is used by characterizing it as playing the same role as a given term in the home language. It is important to see, however, that this is but a special case of functional classification, a classification that ' ". . ." means . . .' also effects when both items are in the home language by the device of linguistic types.

Meaning, then, is an intralinguistic matter, not a word-world relation. But given that this is indeed the case, we are left with a nest of puzzles. How do meanings get hooked up to the world? How are concepts formed and languages learned? The empiricists had ready answers to these questions in terms of their relational theory of meaning and their notion of ostensive definition. These explanatory routes being blocked, meaning seems to have been severed from the world and language learning rendered totally mysterious. Sellars owes us an account of concept formation. The only alternatives seem to be *concept empiricism* and *innatism,* but Sellars hopes to fashion a mediating account that is consistent with his holistic theory of meaning but enables him to do justice to the empirical origins of our understanding of the world.

As was intimated above, Sellars rejects outright the view that concepts are derived piecemeal from experience by some kind of abstractive process (a view we called 'concept empiricism') and his reasoning focuses on the ambiguity in the word 'experience'. If we mean by this the full-blown experience of objects as, for example, red and triangular, this obviously presupposes that we already have the concepts; if, on the other hand, we mean by 'experience' unconceptualized sensation, then the objection is that it alone cannot give rise to these concepts because sensation does not antecedently have their logical space even undiscriminatingly. In short, concept empiricism is seen to be incoherent once we recognize that "instead of coming to have a concept of something because we have noticed that sort of thing, to have the ability to notice a sort of thing is already to have the concept of that sort of thing, and cannot account for it." (EPM, 176.) Moreover, it is not simply the case that concepts are not abstracted piecemeal from experience; they are not arrived at piecemeal from any source at all. One can be said to have a given concept only to the extent that he has the whole system of concepts of which that one is an element. Concepts are essentially systematic, so instead of the dominant atomistic picture of *concept formation* we should shift to the more holistic picture of *adopting a conceptual framework.* However, we are still in the dark about this process and the empirical constraints thereon.

When this problem is transposed onto the linguistic level (for acquiring concepts—in the full sense—just *is* a matter of learning a language), what is at issue is an alternative to the simplistic notion of ostensive definition as an account of language learning. But given that "to have one concept is to have them all" or "to know the meaning of a word is to know a language," there seems to be no way to break into the circle and innatism looms as the only available explanation.

A recourse to innatism, however, may be premature. Sellars urges us to explore the possibility that by attending to the role of social conditioning in language acquisition we may be able to avoid the atomism of ostensive definition and the unexplained holism of innatism. Are not children brought to a language by first being trained by those who already experience the world in terms of that language to *respond,* for example, to red objects in sunlight by *uttering* or being disposed to utter 'this is red'? Only after a long period of training not only with regard to this and other color words but also with regard to a whole network of concepts involved in color recognition can the child finally be said in a given instance to be truly *saying* (as opposed to uttering) 'this is red'.

Hence, Sellars maintains that "even such simple concepts as those of colors are the fruit of a long process of publically reinforced responses to public objects (including verbal responses) in public situations." (EPM, 176.)

An analogy may help. What exactly is involved in learning to tell time, i.e., learning to read the clock? Surely one cannot be said to learn to read, first, six o'clock, then twelve o'clock, then a quarter after nine and so forth until by adding up all these piecemeal readings one acquires by sheer addition the ability to read off all the times from the clock. This account would suggest that to the question "Can you tell time?" the answer "Well, some of them" would be appropriate. A more plausible account suggests itself. A person is trained to respond with "six o'clock," "twelve o'clock," "a quarter after nine," and so forth given the appropriate positions of the hands of the clock, until he gradually comes to get the hang of the symbol system so that he can go on. Only then can he be said to be able to tell time; only then is his utterance of "It's six o'clock" a matter of reading the clock. In a sense, we cannot tell any times unless we can tell them all. So also with language acquisition. An account in terms of learning to say this word and then that until all the sayings add up to knowing a language is implausible. Rather, the child is trained to utter appropriate words and strings of words until he gets the hang of the symbol system so that he can go on. Only then can he be construed as truly being able to *say* the first word he *uttered*.

Just as the ability to tell time is not built up from individual tellings, so the ability to speak a language is not the additive result of individual speakings. Rather, what is involved in both cases is the gradual introduction through training to a whole system. Furthermore, this account of language acquisition presupposes that the language is already known (the truth the innatists misconstrue), not of course by the learner but by the community which is doing the training. At this point Sellars bows in the direction of Wittgenstein by acknowledging that "it is the linguistic community as a self-perpetuating whole which is the minimum unit in terms of which conceptual activity can be understood." (LTC, 100.) To the objection that although this may suffice as an account of language acquisition or concept formation in the present surely it cannot account for the historical origin of language or conceptual activity, Sellars would simply agree. The latter issue is one for the theory of evolution in its social dimensions that is still in its embryonic stages.

(b) Justification.

While their divergence on the question of an atomistic versus a holistic theory of meaning is important, the issues that really divide the foundationalists and the coherentists are those bearing on justification.

Are there noninferential, self-justifying beliefs that function as the foundations of empirical knowledge or not? Whereas with regard to meaning and truth Sellars can be seen to take one side or the other, with regard to justification he fashions a complex middle position.

Sellars is neither a foundationalist nor a coherentist in the classical senses sketched in the introductory section of this essay. He clearly is not a foundationalist. In fact, his many-faceted attacks on what he calls "the myth of the given" have inextricably linked his name with the rejection of foundationalism in all its forms. He rejects the notion of self-justifying beliefs that function as the foundation of our knowledge. There are no self-authenticating, nonverbal episodes, and those reports that do qualify as observation statements derive their epistemic authority from the knowledge of other related facts. On the other hand, he is clearly no coherentist. Sellars does not maintain that all knowledge is inferential; he singles out perceptual and introspective reports as instances of noninferential knowledge.

In fact, Sellars sees both the foundationalist and the coherentist positions as similarly infected by "the myth of the given."

> One of the forms taken by the Myth of the Given is the idea that there is, indeed *must* be, a structure of particular matter of fact such that (a) each fact can not only be non-inferentially known to be the case, but presupposes no other knowledge either of particular matter of fact, or of general truths; and (b) such that the non-inferential knowledge of facts belonging to this structure constitutes the ultimate court of appeals for all factual claims—particular and general—about the world. It is important to note that I characterized the knowledge of fact belonging to this stratum as not only non-inferential but as presupposing no knowledge of other matter of fact whether particular or general. It might be thought that this is a redundancy, that knowledge (not belief or conviction, but knowledge) which logically presupposes knowledge of other facts *must* be inferential. This, however, as I hope to show, is itself an episode in the myth. (EPM, 164.)

In running together the notions of inference and presupposition, both the foundationalists and the coherentists link together the notions of *noninferential* and *self-justifying*. The foundationalist focuses on the fact that not all knowledge can be inferential (with which Sellars agrees) and concludes from this that there must be some self-justifying instances of knowledge (which does not follow), while the coherentist focuses on the fact that no knowledge is self-justifying (with which Sellars agrees), from which he concludes that all knowledge is inferential (which does not follow). Sellars maintains that the conviction underlying both positions, namely, that all knowledge that logically presupposes other knowledge *must* be inferential, is itself an episode in the myth of the given. He will attempt to keep these notions distinct in order to construct a theory of justification in which noninferential knowledge but not self-justifying knowledge will play an important role.

We will approach Sellars' account of justification through his critique of foundationalism. The aim of the foundationalists' infinite-regress argument as it bears on justification is to secure acceptance of the notion of self-justified instances of knowledge. As to the specific character of these instances, one is presented with two alternatives. One could go the route of (1) instances of knowing more basic than believing or (2) instances of self-justified beliefs. Sellars rejects both, and thus he rejects the infinite-regress argument that lies at the heart of foundationalism. However, this is not to say that he rejects the infinite-regress argument when it is put in inferential/noninferential terms instead of other-justified/self-justified terms. One of his main points is to argue that these are separate issues.

Sellars accepts the classical definition of knowledge, which implicitly eliminates the first option of the foundationalist.

> The explication of knowledge as 'justified true belief' though it involves many pitfalls to which attention has been called in recent years, remains the orthodox or classical account and is, I believe, essentially sound. (SK, 332.)

If knowledge is a special case of belief, obviously there can be no instances of knowing more basic than believing. Since one of the principal thrusts of Sellars' theory of cognition was to establish the truth of this claim, his rejection of this first foundationalist alternative lends itself to detailed discussion.

This first form of foundationalism, more specifically, appeals to a level of cognition unmediated by concepts, a subconceptual awareness of facts, that would be self-justifying and would function in the justification of our beliefs. Sellars depicts the position thus:

> Now many philosophers have thought that the epistemic authority of certain *beliefs* is grounded in the fact that what the beliefs *believe* to be the case has been *directly apprehended* to be the case. Thus, the idea that certain facts are directly apprehended and, in particular, the idea that certain states of one's mind are known by virtue of being directly apprehended has been thought to explain how certain beliefs acquire an epistemic authority which is not a matter of their inferential relations to other beliefs. Thus, on directly apprehending that I am believing Albuquerque to be the capital of New Mexico, I may come to believe *that I believe* that Albuquerque is the capital of New Mexico. This meta-belief would acquire its epistemic authority from the direct apprehension of the fact which makes it true. (GEC, 617.)

What is involved here is the notion of *direct apprehension of facts*. Sometimes the purported directly evident facts are taken to be perceptual but more often than not they are regarded as Cartesian-like instances of what is going on in one's mind at the present moment. In both cases they are alleged to be directly apprehended.

Sellars takes exception to both aspects of this purposed cognitive ability. What sorts of entities are *facts*? Are they independently real entities, or are they conceptual in nature? The ties between ''fact'' and ''truth'' would seem to suggest that they belong to the conceptual order. Furthermore, what is this *direct apprehension*? Although 'apprehend' is an achievement word, there is certainly logical room for 'ostensibly apprehending' that does not imply achievement. Accordingly, the distinction between 'apprehending' and 'seeming to apprehend' calls for a criterion that this account in no way provides. Hence, Sellars concludes: ''I suspect that the notion of a non-conceptual 'direct apprehension' of a 'fact' provides a merely verbal solution to our problem; the regress is stopped by an ad hoc regress-stopper; indeed, the very metaphors which promised the sought for foundation contain within themselves a dialectical movement which takes us beyond them.'' (SK, 339.)

This leaves us with the second alternative of the foundationalist, i.e., self-justifying, beliefs. Sellars rejects this notion also, at least in the strong sense that the foundationalist has in mind. While he is willing to defend an account that involves 'basic beliefs' in a weaker sense (given a specific conceptual framework or set of presuppositions, this kind of belief can be said to be noninferentially warranted), he maintains that the notion of beliefs that are *self-justified* trades on a falsely atomistic conception of belief. Individual beliefs are neither meaningful nor justified in isolation from the system of which they are a part. In thus rejecting both alternatives, Sellars rejects the infinite-regress argument as it bears on justification.

If it is his rejection of this infinite-regress argument that separates Sellars from the foundationalist, it is his acceptance of a similar one that separates him from the coherentist. He disagrees with the coherentist's claim that all knowledge is inferential because he accepts the argument that if some instances of knowledge are inferential, in order to get started at all, there must be some noninferential instances of knowledge. It remains to be seen how this notion of noninferential knowledge avoids the myth of the given and fits into his general theory of cognition.

Sellars maintains that there are both noninferential perceptual beliefs and noninferential knowledge of our own mental states, but in neither case is the belief in question self-justifying. First, the perceptual situation:

> Jones thinks out-loud: Lo! Here is a red apple. Now to say that this visual thinking-out-loud that something is the case is epistemically *justified* or *rea-*

sonable or has authority is clearly *not* to say that Jones has correctly inferred from certain premises, which he has good reason to believe, that there is a red apple in front of him. For we are dealing with a *paradigm* case of non-inferential belief. *The authority of the thinking accrues to it in quite a different way. It can be traced to the fact that Jones has learned to use the relevant words in perceptual situations.* (SK, 324.)[9]

Jones, as a competent speaker of the English language, has been trained to respond 'Here is a red apple' to specific visual stimulation, and his response is direct in the sense that it is not inferred from other premises. The *authority* of the response—which it must have to count as knowledge—is ultimately traceable to the reliability of the training and to the resultant fact that one can reliably infer the presence of a red apple from the fact that Jones makes this report.

More must be involved, however, if Jones' report is to count as an expression of knowledge: it must not only *have* authority, but that authority must be recognized by Jones himself. In order for 'Here is a red apple' to express observational knowledge for Jones, he must know that tokens of 'Here is a red apple' are in fact symptoms of the presence of red apples in conditions that are standard for visual perception. In order for his perceptual report to be an instance of knowledge, Jones must be *capable* of reasoning—I just had the thought that-p in appropriate circumstances, so there is a good reason for me to believe that-p. But this is not to say that he originally *inferred* that there was a red apple in front of him but only to say that he must now be capable of inferring that there is *indeed* a good reason to so believe.

The same holds true for introspective reports. Just as Jones was trained to respond directly and reliably to perceptual objects, so he was trained to respond directly and reliably to his own thoughts, i.e., his short-term propensities to say that-p. He can give reliable self-descriptions of what is going on in his own mind without inferring the information from his own overt behavior or from anything else. And, Sellars concludes, "Would not the fact that such responses are *reliable* constitute the core of the explanation of non-inferential knowledge of what one is thinking (in the proximate propensity sense), as the existence of reliable verbal responses to perceptual things is the core of the explication of non-inferential perceptual knowledge." (SK, 327.)

On Sellars' account, the conceptual framework of ordinary language into which we are all initiated at our mother's knee has as principles that are partially constitutive of it those of the form 'judgments that are P_1 are likely to be true' and 'judgments that are P_2 are likely to be true' where P_1 bears on perceptual and P_2 on introspective reports. Our concrete reports are justifiable in terms of these principles, and even these principles are not self-justificatory but are justified by their coherence with other elements in the conceptual framework and by the relative adequacy of the framework itself. It must be noted that although these principles together with the *ceteris paribus* clauses that are also part of the conceptual framework function in the justification of our concrete beliefs, they are not premises from which these beliefs are inferred in concrete contexts (cf. GEC, 621-24).

Sellars summarizes all these points with reference to the original perceptual example of the red apple.

> Jones sees there to be a red apple in front of him. As we have explained, given that Jones has learned how to use the relevant words in perceptual situations, he is justified in reasoning as follows:
>
>> I just thought-out-loud 'Lo! Here is a red apple;
>> (no countervailing conditions obtain);
>> So, there is good reason to believe that there is a red apple in front of me.
>
> Of course, the conclusion of this reasoning is not the *thinking* in his original perceptual experience. Like all justification arguments, it is a higher order thinking. He did not originally *infer* that there is a red apple in front of him. Now, however, he is inferring from the character and context of his experience that it is veridical and that there is good reason to believe that there is indeed a red apple in front of him.
>
> Notice that although the justification of the belief that there is a red apple in front of (Jones) is an inferential justification, it has the peculiar character that its essential premise asserts the occurrence of the very same belief in a specific context. It is this fact which gives the appearance that such beliefs are *self*-justifying and hence gives the justification the appearance of being non-inferential. (SK, 341-42.)

Hence, these perceptual beliefs are noninferential and only appear to be self-justifying, while their justification is ultimately inferential and only appears not to be so. Although this particular example bears specifically on perceptual beliefs, Sellars maintains that the same kind of analysis can account not only for our noninferential knowledge of our mental states but even for the epistemic authority of our memory beliefs (cf. SK, 345).

The overall account of justification, then, is an interesting amalgam of both foundationalist and coherentist strains. Its structure can be characterized in this way; given our ordinary conceptual framework, there are basic beliefs both of a perceptual and of an introspective kind that are noninferential in form and that are warranted in specific concrete circumstances. Although noninferential, they are not self-warranting or self-justifying, for their justification is proximately a matter of their being licensed by certain constitutive principles of our conceptual framework and ultimately a matter of the acceptability of the framework as a whole. Sellars sees this account as "reconciling the claims of those who stress warrantedness grounded on explanatory coherence with the claims of those who stress the non-inferential warrantedness of certain empirical statements.'' (GEC, 621.)[10]

Against this background Sellars' classic summary of his own position becomes readily intelligible.

> If I reject the framework of traditional empiricism, it is not because I want to say that empirical knowledge has *no* foundation. For to put it this way is to suggest that it is really 'empirical knowledge so-called', and to be put in a box with rumours and hoaxes. There is clearly *some* point to the picture of knowledge as resting on a level of propositions—observation reports—which do not rest on other propositions in the same way as other propositions rest on them. On the other hand, I do wish to insist that the metaphor of 'foundation' is misleading in that it keeps us from seeing that if there is a logical dimension in which other empirical propositions rest on observation reports, there is another logical dimension in which the latter rest on the former.
>
> *Above all,* the picture is misleading because of its static character. One seems forced to choose between the picture of an elephant which rests on a tortoise (what supports the tortoise?) and the picture of a great Hegelian serpent of knowledge with its tail in its mouth (where does it begin?). Neither will do. For empirical knowledge like its sophisticated extension, science, is rational not because it has a *foundation* but because it is a self-correcting enterprise which can put *any* claim in jeopardy, though not *all* at once. (EPM, 170.)

There is, then, a point to the concerns of both the foundationalist and the coherentist, but each loses sight of what is legitimate in the other's position. Even more importantly, however, both factions share an impoverished picture of knowledge as an abstract structure existing in the instantaneous present rather than seeing knowledge as concretely embedded in an ongoing temporal process of inquiry. Only the latter perspective provides sufficient scope for a full understanding of human understanding.

(c)   Truth.

Sellars' account of justification traded heavily on the notion of 'reasonable' or 'reliable' belief, where this notion was understood in terms of 'likely to be true'. His account, then, is essentially incomplete without a full discussion of the concept of truth. Whereas Sellars' views on meaning were seen to be in the coherentist tradition and his views on justification to be an amalgam of the two traditions, his views on truth (inasmuch as he does see 'correspondence' as playing a central role) adhere more closely to the foundationalist perspective. But the way in which correspondence is involved in truth is much more complicated than most correspondence-theorists think.

Any account of truth must carefully distinguish the issues directly bearing on the *meaning* of truth from those other issues that bear on truth's *properties* or truth's *criteria*. Sellars is careful to do just that in ascribing to a semantical account of truth's definition but to a much more diversified account of truth's properties and criteria. Since he does accept a semantical account of truth's meaning it is important to note that he sees this account as *general* in that it ranges over empirical, mathematical, and moral truths, and as *neutral* with regard to the real controversy between the adherents of correspondence, coherence, and pragmatic theories. This does *not* mean that he thinks that there are no real differences among kinds of truths and no real issues at stake in these philosophical disputes but rather that these difficulties and issues have to be properly situated in domains other than that of truth's definition.

What, then, does it mean to say that a given proposition is true? At first blush it would seem that a semantic theory is a dead end inasmuch as it bears on linguistic rather than conceptual entities, and it is to the latter that 'true' and 'false' primarily apply. The general response would be that we have only to acquiesce in Sellars' account of conceptual items as methodologically parasitic on linguistic ones to share his confidence that by focusing on the semantic theory as it bears on overt discourse we can get an account of the meaning of truth that can be extended to acts of thought and what is thought in those acts (cf. TC, 200). However, something more specific must be added because the fact that any linguistic approach to this issue seems committed quite counterintuitively to rendering the concept of truth language-relative from the very beginning would seem to be a sufficient indictment of such an approach. Sellars avoids this objection by invoking the previously introduced notion of linguistic type (via the dot-quote convention) to capture what is sound in the thesis that the truth of statements in a language is to be defined in terms of the truth of propositions without compromising the methodological priority of the linguistic approach (cf. NI, 313-17).

Sellars, then, gives a semantic account of the meaning of truth.

'True' then means *semantically* assertible (S-assertible) and the varieties of truth correspond to the varieties of semantical rule.

From this point of view

the •snow is white• is true

has the sense of

the •snow is white• is S-assertible;

and the implication

that snow is white is true → snow is white

is not an element of an *extensional* definition of 'true', a recursive listing of truth conditions, as, in effect it is on Carnap's account, but is rather a consequence of the above *intensional* definition of 'true', in the sense that the assertion of the right hand side of the implication statement is a *performance of the kind authorized by the truth statement on the left. (SM*, 101.)

There are several points to note in this account. In the first place, this definition satisfies the classical standard inasmuch as it yields Tarski-equivalences as its consequences. Secondly, although there may be some point to categorizing it as an "inference ticket" account of truth, one must be careful to distinguish the inference pattern

the •snow is white• is true,
so, snow is white

from the radically different inference represented by the following sequence:

If it is day, it is light;
it is day;
so, it is light.

The difference is that in the latter case 'it is light' is warranted by a leading principle (*modus ponens*) that does not occur *in the sequence,* whereas in the former 'truth inference' the premise is a statement which *of itself* authorizes the consequence (cf. *SM*, 102). Thirdly, although this is similar to the 'warranted-assertability' theory of truth, Sellars cautions us that the difference is all-important if we are to avoid the confusion of truth with probability (cf. NI, 318). Fourthly, it is important to be clear about the fact that this is an account of *what 'truth' means* and thus that "*all* true statements of whatever kind are true in the same sense of true." (TC, 223.)

This explication of truth as S-assertability inevitably raises the question, "assertability by whom"? By answering this question, we can get clear about two other notions that are in the neighborhood. The principal answer is—"by *us*"; *truth simpliciter* is a matter of S-assertability in *our* conceptual framework. This construal of truth simpliciter suggests two other notions. We have already alluded to the fact that there is a weaker notion, which we will call *relative truth*, i.e., a true sentence in L, that is to be explicated in terms of truth simpliciter according to the schema

'. . .' (in L) is true ↔ '. . .'s (in L) are •. . .•s, and •. . .•s are true.

Truth simpliciter, of course, is relative in its own way inasmuch as the above schema made explicit becomes

'. . .' (in L) is true ↔ '. . .'s (in L) are •. . .•s, and •. . .•s are S-assertible propositions belonging to our conceptual structure.

Given this, we need only reflect on the fact of conceptual change and on our concern to know *the* truth at least in the factual domain to come up with a definition of *ideal truth* in terms of S-assertability in an ideally adequate conceptual framework (cf. *SM,* 131-34).

In addition to this generic definition of truth and the related notions of relative and ideal truth, there are the specific notions of mathematical truth, moral truth, and factual truth. Each of these specific kinds of truth has its own distinctive *properties* that enter into each specific concept. Mathematical truth involves the notions of coherence and provability, while the properties of moral truth have always been subject to philosophical debate (Sellars himself taking the view that they really are the extensions of matter-of-factual truths into the domain of intentions and purposes). But, following Sellars, I will focus attention on factual truth because it is with regard to the issue of the specific properties of factual truth that the notion of *correspondence* significantly appears in Sellars' account.

Given his semantic theory of truth, the objection that, whatever its merits, it is inadequate to handle the notion of factual truth has a certain initial plausibility. For the point of factual propositions is to disclose the makeup of the world and the semantic theory makes truth simply a linguistic matter. Just as meaning only apparently involved a word-world relation but was really nonrelational, so also truth only apparently involves a word-world relation but is really nonrelational. Since neither meaning nor truth is defined in terms of a real relation between language and an independent world, we seem condemned to the coherentist account of a linguistic idealism that, whatever be its adequacy for mathematics and morals, is clearly inadequate to the notion of factual truth.[11]

At this point Sellars has recourse to the notion of *picturing.* Picturing as a property of factual truth *is* a real relation between linguistic items and the world and as such enables Sellars to escape linguistic idealism by providing him with an Archimedean point outside not only our present conceptual system but even the whole series of conceptual systems in terms of which to define the limit to which members of this series converge.

Accepting the view that different kinds of statements have different roles, to the question—"What is the basic job of factual statements?" Sellars maintains: "The answer is, in essence, that of the *Tractatus* (i.e., to compete for places in a picture of how things are, in accordance with a complex manner of projection)." (NI, 318.) The S-assertability of matter-of-factual propositions is a matter of their being candidates for correct pictures of the world.

Since picturing is a relation between linguistic items and nonlinguistic ones, it is important to get clear about the status of this relation.

A statement to the effect that a linguistic item pictures a non-linguistic item by virtue of the semantic uniformities characteristic of a certain conceptual structure is, in an important sense, an object language statement, for even though it mentions linguistic objects, it treats them as items in the order of causes and effects, i.e., *in rerum natura,* and speaks directly of their functioning in this order in a way which is to be sharply contrasted with the metalinguistic statements of logical semantics, in which the key role is played by abstract singular terms. Thus, it is essential to note that whereas in

'a' (in L) denotes O

the 'o' in the right hand side is a meta-linguistic expression, in

'a's (in L) represent O

it is not. (*SM*, 137.)

The point here is that the relation between a conceptual picture and the object it pictures is a factual relation between two objects in the world, i.e., between natural-linguistic objects and those nonlinguistic objects that the former qua semantical items are about. Picturing is a complex matter-of-factual relation between objects and must be carefully distinguished from the pseudo-relations of meaning, denotation, and truth.

Some specification must be introduced. It is not all factual truths that picture but a specifiable subset of these. In the first place, Sellars is talking about *first-level* matter-of-factual discourse because he construes lawlike statements as material rules of inference. Secondly, it is *atomic* rather than molecular first-level matter-of-factual statements that make up these pictures of the world. Molecular statements have their own specific way of being S-assertible, i.e., they pick out sets of pictures and are true if the set includes the correct picture and false if it does not. More specifically, then, Sellars' position is that "the fundamental job of singular first level matter-of-factual statements is to picture, and hence the fundamental job of referring expressions is to be correlated *as simple linguistic objects* by matter-of-factual relations with single non-linguistic objects." (*SM*, 124.) It is most important to note, moreover, that picturing is not restricted to 'descriptive' as opposed to theoretical statements. If we are to avoid instrumentalism in science, singular theoretical statements just as much as what we ordinarily call singular descriptive statements are to be seen as candidates for places in the ultimately correct picture of how things are (cf. SRI, 369).[12]

Much more needs to be said about this relation of picturing and its role in Sellars' full account of truth. In the first place, pictures can be correct or incorrect.

Pictures like maps can be more or less adequate. The adequacy concerns the 'method of projection'. A picture (candidate) subject to the rules of a given method of projection (conceptual framework), which is a correct picture (successful candidate), is S-assertible with respect to that method of projection. (*SM*, 135.)

Although the concept of a first-level matter-of-factual truth is not identical with that of a correct picture (because the former is a matter of the correctness of an assertion, whereas the latter is a matter of the correctness of projection), there is an obvious tie between the truth of first-level matter-of-factual statements and the correctness of the pictures involved. It is important to get clear about the nature of this tie.

Sellars is quite explicit about the relation between the two concepts.

> Linguistic picture-making is not the performance of asserting matter-of-factual propositions. The *criterion* of the correctness of the performance of asserting a basic matter-of-factual proposition is the correctness of the proposition *qua* picture, i.e., the fact that it coincides with the picture the world-cum-language would generate in accordance with the uniformities controlled by the semantical rules of the language. Thus, the *correctness* of the picture is not defined in terms of the *correctness* of a performance but vice versa. (*SM*, 136.)

Picturing, then, enters into the *specific* definition of matter-of-factual truth and is in some sense a criterion thereof. Before we broach the issue of the sense in which it is a criterion, we need to get a little clearer about this relation of picturing itself.

As an approach to the question of the sense in which linguistic pictures can be correct or incorrect, it may prove helpful to reflect on the simpler cases of geometrical projection, mapping, and computer scanning. The sense in which one geometrical figure is a correct projection of another is rather straightforward, and cartographical correctness simply involves a more complicated form of spacial projection. In both cases the rules of projection that determine correctness are commonly understood. The example of the robot is closer to home. We can imagine a robot so wired as to emit rays that are reflected back to it in ways that project the structure of its environment on its tapes. The input registers on both spatial and temporal axes, and the information is duly recorded. In this case, "it makes perfectly good sense to say that as the robot moves around the world the record on the tape contains an ever more complete and perfect map of its environment; in other words, the robot comes to contain an increasingly adequate and detailed *picture* of its environment in a sense of 'picture' which is to be explicated in terms of the logic of relations." (BBK, 53.) The robot contains a picture of the world in the sense that there is a real isomorphism between the patterns on the tape and the structure of its environment. The rules of projection in this case are understood in terms of the natural laws that, in conjunction with the wiring diagram of the robot, govern the imprinting of the patterns on the tape.

Sellars feels that the notion of a 'linguistic picture' can be understood along the same lines. He focuses on elementary statements spontaneously thought-out-loud in an attempt "to see whether, on certain idealized assumptions, a mode of picturing can be defined with respect to overt discourse that might be extended to acts of thought in their character as analogous to statements in overt discourse." (TC, 216.) To begin he returns to the Tractarian setting.

> The natural-linguistic objects which, by virtue of standing in certain matter-of-factual relationships to one another and to their non-linguistic objects, constitute a picture of them in the desired sense, are the linguistic counterparts of non-linguistic *objects* (*not* facts), and it is not too misleading to speak of them as names. . . .
>
> Let me emphasize, however, that in my account the *manner* in which the names occur in the 'picture' is not a conventional symbol for the *manner* in which objects occur in the world, limited only by the abstract condition that the picture of an n-adic fact be itself an n-adic fact. Rather, as I see it, the manner in which the names occur in the picture is a projection, in accordance with a fantastically complex system of rules of projection, of the manner in which the objects occur in the world. (TC, 215.)

So, Sellars adopts the Tractarian view that it is configurations of names that picture configurations of objects, but instead of the simple condition that the picture of an n-adic fact be itself an n-adic fact, he adopts a more complex condition to the effect that "(natural linguistic objects) O_1', O_2' . . . O_n' make up a picture of (objects) O_1, O_2, . . . O_n by virtue of such and such facts about O_1', O_2' . . . O_n'." (TC, 215.)

Now there are important differences between our case and that of the robot. In the case of the robot, the isomorphism is between its 'inner patterning' and the patterns of objects in the world. But in our own case, we do not have access to this inner patterning (thoughts) except through overt discourse, so picturing must be primarily approached in terms of an isomorphism between items in overt discourse and the objects that they are about. Secondly, in contrast to the robot case, there is considerable unclarity about the sense in which linguistic pictures are brought about by the objects pictured. In the case of the robot, the bringing about is mechanical, but in the linguistic case, the bringing about of the uniformities is a much more complicated matter, involving rules of criticism as they bear on language-entry transitions, interlinguistic moves, and language-exit transitions. The rules of projection that generate the isomorphisms between verbal responses and objects in the world involve the mediation of a complex process of training.

Sellars attempts one final modeling of this picturing relation in terms of a superinscriber who speaks by inscribing statements in wax. Let us suppose that he has a system of coordinates metrically organized in terms of steps (spatial grid) and heartbeats (temporal grid) and that he uses a coordinate language in which names are ordered sets of numerals (three for space; one for time) that are assigned to events on the basis of measurement. The superinscriber can then go from a this-here-now statement to one in which the events in question are referred to by a coordinate name, and these inscriptions will reflect in their multiplicity the multiplicity of heartbeats and steps that separate the events that are known to be referred to by the inscriptions (cf. TC, 219-21).[13] While this model is complicated, it is still far less complicated than the real case Sellars is trying to elucidate. But whatever the complications of the actual process, to the degree that the model of the robot and the superinscriber are at all appropriate, Sellars feels that in a general way he has indicated "how a structure of natural-linguistic objects might correspond by virtue of certain 'rules of projection' to a structure of nonlinguistic objects." (TC, 222.) This is the salvageable core of the correspondence theory of truth.

It is significant to note that "to say that a linguistic object *correctly* pictures a nonlinguistic object in the manner described above is not to say that the linguistic object is *true*, save in that metaphorical sense of 'true' in which one geometrical figure is said to be a true 'projection' of another if it is drawn by correctly following the appropriate method of projection." (TC, 222.) The truth of any assertion is still a matter of what is licensed by the semantical rules of a given conceptual system, but the adequacy of this overall conceptual system is a matter of the correctness as pictures of the singular first-level matter-of-factual statements it licenses.

This brings us finally to the central *role* of picturing in Sellars' account of truth. He refers to the correctness of the proposition qua picture as the *criterion* of the correctness of the performance of asserting singular matter-of-factual propositions. By this, Sellars does not mean that it is by noticing the correctness or incorrectness of the picturing relation that we can judge as to the truth or falsity of the proposition but only that the correctness or incorrectness of the picturing is the *defining condition* of the truth or falsity of singular first-level matter-of-factual propositions and of the conceptual system that licenses them. The correctness of the performance can be defined in terms of the correctness of the picturing. Moreover, even though it cannot function as a manifest criterion, the concept of picturing is far from idle in Sellars' account. On the contrary, the picturing relation is of crucial importance for him because it is in terms of it that he can give content to and thereby render intelligible the notion of *degrees of adequacy of conceptual frameworks* and the limit notion of *ideal truth*.

Since the truth of a given assertion is something that is determined from within a conceptual framework by reference to its system of semantical rules, we seem forced to choose between the view that there is but one conceptual framework and the view that truth is totally relative. Sellars maintains that this is a false dichotomy and that by recourse to the role of picturing in his account he can render intelligible the claim that "one conceptual framework can be more adequate than another" and then show how "this fact can be used to define a sense in which one proposition can be said to be 'more true' than another." (*SM*, 134.)[14]

'Degrees of truth', then, are a function of 'degrees of adequacy', and we can get a handle on this latter notion by viewing our conceptual structure as but one stage in an evolving series of conceptual frameworks that are, with respect to the pictures they generate, increasingly adequate. We can view our propositional claims as "truer" than their counterparts in less adequate conceptual frameworks and "less true" than some of their potential successors. We can even go on to conceive of a conceptual framework that enables us to form ideally adequate pictures of objects; this limit conceptual framework Sellars refers to as "Peirceish" or CSP (conceptual structure Peirceish).

The crucial point for Sellars is his contention that it is only in terms of picturing that content can be given to the 'degrees of adequacy' and the 'regulative ideal' invoked above. Picturing is the "missing ingredient the absence of which from Peirce's account of truth leaves the 'would-be' of the acceptance 'in the long run' of propositions by the scientific community without an intelligible foundation." (*SM*, vii.) Peirce's own account is seen to be at best metaphorical because "by not taking into account the dimension of 'picturing', he had no Archimedean point outside the series of actual and possible beliefs in terms of which to define the ideal limit to which members of this series might approximate." (*SM*, 142.) Sellars has such an Archimedean point that, although it cannot provide us with a decision procedure, can give content to the notion of a progressive series.

There is one final objection to this account. How can we even speak of objects that are either less, more, or even ideally pictured by the elementary statements in a series of conceptual frameworks, since the very meaning of concepts that determine objects is a framework issue? How can we talk of transframework objects? Sellars provides a very general answer to this crucial objection.

> The purely formal aspects of logical syntax, when they have been correctly disentangled, give us a way of speaking which abstracts from those features which differentiate specific conceptual structures, and enables us to form a concept of a domain of objects which are pictured in one way (less adequate) by one linguistic system, and in another way (more adequately) by another. And we can conceive of the former (or less adequate) linguistic system as our current linguistic system. (*SM*, 139-40.)[15]

Since meaning is a matter of linguistic role, Sellars maintains that we can identify similar roles across conceptual frameworks by attending to the purely formal aspects of logical syntax. In this way we can isolate counterpart concepts and thus talk meaningfully of conceptual development and the progress toward truth.

This concludes the treatment of Sellars' theory of knowledge. The overall account can be viewed as an attempt to provide an alternative to the dominant pictures of knowledge, i.e., the picture of an elephant resting on a tortoise and the picture of a serpent with its tail in its mouth. He has clearly sketched a real alternative. It remains to be seen whether or not it is the account that would be chosen in the long run.

NOTES

[1] Several of the introductory paragraphs of this essay are drawn from my earlier paper, "Foundations of Empirical Knowledge—Again," *New Scholasticism* 50 (1976): 1-19. Although the positive views expressed in that paper are in several important respects quite different from those of Sellars, it is that case that both epistemological positions occupy a similar position between the foundationalist and the coherentist pictures of knowledge.

[2] Sellars' strategy here can be considerably illuminated by viewing it in the light of his father's (Roy Wood Sellars) much earlier attempt to articulate a 'direct though mediated' theory of knowledge as a mean between the completely unmediated accounts put forward by the New Realists and the inferential accounts of those he referred to as the representational wing of the Critical Realists. For an account of Roy Wood Sellars' position, see my *Mind and Nature: A Study of the Naturalistic Philosophies of Cohen, Woodbrige and Sellars* (Notre Dame: University of Notre Dame Press, 1969), pp. 156-66.

[3] Roderick Firth has argued that although our ordinary concept of 'looks red' is parasitic on the concept 'is red', nevertheless, there is a more primitive form of the concept of 'looks red' that is logically prior to 'is red' (in the sense that no contrast is involved), and it is this primitive concept that the language-learning child expressed by 'red'. Moreover, Firth argues, there is no need to suppose that the child loses this concept when he acquires the mature notion of 'looks red', and thus the primitive notion is still available for epistemological purposes. For Sellars' discussion of this "ur-concept of 'looks red' " see his GEC, 614.

[4] In the latter paper, Sellars responds to a series of criticisms of transcategorial analogies put forward by Bruce Aune.

[5] This myth occupies a central place in Sellars' theory of knowledge, and its precise methodological role is far from simple. Its primary point is not historical but conceptual, but the conceptual point it makes is such that it does have historical implications. Part of the import of this story of the development of our knowledge of our mental states is to exclude as unintelligible other stories that might be told. And the story it tells is not simply a matter of unrecoverable history, for it is one which is recapitulated wherever children mature into rational adults.

[6]Sellars gives a more detailed account of the kind of conditioning involved in acquiring the ability to use the language of thoughts in a reporting capacity in his unpublished correspondence with Hector Castañeda.

The important thing to note is that the core of Dick's learning to report what he is thinking is a matter of his acquiring a tendency (ceteris paribus) to respond to his thoughts that-p by saying 'I am thinking that-p'. Everything hinges on the force of the word 'respond' in this connection. It is being used as a technical term borrowed from learning theory. The following diagram will help clarify matters—

$$M\theta_i \cdot \rightarrow \cdot MV_i$$
$$\theta_i \uparrow$$

where θ_i is a thought that-p, $M\theta_i$ is a meta-thought •I am thinking that-p• and MV_i is a meta-statement 'I am thinking that-p.'

The connection between θ_i and $M\theta_i$ is *in the first instance* a *conditioning* and not an *inference*. As such it presupposes neither an awareness on Dick's part that he is thinking that-p nor any recognition on Dick's part that the circumstances are such as would usually involve his thinking that-p. It requires only that the reinforcer (applauder), in this case Jones, correctly infers that Dick is thinking that-p and, given that Dick *happens* to say 'I am thinking that-p', applauds. Needless to say, Dick will be most unlikely simply to *happen* to say 'I am thinking that-p'. He can be led to say it, for example, by asking him 'What are you thinking?' (remember that Dick knows the theory). But we need not suppose that he painstakingly argues to the conclusion 'I am thinking that-p'. All we need suppose is that circumstances can be arranged which bring about the joint occurrence of a thought that-p and a saying of 'I am thinking that-p' with sufficient frequency for conditioning by reward (applause) to occur. Thus the decisive feature is that the connection between θ_i and ($M\theta_i \rightarrow MV_i$) is a direct nonrational S-R connection. Certainly this S-R connection exists within a rich conceptual context, but unless it existed as an S-R connection there could be no direct non-inferential self-knowledge. (*Correspondence between Hector Castañeda and Wilfrid Sellars on Philosophy of Mind,* unpublished manuscript, 1961-1962, p. 5.)

[7]I will concentrate on Sellars' account of 'means' or 'stands for', but it should be pointed out that he has an account of 'denotes' that is in the same spirit. The difference between ' ". . ." (in L) stands for ____' and ' ". . ." (in L) denotes ____' is not a matter of what goes on the right hand side of the schema, for in each case it is an expression for a sense; neither case is to be construed as (linguistic) R (nonlinguistic). Rather the difference is in the diluted character of 'denotes' as contrasted with 'stands for', i.e., 'denotes' invokes a weaker sense of 'plays the same role as'. More specifically, 'Plato (in E) denotes the teacher of Aristotle' is to be parsed as "for some S, 'Plato' (in E) stands for S, and S is materially equivalent to •the teacher of Aristotle•." Cf. *SM,* 84-86.

[8]For a full account of the convention of dot-quotation, see Michael Loux's study on the ontology of Wilfrid Sellars in this volume.

[9]For a more detailed discussion of the manner in which perceptual reports acquire epistemic authority, see EPM, 167-69.

[10]Inasmuch as he accepts the distinction between basic and derived propositions but sets it against the background of an overall coherentist account, Sellars views his position as assimilating much of what is sound in the analyses of Firth and Chisholm into a more comprehensive framework.

[11]It is important to note here the consistency in Sellars' analyses of meaning, denotation, and truth. The 'means', 'stands-for', and 'corresponds-to' rubrics

do not specify word-world relations but rather interlinguistic classifications. On this point, see his TTC, 334-36.

[12]This point is discussed in some detail in Gary Gutting's paper on Sellars' philosophy of science in this volume.

[13]Sellars goes into much more detail about assumptions that would have to be made to render this example intelligible.

[14]Distinguishing between the conceptual structure to which a proposition belongs and the conceptual structure with respect to which its truth is defined, Sellars introduces some further notions. First, he defines a sense in which a proposition in our current conceptual structure (CSO) can be said to be true quoad an earlier conceptual structure (CS_1), i.e., the notion of 'true quoad CS_1' as distinguished from the notion 'true in CS_1'. Secondly, he defines a sense in which a proposition in our (or any) conceptual structure can be said to be true quoad an ideally adequate conceptual structure (CSP), i.e., the notion 'true quoad CSP' as distinguished from the notion 'true in CSP'. Cf. *SM*, 134, 141.

[15]Sellars does develop this suggestion in a little more detail:

Are the individual variables we use tied exclusively to the individual senses of our current conceptual structure? Are the predicate variables we use tied exclusively to our conceptual resources? It is obvious that the only *cash* we have for these variables is to be found in our current conceptual structure, but it is a mistake to think that the substituends for a variable are limited to the constants which are here-now-possessions of an instantaneous cross-section of language users. The identity of a language through time must be taken seriously, and a distinction drawn between the *logical* or 'formal' criteria of individuality which apply to any descriptive conceptual framework, and the more specific (material) criteria in terms of which individuals are identified in specific conceptual frameworks; and similarly, between the logical criteria which differentiate, say, n-adic from m-adic predicates generally, from the conceptual criteria (material rules) which give distinctive conceptual content to predicates which have the same purely logical status. (*SM*, 139-40.)

Ontology

Michael J. Loux

As philosophers, we are frequently confronted with forms of discourse whose legitimacy appears to demand the existence of objects we are reluctant to postulate. It is, for example, tempting to think that the attribution of moral responsibility presupposes the existence of uncaused events; but the notion of an uncaused event, if not incoherent, is puzzling. Again, we are inclined to think that the possibility of distinguishing, as we do, between lawlike and merely casual regularities requires the assumption of necessary connections; but when we examine the events exhibiting lawlike regularities, the necessity escapes us. In these and countless other such cases, unexceptionable ways of talking seemingly presuppose the existence of objects with extraordinary properties. These properties arouse our philosophical suspicions and give rise to a familiar tension. On the one hand we are reluctant to postulate extraordinary objects; but, on the other, we want to preserve the legitimacy of talking and thinking as we do.

This tension is a familiar theme in the writings of Wilfred Sellars; and wherever it appears, Sellars is anxious to reconcile the opposing forces behind the tension. The drive to keep ontological presuppositions to a minimum, he insists, is perfectly compatible with the attempt to defend the integrity of our conceptual scheme. Nowhere is Sellars' methodological compatabilism more apparent than in his work on the problems of ontology. The basic assumption underlying this work is the view that while the nominalist is right in eschewing abstract entities, the Platonist is right in pointing to the indispensability of talk involving concepts like meaning and exemplification and the apparatus of higher-order quantification. Taken collectively, his writings in this area represent the attempt to show how the forms of discourse that have proved central in the

43

realism-nominalism debate are susceptible of an analysis that demonstrates at once their conceptual autonomy and ontological neutrality. In this paper, I want to examine the strategy Sellars employs in executing this project. The paper divides into three parts. In the first section, I examine Sellars' treatment of abstract singular terms; in the second, his analysis of predication; and in the third, his theories of quantification and existence.

<h1 style="text-align:center">I</h1>

The issue of abstract singular terms has always been pivotal in discussions of ontological issues; for prima facie terms like 'triangularity' and 'wisdom' signify abstract entities; but since they have what appear to be essential (i.e., noneliminable) occurrences in true propositions, they seem to commit us to a Platonic ontology. We say, for example, that wisdom is exemplified by Socrates and that triangularity is a shape; and in both cases, it is only natural to assume that we are talking about things quite different from the concrete objects we meet in sense experience. Although there have been philosophers who have simply denied that sentences such as these can ever be true,[1] most nominalists have granted the legitimacy of employing abstract singular terms. They have argued, however, that the surface structure of sentences incorporating abstract singulars is misleading. While they appear to involve a reference to abstract entities, sentences like "Triangularity is a shape" are said to give way, under philosophical ellucidation, to sentences that involve no commitment to peculiar kinds of objects. The general claim here has been that contexts involving an abstract singular term are replaceable, without loss of content, by contexts involving the concrete counterpart of the problematic form. Thus, sentences incorporating the term 'triangularity' give way, under analysis, to sentences incorporating the nonproblematic 'triangular', sentences incorporating the term 'wisdom' to sentences incorporating the term 'wise', and so on.

Now, Sellars wants to claim that this sort of approach is on the right track. What we accomplish by the use of abstract terms we could just as well accomplish by the use of concrete expressions. Nonetheless, he maintains that the approach goes wrong in supposing that one is to analyze an abstract expression in terms of *its own concrete counterpart*. Traditionally, nominalists have worked on the assumption that abstract terms fall within the object language; and, consequently, they have claimed that talk about things like triangularity and wisdom is just a short-hand way of making claims about objects that are triangular and wise. Sellars, however, contends that the use of abstract singular terms is metalinguistic; but he wants to deny that the metalinguistic force of abstract singular terms is that exhibited by the straightforward formal mode utterances philosophers are accustomed to. To bring out the peculiar way in which the use of abstract terms involves talk about language, Sellars develops the notion of a *linguistic type*.[2]

Given the complexity of the notion, the concept of a linguistic type must be approached in stages. We can make a first step toward grasping the notion if we reflect on the fact that different languages incorporate expressions that come to much the same point. Thus, the English word 'man' has its parallel in the French 'homme', the German 'Mensch', the Italian 'uomo', and the Spanish 'hombre'. Stated very roughly, the moves which the relevant languages permit us to make with these terms are quite similar. The words have, for example, the same force in inferential contexts and can be employed in much the same way in linguistic responses to the perceptual environment. Reflecting on these facts, we are tempted to say that these terms are all subject to one and the same set of rules, that they all play one and the same linguistic role.[3]

Now, we can imagine an individual who, impressed by these considerations, proposes a convention according to which we can refer to 'man's, 'homme's, 'hombre's, and all other expressions exhibiting the linguistic role in question without going through the tedious business of listing examples from the various historical languages. The convention he proposes involves extending the normal convention for quoting in such a way that a quoted term can apply across language barriers. The application of the quoting device to a term X typically has the effect of creating a new term, a metalinguistic term, which applies to only expressions within the base language (the language in which we are quoting) and among these expressions only to tokens of the expression to which quotation has been applied. According to the proposed extension of the convention, quoting would create metalinguistic terms that apply outside as well as within the base language so that a quoted term would apply to all expressions that, in their own languages, play the same linguistic role that the quoted term plays in the base language. Thus, our innovator would have us apply quotation to the English word 'man' to create a term, specifically a common nounn by means of which we can refer to all those expressions in historically different languages that play the role played in English by 'man'. Since the extended use of quotation would form common nouns, 'man' (in its new use) would admit the plural as well as the definite article. We can imagine our innovator exploiting these features of quoted terms in summarizing the implications of his convention. He would say that the French 'homme', the Spanish 'hombre', and the German 'Mensch' are all 'man's, that they all exhibit the 'man'. Putting a label on this interlinguistic expression, he might say that all these terms are materially different embodiments of one and the same linguistic type, the 'man'.

We can clarify the nature of this innovation if we reflect on Sellars' revealing account of Tess.[4] Sellars has us imagine that Texans play a game involving automobiles and counties, a game they call Tess. Now, we who play chess watch the Texans as they are engaged in Tess; and we are surprised to see how Tess has its parallels in our chess. These parallels, we soon note, pervade the whole structure of the game; and this leads us to conclude that Tess and chess can be construed not just as two different games with important similarities but as materially different ways of playing one and the same game. Having concluded this, we might decide to call Volkswagens qua functioning in Tess pawns, Rolls Royces qua functioning in Tess kings, and so forth. The effect of such a move would be an extension of the terms 'pawn', 'king', and so forth. Originally, we who play ordinary chess limited our use of the term 'pawn', for example, to objects of the familiar size and shape; but in extending the term to Volkswagens as they function in Tess, the material requirements for pawns become less exacting, less determinate. The decisive criteria for being a pawn now hinge on whether or not the object satisfies certainly abstractly formulated rules for moving pieces in a game.

In the same way, according to the preinnovative or ordinary use of quotation, the material requirements for being a 'man' were fairly detailed. An object had to be of a certain fairly determinate auditory or visual shape: it had to sound such and such or look such and such. But with the extension of the quoting device, the material requirements for being a 'man' become less determinate. Objects with a very different sound and look ('Mensch' and 'homme') are now to count as 'man's. Given the extension of quotation, the decisive criteria for being a 'man' now turn only on the linguistic role of an expression. As long as it plays the relevant role, it is a 'man'; its matter does not matter.

Now, we can imagine our innovator foreseeing the possible confusions his extension of quotation would occasion. Confronted with a use of 'man', people might wonder whether the term was functioning in the preinnovative or postinnovative fashion. In an attempt to forestall such confusions, our innovator might suggest that we reserve the apparatus of quotes for preinnovative quotation and that we employ a different set of markers, say dots, to signal the interlinguistic flavor of postinnovative quotation. Thus, whereas 'man' would apply only to English terms of the same design as the quoted term, •man• would be a common noun true of 'homme's, 'Mensch's, and, generally, all terms exhibiting the linguistic type, the 'man'. Nor would the need for this sort of move destroy the parallel with Tess; for in the same way, we could (and probably would) decide to forestall confusions by reserving the term 'pawn' for pawns in ordinary chess and coin a new word, say 'prawn', to apply to both pawns in chess and their counterparts in Tess.

I have spoken of the quotation marking the various exemplars of a linguistic type as a possible innovation. The suggestion has been that we are still awaiting the incorporation of a device to this effect into our conceptual scheme. The central theme of Sellars' ontology is that the sort of interlinguistic reference outlined above already is an essential ingredient in our conceptual scheme. Although their surface grammar suggests something quite different, abstract singular terms are devices for marking linguistic types; and although the use of dot quotation is not, as such, a fully articulated convention, Sellars contends that it is a fruitful device for reconstructing the depth grammar of abstract terms. Thus, while 'triangularity' appears to be an expression signifying a nonlinguistic object, it is really a device for marking the linguistic type realized by the English concrete term 'triangular', the German concrete term 'dreieckig', and so forth. Employing the dot-quoting device, we can say that 'triangularity' is equivalent to the singular term 'the •triangular•'; but, then, it becomes clear that it is only superficially that 'triangularity' is an object-language term. Under philosophical elucidation, it gives way to an expression that falls within the metalanguage of dot quotation.

But, of course, this can hardly be the end of the story; for although this account enables us to eliminate the abstract singular term 'triangularity', it saddles us with the singular term 'the •triangular•'; and, at first glance, this expression seems equally as blatant in its reference to an abstract entity. Admittedly, 'the •triangular•' does not introduce a nonlinguistic object; but my account suggests that it refers to a linguistic type and that this is an abstract entity—a universal—in its own right. As I have described them, linguistic types have different embodiments or realizations in different languages; and by any traditional criterion, that makes them universals.

Sellars' response here is that we can get below the notion of a linguistic type. We can show that interlinguistic reference and the subservient dot quotation carry no commitment to a Platonic ontology. The crucial move here is Sellars' analysis of the form exhibited by 'the •triangular•'. 'The •triangular•' appears to be a singular term referring to a one over and against a many, the one •triangular• that the many individual •triangular•s exhibit; and Sellars' talk about linguistic types only reinforces the temptation to construe a term like 'the •triangular•' in this way. Sellars wants to say, however, that talk of linguistic types is only a *façon de parler*. A term like 'the •triangular•' does not introduce numerically one thing; it is, he tells us, a *distributive singular term*.[5]

According to Sellars, a distributive singular term is an expression, typically of the form 'the K' which, while appearing to signify some one object, the K, is really just a device for referring to individual K's. Sellars' example of the distributive singular term is the expression 'the lion' as it occurs in 'The lion is tawny'. At first glance, this singular term appears to be a device for referring to a universal; but a moment's reflection shows that it cannot be playing that role. The proposition in question is true; but if 'the lion' took as its referent some universal, the proposition would be false. No universal is tawny; it is individual lions that are tawny. Thus, while 'The lion is tawny' appears to be a claim about a universal, it is really a claim about individual lions. The use of distributive singular terms is widespread; the following all incorporate expressions of this sort:

(1)   The Eskimo builds igloos.
(2)   The sea lion eats fish.
(3)   The Ferrari is a fast car.
(4)   The oak tree is deciduous.
(5)   The halfback carries on the draw play.

In all these cases, we employ the institutional 'the' to form a singular term by means of which we can refer to the individuals of some sort or kind. In general, then, where we apply the institutional 'the' to a common noun, 'K', to form a distributive singular term, contexts involving the resulting expression, 'the K', are replaceable by contexts involving the plural form of the enclosed common noun, 'K's'. Thus, 'The lion is tawny' becomes 'Lions are tawny'. The subject of the distributive singular term is hardly exhausted by these remarks. A more detailed account would focus on the fact that distributive singular terms generally mark a context where a noncontingent claim is being made as well as the fact that the shift from contexts incorporating 'the K' to contexts involving 'K's' forces modifications in the remainder of the proposition involved. But for our purposes, these points are sufficient.[6]

For our concern is to show that while terms like 'the •triangular•' appear to refer to universals, they are actually devices for referring to individual •triangular•s. Sellars' claim is that 'the •triangular•', like 'the lion', is a distributive singular term. It is an expression that enables us to make claims about the various materially different items that, in virtue of their linguistic role, qualify as •triangular•s. But which items are these? One might want to say that the relevant items are the English word 'triangular', the German word 'dreieckig', and so on. The difficulty is that words are subject to the distinction between types and tokens. To say that '•triangular•' is a common term true of the relevant types gets us no further toward eliminating the commitment to

Platonism. The English type 'triangular', for example, is instanced by its various tokens and must itself be construed as a universal. Sellars sees this point and claims that '•triangular•' is a common noun true of the different tokenings that are English 'triangular's, German 'dreieckig's, and so on. But, then, all contexts involving the singular term 'the •triangular•' can be replaced by contexts involving a common noun '•triangular•' that commit us, at most, to the existence of individual vocalizings and inscribings.

Thus, there are two stages in Sellars' analysis of abstract singular terms. In the first stage, we make explicit the interlinguistic reference at work in the abstract form. Here, we employ the singular term built by the application of the institutional 'the' to the common noun formed by dot quoting. This singular term appears to commit us to the existence of a new abstract entity; but employing the strategy of distributive singular terms, we can reduce the relevant singular terms to common nouns true only of individual linguistic tokens. Thus, in the case considered, we have the three forms:

triangularity → the •triangular• → •triangular•s

In other cases, the same general pattern emerges. Thus,

redness → the •red• → •red•s
mankind → the •man• → •man•s
that 2 + 2 = 4 → the •2 + 2 = 4• → •2 + 2 = 4•s

But while agreeing that this strategy is ingenious, we are tempted to object that it is simply wrongheaded. What reason is there to believe that talk about triangularity or mankind has anything whatever to do with talk about tokenings of •triangular•s or •man•s? If talk about triangularity or mankind is talk about objects at all, surely those objects are nonlinguistic. The only way of meeting this objection is by examining the various kinds of contexts where abstract terms occur. Sellars' claim that the use of abstract terms is implicitly metalinguistic is to be tested by its ability to shed light on the propositions in which such terms play a role.

There are a large number of contexts where abstract singular terms appear. I shall consider three such contexts. The first we can call the categorizing context. Examples are:

(1) Triangularity is a quality.
(2) Mankind is a kind.
(3) That 2 + 2 = 4 is a proposition.

On the surface, at least, (1) to (3) appear to be propositions in which we refer to an abstract entity and subsume it under a very general ontological category.

The second context I want to examine I call the exemplification context. Here, we are, to all appearances, saying that one or more individuals have, possess, exhibit, or exemplify some abstract object. Examples are:

(4) Socrates exemplifies wisdom.
(5) Socrates and Plato exhibit the relation of historical proximity.

Finally, I shall examine the use of abstract singular terms in semantic contexts, contexts where we say what a linguistic expression means or stands for. Examples:

(6) 'Rouge' stands for (expresses) redness.
(7) 'Hombre' stands for (expresses) mankind.
(8) 'Deux et deux font quatre' stands for (expresses) the proposition that two plus two equal four.

A mere rehearsal of these examples should give one pause; for while nominalists are generally willing to grant the legitimacy of employing abstract singular terms in some contexts, the examples listed above include propositions very few, if any, nominalists would be willing to grant. (1) to (8) are propositions that roll most naturally off the tongue of the realist. As I have suggested, it is characteristic of Sellars' method to insist that realism embodies important insights, insights that even a nominalistic ontology must accommodate. Indeed, Sellars would construe it as the strongest possible recommendation for his account if he can provide a natural reconstruction of the sorts of claims that make up the substance of a Platonic metaphysics. Such a reconstruction would enable us to preserve the genuine insights of the Platonic tradition without its cumbersome ontological presuppositions.

Let us begin with examples (1) to (3), propositions exhibiting what I have called the categorizing context. Very generally, Sellars wants to construe such examples as pseudomaterial mode propositions. While they appear to be cases where we are specifying the kind to which an abstract object belongs, they are actually propositions in which we characterize the grammar or syntax of interlinguistic expressions.[7] The major obstacle to such an analysis is presented by the predicates in each of our examples. Employing the pattern set out earlier, we can reduce the abstract forms in (1) to (3) to common nouns formed by dot quotations; but, then, how are we to take the term 'quality', 'kind', and 'proposition'? They appear to be expressions holding true of nonlinguistic objects so that to construe them as expressions predicable of dot-quoted expressions would seem to involve a category mistake. Sellars' response here is that these terms are the material mode counterparts of expressions specifying the various syntactical categories. As we move from the material to the formal mode, they give way to terms like 'adjective', 'common noun', and 'declarative sentence'. Thus, the examples listed above reduce as follows:

(1) Triangularity is a quality—The •triangular• is an adjective—•Triangular•s are adjectives.

(2) Mankind is a kind—The •man• is a common noun—•Man•s are common nouns.

(3) That 2 + 2 = 4 is a proposition—The •2 + 2 = 4• is a declarative sentence—•2 + 2 = 4•s are declarative sentences.

Sellars' reconstruction of exemplification talk is a bit more complicated. Let us confine ourselves to (4). (4), Sellars wants to say, is equivalent to

(4') Wisdom is true of Socrates.

Now, (4') gives the appearance of incorporating the abstract singular term 'wisdom' and suggests the sort of treatment we are, by now, accustomed to. Sellars denies, however, that 'wisdom', as it appears in (4'), is playing the role abstract terms normally play. Thus, it is not to be analyzed in terms of the concrete term '•wise•'. We have the concept of truth at work in (4'), and this notion demands something propositional as its subject. According to Sellars, this something is the propositional function 'that x is wise'. Thus, (4') gives way to

(4'') That x is wise is true of Socrates.

Now, (4'') does incorporate an abstract singular term that is susceptible of the general analysis outlined above. According to that analysis, (4'') is to be read as

(4''') The •x is wise• is true of Socrates.

But this is not the end of the story. The reference in (4''') to a propositional function suggests that 'Socrates' is not being used but mentioned. Following out this suggestion, we arrive at the final reparsing of our original (4) as

(4'''') The result of substituting a •Socrates• for an •x• in an •x is wise• is a true declarative sentence.

Talk about exemplification appears to involve the claim that two objects, one a particular and the other a universal, enter into the nexus of exemplification. What (4'''') shows is that the notion of exemplification is implicitly a metalinguistic concept that signals the possibility of sub-

stituting certain specified expressions for the free variables of propositional functions.[8]

Examples (6) to (8) are also susceptible of treatment in terms of dot
quotation. According to Sellars, when we say 'X' stands for or expresses
F-ness, we are not relating a linguistic expression to a nonlinguistic
object. We are merely classifying 'X' by specifying its linguistic role.[9]
This comes out when we employ dot quotation. Thus (6) becomes

> (6')   'Rouge' stands for (expresses) the •red•;

but when we reflect on the fact that 'rouge', like 'the •red•', is a distributive singular term (effectively, 'the "rouge" ') we see that (6') is really a
stand-in for

> (6'')   'Rouge's stand for •red•s.

(6'') retains the expression 'stands for' ('expresses'), but Sellars argues
that this expression is only superficially relational. In actual fact, it is a
disguised version of the copula 'is', so that (6'') yields

> (6''')   'Rouge's are •red•s.

Thus, to say what a term stands for or expresses is merely to classify it
functionally, to say that it is a term that plays the role of some other
term. Technical semantics aside, the typical context where this use of
language occurs is in the characterization of the meanings of words; and,
according to Sellars,

> (6)   'Rouge' stands for (expresses) redness

is logically equivalent to the more familiar

> (9)   'Rouge' means red.

To state the meaning of a word, then, is to classify it functionally.
Typically, this classification is effected indirectly. We tell someone how
a term is to be used by providing him with some other term whose use he
is presumably familiar with. The term to be explicated, we tell him, has
the same use as the familiar term. Thus, in (9), we identify the role of
'rouge', a term our audience does not understand, by exhibiting the term
'red', which it does understand. The former, we say, has the same force
as the latter. But, then, the term 'means' has the same ontological
neutrality as its more technical counterparts 'stands for' and 'expresses'. When we state the meaning of a term, we are not relating the term to
some abstract entity; we are merely characterizing the term as one that
plays the same role as some other term that our audience, in virtue of its
knowledge of the base language, already understands.

But this talk of roles is likely to make us uneasy; for the way it functions in the previous paragraph and, generally, throughout this section suggests that perhaps Sellars has not really succeeded in eliminating all abstract objects. To bring out the full force of this difficulty, we should ask how one identifies an expression that is, say, a •triangular•. The answer suggested by our account is that a term is a •triangular• if it plays in its own language the role played in our language by 'triangular'; but, then, Sellars' account eliminates one abstract term only by introducing another—the linguistic role exhibited by 'triangular'. It should be obvious that the account can eliminate this new abstract term only by introducing another and so on ad infinitum. Each application of Sellars' schema for eliminating abstract singular terms seems to leave us with one more abstract singular term to eliminate.

Sellars never confronts this issue directly, so at most I can indicate how I think he would respond here. The difficulty has its origin in the belief that the only available technique for identifying •triangular•s consists in referring to an abstract entity. Phrased in another way, the assumption is that we can specify what a •triangular• is only by employing the singular term 'the linguistic role of "triangular" '. What are we to make of this assumption? This question gives rise to another. What is involved in talking about linguistic roles? This much is clear. Philosophers introduce the notion of a linguistic role into the theory of meaning because they want to direct our attention to the various uniformities attaching to the use of a term. They want, that is, to disabuse us of the model: one word—one thing. Thus, talk of roles has point only to the extent that we can make remarks about the things one can and cannot do with the use of a term, only to the extent that it is possible to specify general rules indicating what is and what is not permitted with the term in the large variety of contexts where it can appear. But this means that the use of the singular term 'the linguistic role' is not essential in the identification of a term across languages. It is merely a short-hand technique for referring to the very complex set of rules underlying the use of the term. To specify the range of a dot-quoted term, then, we need not refer to an abstract entity.[10] What we must do is to specify the rules governing the use of a term in the base language, in this case, 'triangular'. For Sellars, to specify such meaning rules involves specifying how 'triangular' functions in (1) inferential contexts, (2) responses to perceptual situations, and (3) contexts where we move from speech to action. Now, to generate the notion of a •triangular•, we need merely generalize. Any term which, within the context of its language, functions as 'triangular' does in English is a •triangular•.[11]

Thus, no reference to abstract entities is involved in identifying a linguistic type. What is essential, however, is the reference to norms, to what we are, given the language, permitted to do with a term. It is here that Sellars thinks he differs most markedly from classical nominalists. They thought that a term like 'triangularity' is to be analyzed in terms of the concrete object-language term 'triangular'. But, according to Sellars, this is to miss the normative force implicit in 'triangularity'. Abstract singular terms signal talk of what the language allows us to do with linguistic expressions. To miss this, as classical nominalists did, is, Sellars claims, to commit a mistake analogous to the naturalistic fallacy. It is to try to derive an abstract singular term, a term with normative force, from terms (like 'triangular') that are completely lacking in such force.[12]

II

But Sellars' treatment of abstract singular terms is at most a first step toward combatting Platonism. Sellars contends that contexts incorporating abstract singular terms of the form 'F-ness' give way, under analysis, to contexts incorporating general terms of the form '•F•'. Put in another way, his analysis replaces singular terms by predicate expressions. Now, while the use of abstract singular terms has been one source of Platonism, the notion of predication has also figured prominently in the realism-nominalism debate. Philosophers from Plato onwards have contended that predicates designate or refer to universals. If Sellars' treatment of abstract singular terms meets the Platonist on one front, it merely plays into his hands on another.

Sellars' general response here is that predicates have no referential force, that they are what the medievals called *syncategorematic terms*. But if we are to see this response in its proper perspective, we must view it in terms of Sellars' criticism of opposing theories of predication. First, then, I shall discuss Sellars' treatment of Platonistic theories of predication; afterwards, I shall consider his own analysis of predicates as syncategorematic terms.

In its most extreme form, the Platonistic analysis of predication construes predicates as names of universals. Thus, we are told that 'red' designates a color and 'triangularity' a shape in precisely the way that a proper name designates its bearers. In recent years, this sort of account has been defended by Gustav Bergmann. For Bergmann, a sentence like 'This is red' contains two names, 'this' and 'red'. The name 'this' designates a particular, and the name 'red' the universal color that numerically different objects can possess or exhibit.[13]

In criticizing Bergmann, Sellars tries to show that this account of predication rests on what Wittgenstein terms a steady diet of one (here, the wrong) kind of example. Bergmann invariably takes as his examples propositions in which the predicate term is a color word. Now, color words are syntactically ambiguous; and, according to Sellars, it is precisely because he has been misled by this syntactical ambiguity that Bergmann presents the sort of account he does.[14]

The principle underlying Sellars' attack on Bergmann is the claim that a name can always be truly applied to its bearer, so that where 'N' is a name and *a* its bearer, the proposition that *a* is N is true.[15] Applying this principle to the case of predicates, Sellars argues that a predicate term 'F' cannot be truly applied to the alleged universal exhibited by all F-things. To bring this out, Sellars asks us to consider the following:

> This is triangular.

Here, there is no temptation to take 'triangular' as the name of the universal that triangular objects supposedly exhibit. The reason, of course, is that we have at our disposal the singular term 'triangularity'; and if any term names the relevant universal, it is this term. When we apply the principle stated above, we see that to construe 'triangular' as also naming that universal is to commit ourselves to the claim that triangularity is triangular; and pace Plato, that claim is either ill-formed or false.

When we turn to color words, however, the distinction between adjective or predicate term and name or singular term does not so obviously force itself upon us. Thus, at first glance, it appears that one and the same term 'red' is at work in

> (1)   This is red.

and

> (2)   Red is a color.

Viewing the issue in this way, we are, like Bergmann, tempted to say that since in (2) 'red' is functioning as a name, it is playing the same role in (1). But if we think back to 'This is triangular', we see that this sort of account is mistaken; for 'red' in (1) is syntactically of the same form as 'triangular' in our earlier example. If the latter is not suited to name the relevant shape, neither can 'red' name the relevant color. The point here is that 'red' is ambiguous. It is at least two different terms wrapped into one—a general term or adjective and a singular term or name.[16] In (1) it is functioning as a general term and in (2) as a singular term; but, of course, it is only when functioning as a singular term that it can serve to name the alleged universal.

But while the syntactical difference between terms like 'triangular' and 'triangularity' is an obstacle to construing predicates as names of universals, there remains the possibility of introducing a weaker sort of referential tie between predicates and universals. The notion of such a tie appears first in Aristotle's account of paronymy, is articulated in medieval doctrines of connotation, and reemerges in P. F. Strawson's doctrine of predication. On this view, predicates do not name universals; they *consignify* or *connote* them. As Strawson puts it, predicates "introduce" universals in the assertive rather than nominal style.[17] Roughly, the view is that while a term like 'triangular' primarily designates the various triangular objects, it designates them by pointing to the universal they have in common. Thus, we have a referential tie between term and object such that a term and an object can enter into this tie even though the term is not truly predicable of the object. Effectively, this view wants to construe predicates of the form 'F' as equivalent to 'object having F-ness', 'Triangular', for example, means 'object having triangularity'; but, then, even though 'triangular' is not predicable of triangularity, it can be said to signify or designate that abstract entity.

When the view is stated in these terms, it becomes clear how Sellars would respond. This account of predication rests its case for construing predicates as referentially tied to universals on two facts: (1) the fact that language allows us to move from expressions of the form 'F' to expressions of the form 'object having F-ness' and (2) the fact that the use of expressions of the form 'F-ness' commits us to the existence of entities over and above the various concrete particulars. But while Sellars is willing to grant the possibility of interchanging linguistic forms that is specified in (1), he sees this possibility as offering no consolation for the Platonist; for as his analysis of abstract singular terms shows, the use of terms like 'triangularity' does not, contrary to (2), carry any interesting ontological force.[18]

Both of the views I have so far considered construe the referents of predicates as, to use Fregean jargon, complete or saturated entities. Thus, whether the talk has been in terms of naming or connoting, the claim has been that the universal that is the referent of a predicate can also be designated by a singular term. On both views, then, the universal referred to by 'triangular' can also be the referent (although perhaps in a different way) of the abstract singular term 'triangularity'. But to mention Frege suggests a rather different account of predication. On Frege's view, predicates refer to "things" other than particular objects; but those things are unsaturated or incomplete: they cannot be the referents of expressions that are syntactically suited to function as logical subjects in predication.

The Fregean approach to predication is defended in some of Peter Geach's early work.[19] Geach notes that we can move from sentences like

(1)   Socrates and Plato are both men

and

(2)   *a* and *b* are both triangular

to sentences like

(1')   Socrates and Plato are both something

and

(2')   *a* and *b* are both something.

According to Geach, the reference in (1') and (2') to *the something that the relevant objects are* involves a commitment to the existence of entities over and above those objects; but, then, given the possibility of moving from (1) and (2) to (1') and (2'), this establishes the ontological involvement of predication. The use of predicates, he concludes, commits us to the existence of a new class of things. Geach calls these things properties and construes them along the lines of Fregean concepts, telling us that they are what an object can either be or fail to be.

Now, Sellars agrees that we can make the moves Geach points to; but his own contention is that those moves signal nothing of ontological significance.[20] Later we shall examine Sellars' account of the logic of 'something'; but for the present, we can say that, according to Sellars, the claim, to stick with (1), that Socrates and Plato are both something is true just in case it is possible to specify some predicate term that holds true of both Socrates and Plato. To make this claim is like writing

> The blank in 'Socrates and Plato are both _____' can be filled in to yield a true sentence.

Thus, the possibility of moving from (1) to (1') does not point to the existence of some entity (even if unsaturated) that Socrates and Plato both exhibit. The temptation is to construe the relevant transformations as making explicit the nonlinguistic entities whose existence is presupposed by the use of subject-predicate language; but if Sellars is correct, those transformations do not take us outside the web of language.

But while Sellars' criticisms of Platonistic theories of predication carry force, the fact remains that predicate terms play a role in our language. If the nominalist cannot explicate this role, then his account can hardly prove adequate. Traditionally, nominalists have wanted to say that predicates are merely syncategorematic terms. They introduce no new entities but merely serve to modify the signification or reference of genuinely referential expressions. While Sellars agrees with this general claim, he insists that it needs to be filled in. What must be determined is *how* predicates modify names. In this connection, Sellars appeals to a doctrine of predication he claims to find in the *Tractatus*.[21]

The passage Sellars emphasizes in outlining this doctrine is 3.1432, where Wittgenstein says:

> We must not say: "The complex sign 'aRb' says 'a stands in the relation R to b' "; but we must say, "That 'a' stands in a certain relation to 'b' says that aRb."

Sellars construes Wittgenstein to be saying here that what is required to make the claim that two objects are related is not the coupling of their names with some further expression, a relational predicate; what is required is that we write or utter those names in a certain relation. As things actually stand, this relation is effected by writing the relational predicate between the names; but according to Sellars' Wittgenstein, the relation could have been effected without any additional sign designs so that relational predicates are dispensable as a separate class of linguistic terms. Now, Sellars contends that the tractarian account of nonrelational predicates is essentially the same. To make an assertion about an object, we need not attach a further expression to the name of that object; we could merely utter or write the name in some particular style. How the name is tells us how the corresponding object is. In a subject-predicate language, the "how" of a name is captured by writing or uttering the name along with a predicate term; but, Sellars has Wittgenstein insist, this is merely a matter of practical convenience. Nonrelational predicates are also dispensable.

To bring out the force of this account, Sellars describes an imaginary language which he calls Jumblese. Jumblese contains no separate words to correspond to our predicate expressions. In Jumblese, one says how an object is or that several objects are related by uttering or writing the relevant names in a certain style or relation. Sellars concentrates on written Jumblese and employs the notion of different type fonts to capture the notion of different styles of name use. Thus, where we write

Socrates is wise,

in Jumblese, one employs a certain type font and writes, for example,

Socrates

Again, where we write

Socrates is courageous,

Jumblese dictates the use of a different type font to yield

Socrates

Likewise, with relational predicates. Where we write

Socrates is older than Plato,

speakers of Jumblese write the relevant names in a certain relation. Thus,

>   Socrates   Plato

and, in the case of our

>   Plato is taller than Socrates,

those speaking Jumblese might write

>   Plato
>   Socrates

Sellars calls Jumblese a logically perspicuous language. The point is that Jumblese contains among its sign designs only expressions functioning as names. If one were to examine the sign designs of Jumblese, one would not be tempted to look for entities where there are none. Subject-predicate languages, on the other hand, are unperspicuous. For practical reasons, the conventions employed in subject-predicate languages for the various styles of name introduction and the various forms of name relations involve a whole new set of sign designs. These are the predicate terms that send Platonists in search of special sorts of entities. These sign designs, of course, do not play any referential role. Thus, the 'is wise' of

>   Socrates is wise

does not name any entity; its effect is merely to yield, when coupled with a name like 'Socrates', a particular style of name introduction. Thus, where the Jumblies write 'Socrates' in a particular type font, we write the name to the right of the mark 'is wise'. Similarly,

>   Socrates is older than Plato,

appears to involve three categorematic terms, 'Socrates', 'Plato' and 'is older than'; but actually we have only the two names written in a certain relation, the relation of having 'is older than' between them. The occurrence of that relation tells us, given the conventions governing English, that the relevant objects are, in turn, related in a particular way.[22]

Thus, Sellars finds in the *Tractatus* a model for clarifying the nominalistic claim that predicates are syncategorematic expressions. It is important, however, to see the force of Sellars' appeal to the *Tractatus* here. Sellars does not employ the model to "deduce" the truth of nominalism. As he employs it, the model is merely meant to *exhibit* the ontological neutrality of predication. Effectively, the model shows us that if we are to determine the extent of our ontological commitments, we must look not to the stock of predicates but to the category of names.

But notice, the tractarian model by itself does not dictate which singular terms are to be construed as names, so it is neutral as between nominalism and Platonism. But although the model in isolation is neutral, it reinforces the nominalism of Sellars' system when it is coupled with his analysis of abstract singular terms. The effect of that analysis was to show that singular terms that purport to designate abstract entities do not name objects at all but are merely ways of talking about particular linguistic episodes. If Sellars is right on that point, if the only names are expressions referring to individuals, the tractarian model of predication tells us that we need not look elsewhere in determining our ontological commitments.

But one might wonder whether the model tells us even this much, for it might seem that the model could be turned upside down. Thus, one might argue as follows:

> It is possible to imagine a language equally as powerful as our own but completely lacking in names. Where we use names, the speakers of our imaginary language would merely utter or write expressions from the stock of predicates in one of a variety of styles. Admittedly this language would be incomparably more complicated in its conventions than our own language and, perhaps, more complicated even than Jumblese; but clearly the notion of this sort of language is coherent. Granting that, the language has as much right to the title, "logically perspicuous language," as Sellars' Jumblese, with the consequence that Sellars' model can have absolutely no ontological force.

Sellars' response to this objection would, I take it, be to grant the possibility of constructing a language without a special class of sign designs for names but to demand the point of such an enterprise; and surely he would be right in this demand. There can be no doubt that the use of names to refer to objects carries ontological commitment. Given this fact, the possibility of eliminating names as a special class of sign designs is gratuitous. Whatever conventions we would employ to achieve what we now achieve by using names would, if we were to capture the point of names, carry that same ontic import. The absence of the relevant sign designs would be beside the point. However, in the case of predication we have, if Sellars is correct in his criticism of opposing views, no reasons for believing that predicates introduce a special class of entities. The task, then, is to try to explain why, given their ontological neutrality, predicates appear in language as a set of sign designs on an equal footing with names. It is in this and only this connection that Sellars appeals to the tractarian account of predication.

I have suggested that this account of predication is in basic harmony with Sellars' account of abstract singular terms. Taken together, I have suggested, the two accounts seem to provide the basis of a coherent and even plausible version of nominalism. However, if we look more closely at the matter, we are likely to be uneasy with this suggestion. I began this section of the paper with the reminder that Sellars' analysis of abstract singular terms replaces expressions of the form 'F-ness' with expressions of the form '•F•'. At that point, the concern was that perhaps the use of predicate expressions in that and an infinity of other contexts carried commitment to Platonism. The subsequent analysis has shown that such worries were unfounded; but while that analysis has removed one set of worries, it gives rise to new worries. I have said that a logically perspicuous language will contain no predicate terms; but given Sellars' analysis of abstract singular terms, this entails that a logically perspicuous language cannot have any terms that play the role of our 'triangularity'. This expression is equivalent to 'the •triangular•'; and in a language without any special sign designs to play the role of predicates, that distributive singular term cannot be formed.

Now, some nominalists might find this a comforting result. If the logically perspicuous language is one where abstract singular terms can play no role, then so much the better for nominalism. The appeal to abstract entities, one might conclude, has its basis in merely superficial grammatical features of logically unperspicuous languages. It tells us a great deal about Sellars' method to discover that this is not his response. He contends that the forms of discourse that give rise to the realist position must be taken seriously. The fact simply is that there are truths about triangularity, mankind, and the proposition that $2 + 2 = 4$. The philosopher has to start here. He must explain, not reject, the datum. According to Sellars, if a language is such that we cannot express the relevant truths in it, then we are justified, on that ground alone, in concluding that it is not a logically adequate language.

The task, then, is to revise the original analysis to take account of the role attributed to predication. We must modify that analysis to make it possible even for those who speak Jumblese to make remarks about kinds, propositions, and qualities.[23] The basic move Sellars makes here is to note that while Jumblese has no expression to correspond to our predicate term '•triangular•', it does incorporate propositional functions. Thus, where we have the function

x is wise,

speakers of Jumblese write the variable 'x' in the style corresponding to our 'is wise' style of name use. Thus,

      x.

But, then, just as we can form propositional functions incorporating dot-quoted terms, thus,

      x is a •triangular•,

so too the Jumblese have a propositional function with exactly the same force. Thus, perhaps,

      x.

Sellars exploits this similarity. He tells us that a distributive singular term like 'triangularity' is not, as the provisional account in the first part of this paper suggests, equivalent to the distributive singular term 'the •triangular•', but rather to a distributive singular term formed out of the propositional function corresponding to this. Sellars complicates the pattern a bit by introducing two new symbols into the metalanguage of dot quotation. Thus, he introduces INCON and PRECON to function as metalinguistic variables that take as their substituends, respectively, dot-quoted individual constants and dot-quoted predicate constants. But employing these variables, it turns out that 'triangularity' is equivalent to

      the (•triangular•INCON)

and 'mankind' to

      the (•man•INCON).

This modification of the original analysis forces us to revise the translations we outlined in the first Part. Sellars himself never tells us how these revisions are to go; but it does not take much imagination to see that whereas, on the original model,

      Triangularity is a quality

is implicitly a remark about interlinguistic adjectives, the amended account forces us to see it as a remark about propositional functions. Thus, perhaps, our original translation of this sentence as

      •Triangular•s are adjectives

should be replaced by

      (•Triangular•INCON)s are adjective attributive

or something to the same effect. The other translations must be modified in a corresponding way.

III

The issues discussed in the first two sections of this paper have a traditional ring to them. Philosophers as far back as Plato worried about the ontological status of predication; and the issue of abstract singular terms is already a clearly articulated problem in the writings of Aristotle. Of more recent vintage are the ontological questions associated with the apparatus of quantification. Indeed, to mention these questions is to call to mind the name of W. V. Quine, who has claimed that his slogan, "To be is to be the value of a bound variable," provides a criterion for determining the ontological presuppositions of what we say.[24] The criterion supposedly enables us to determine the range of entities to which we are committed by the espousal of a particular sentence in a theory. Let us suppose that we wish to determine the ontic commitment imposed by accepting a certain sentence S. Quine directs us to translate S into the language of quantificational logic. Let us call the results of this translation S'. The next step in determining the ontic import of S consists in specifying the truth conditions for S'. Quine's criterion tells us that S presupposes the existence of all such entities as much be counted among the values of the bound variables of S' if S' is to come out true.

Quine originally thought it possible to reconstruct logic and mathematics in such a way that neither involves quantification over variables whose values are abstract objects. More accurately, he thought a reconstruction of logic and mathematics along these lines was possible or, at least, a project worthy of the philosopher's best efforts. Recently, however, Quine has given up this project. Mathematics, he contends, requires quantification over variables whose values are classes. Without classes, mathematics cannot advance beyond the most elementary parts of simple arithmetic.

While Sellars agrees with Quine that the mathematician and logician must quantify over variables other than individual variables, he does not find this point, by itself, ontologically decisive.[25] In addressing Quine's views, Sellars considers only the so-called existential quantifier. Since Quine's criterion concerns quantification in general, both universal and existential quantification, it might seem that Sellars is not meeting Quine head on. But, of course, the universal quantifier and the so-called existential quantifier are interdefinable. To establish the ontological neutrality of the one is to establish the ontological neutrality of the other. Sellars deals only with the E-quantifier because, under the normal informal reading 'there is . . .' or 'there exists . . .', it seems more clearly associated with ontological commitment. If this informal reading is correct, then to employ the E-quantifier is just to assert the existence of one or more objects.

Sellars' contention is that we need not accept this informal reading. There is nothing, he contends, in the logic of quantification that compels us to construe 'E' as meaning 'there is . . .' or 'there exist . . .'. Granted, as long as we read the E-quantifier in this way, we are forced to accept Quine's criterion of ontological commitment; but Sellars feels that a quite different reading, one that shows the ontological neutrality of the E-quantifier, is equally adequate to the demands of logic. The alternative reading Sellars has in mind harkens back to the foundations of the distinction between the universal quantifier and 'E'. Medieval logicians contrasted the syncategorematic terms 'all' and 'every' not with the phrases 'there is . . .' or 'there exists . . .', but with the syncategorematic term 'some'. Sellars wants to see the same sort of contrast at work in the distinction between the two quantifiers. As he reads it, then, the so-called existential quantifier is not existence-imputing at all. Its force is rather that of 'some'. Thus, the label 'existential quantifier' is misleading, and, according to Sellars, should be replaced by some term like 'particular quantifier' or, to use a logician's term, 'Σ-quantifier'.

But, regardless of the label we apply, Sellars' construction seems to rob the 'E' of the ontological force Quine attributes to it. On Sellars' reading,

(EF)(Socrates is F)

means

Socrates is something;

(EK)(Socrates is a K)

is to be read

Socrates is a something;

and, finally,

(Ep)(p v Jones speaks Jumblese)

comes out as

Something or Jones speaks Jumblese.

But if we read the relevant formulae in this way, they appear ontologically neutral. The formula

(EF)(Socrates is F)

does not assert the existence of a property which stands in some special relationship to Socrates. It merely says that Socrates is something, such as wise, courageous, tall, or well versed in mathematics; and to make that claim is hardly to introduce any peculiar objects.

A critic, however, might be willing to accept Sellars' proposal to read 'E' as 'some' but argue that this is irrelevant to the question of ontological commitment. The point here is that the Quinean criterion did not originate with the ordinary language reading of 'E' as 'there is . . .' or 'there exists . . . .'. On the contrary, that informal reading, along with the criterion of ontological commitment, derives from the logician's account of the truth conditions for statements involving quantifiers. Thus, since Sellars' proposal does not operate at that level, it is quite powerless to show that 'E' does not involve the assertion of existence.

The logistical account the critic has in mind would doubtless be what Quine has called the *traditional* or *referential (objectual)* interpretation of quantification.[26] On that account, a nonnegative Σ-quantification comes out true just in case there is at least one object that satisfies the open sentence following the Σ-quantifier. Thus,

(Ex)(x is wise)

is true just in case there is one object that satisfies the open sentence

x is wise.

But if this sort of account is inescapable, we seem compelled to accept Quine's criterion of ontic commitment and, with it, an ontology of classes.

To establish the ontological neutrality of 'E', then, Sellars must provide an alternative account of the truth-conditions for formulae involving 'E'. Quine himself suggests such an account. He calls it the *substitutional* interpretation of quantification. On this account, a Σ-quantification is true just in case there is a linguistic expression that, when substituted for the variables bound by the Σ-quantifier, makes the open sentence following the quantifier come out true.[27]

Now, although Sellars has not written extensively on this issue, it is fairly clear he would defend this sort of account.[28] As I have explained it, the substitutional interpretation of quantification tells us that the formula

(Ex)(x is wise)

is true just in case some individual constant can replace the 'x' in 'x is wise' to yield a true sentence. If we were to mobilize Sellars' strategy of dot quotation here, we could provide a much more powerful version of the substitutional interpretation. As stated above, the truth conditions for a Σ-quantification are always stated relative to the resources of a given language, the language in which the relevant open sentence is formulated. The difficulty is that we think of the various Σ-quantifications as having a range that is quite independent of the vocabulary of this or that language. Employing dot quotation we could make explicit the interlinguistic flavor of quantification. To make this move, we must employ some symbols we introduced at the end of the previous section. There, we indicated that Sellars wants to add to the metalanguage of dot quotation the expressions 'INCON' and 'PRE-CON'. To these, I shall add 'PROP'. The first two, we noted, are metalinguistic variables that take as their substituends dot-quoted terms. Thus, INCON takes as its substituends individual constants like '•Socrates•' and '•Plato•'; whereas, PRECON takes as its substituends dot-quoted predicates like '•triangular•' and '•courageous•'. In the same spirit, PROP is to be taken as a variable that takes as its substituends dot-quoted propositions like 'the •2 + 2 = 4•'.

Employing these variables, we can state the truth conditions for Σ-quantifications in the following way:

> (Ex)(x is wise) is true just in case some proposition that is a •wise•INCON is true.
> (EF)(Socrates is F) is true just in case some proposition that is a PRECON•Socrates• is true.
> (Ep)(p v Jones speaks Jumblese) is true just in case some proposition that is a PROP v •Jones speaks Jumblese• is true.

But while this interpretation seems plausible in itself and, because of its consequences for ontology, desirable, it is open to an obvious and devastating objection. This objection has its source in the fact that the linguistic resources of language are frequently limited. If we restrict ourselves to the class of names or individual constants, we note that many objects lack names. Indeed, it is possible, and given the limitations of our methods of empirical investigation even likely, that there are whole classes of objects none of which bear names. If we suppose that the class of objects that are blue whales meets this condition, we have a ready refutation of the substitutional account just presented. Clearly,

> (Ex)(x is a blue whale) i.e., something is a blue whale.

is true; but since we have assumed that no blue whales have, in any language, names, the substitutional interpretation forces us to conclude that the formula is false.

Another example brings out the difficulty in a more pointed way. The following formula is true:

> (Ex)(x has no name) i.e., something has no name.

But there cannot, on pain of paradox, be any true proposition that is a

•Has no name• INCON.[29]

The conclusion would seem to be that we must accept the referential interpretation of quantification and, with it, Quine's criterion.

The difficulty I introduce here is nothing new. It is, if one can speak of such, a standard objection. Sellars never addresses the objection directly; but some remarks in an early paper, "Realism and the New Way of Words," suggests a way of handling the difficulty. In that paper, Sellars speaks of what he calls the "language of omniscience." This is an imaginary language that we are to construe our language as evolving toward.[30] It is a language that contains names for all existent objects and predicate expressions (or name styles and name relations) for all the ways in which these objects can individually be or be related to each other. In "Realism and the New Way of Words," Sellars wants to relate the use of the universal quantifier to the linguistic resources of the language of omniscience. The suggestion is that a universal quantifier is true just in case all the substitution instances of the open sentence following the quantifier come out true in the language of omniscience. Now, it is tempting to generalize on this suggestion and to see in it a complete account of the truth conditions for quantificational formulae. To say that a Σ-quantification is true is to say that some substitution instance of the open sentence following the quantifier comes out true in the language of omniscience. Put in another way, we can restate our original formulation of the truth conditions so that the INCONs PRE-CONs and PROPs of that formulation do not take as their substituends expressions from actual, historical languages but rather the linguistic elements belonging to the language of omniscience. But if we modify our formulations in this way, we can make perfectly good sense of true Σ-quantifications involving objects that have no names. Such objects have no names now; but since they do have names in the language of omniscience, the relevant formulae can be true. Likewise, it is clear how

(Ex)(x has no name)

can, without paradox, be true. The statement is true just in case there is some true sentence in the language of omniscience that is a

•Has no name (in the language of 1977)• INCON;

and we both can and must hold that the language of omniscience contains such a sentence.[31]

There is one respect in which my account of Sellars' theory of quantification is inadequate. Although it is true that Sellars wants to construe 'E' as equivalent to 'something' and to present the truth conditions for the formulae of quantification in substitutional terms, he wants, never-

theless, to say that the use of the Σ-quantifier over singular-term variables does have the effect of imputing existence. At first glance, this
seems to be inconsistent; for surely it is the same quantifier that ranges
over predicate variables, class variables, and sentential variables on the
one hand, and individual variables on the other. Why, then, attach
existential force to the quantifier in the later case but not in the former?
To see the rationale behind Sellars' claim here, we have to look at the
differences among the kinds of terms a Σ-quantifier can bind. The use of
a predicate term or sentence, we have said, commits one to the existence
of no special entities. It is, on the contrary, to the category of names that
we must look if we are to determine the extent of our ontological
commitments; but, then, quantification over variables whose values are
names or individual constants will, from an ontological point of view,
differ from quantification over variables whose values are predicates or
sentences. Thus, a formula of the form

(Ex)(x is a man)

is true if and only if the language of omniscience incorporates a true
proposition that is a

•man•INCON.

But this requires that the language of omniscience contain a name that
can have a use in a true proposition; and that condition can be met only if
there actually exists some object for the term to name.[32] Thus, although
the truth conditions for statements incorporating 'E' are always stated in
substitutional and, therefore, ontologically neutral terms, the actual
application of those truth conditions to the case of names forces us to see
the use of Σ-quantification over singular-term variables as existence-
involving. Nor does this concession to Quine offer any consolation to
the Platonist; for, as Sellars has already shown, the category of names
includes only expressions that designate concrete particulars. Expressions like 'triangularity', which appear to be names of abstract
entities, are to be parsed in a way that shows the reference to some
Platonic object to be only apparent. While it may seem, then, that one
can construct Σ-quantifications that appear to commit us to
Platonism—e.g., (Ex)(x is exemplified by Socrates)—the construction
of these formulae is based on a misunderstanding of the logic of abstract
singular terms; and, in any case, such formulae are never true.

We have said that Sellars' interpretation of 'E' is substitutional. This
is not to say that Sellars construes 'E' as a metalinguistic symbol.
Although the truth conditions for formulae embodying 'E' are specified
in the metalanguage, the expression itself falls within the object language.[33] Contrasted with the notion expressed by 'E' or 'something' is

the concept of existence. This is a notion that Sellars does construe as metalinguistic. According to Sellars, to say that Socrates, for example, exists is to make a disguised remark about the dot-quoted expression •Socrates•. Effectively, it is to say that this expression has a use in a true proposition.

To see the plausibility of this account, we must reflect again on the connection in Sellars between existence and namehood. For Sellars, we determine the extent of our ontic commitment by looking to the stock of names. But if we employ this as a clue, it is fairly easy to see how

Socrates exists

is really just a remark about the •Socrates•. Essentially, it is the claim that the •Socrates• is an expression that can play the role of a name. But when is an expression a name? Well, an expression is a name when it can function as the subject of a true subject predicate proposition.[34] Stated with relation to a logically perspicuous language, an expression is a name if it can be employed in a variety of styles or in a variety of relations with other such expressions to make a variety of true assertions about how objects are or are related to each other. But, then, we can say that

Socrates exists

is really the metalinguistic claim that

(E PRECON)(PRECON•Socrates•)

is true.[35]

But if this sort of account is correct, then Quine's criterion of ontological commitment ultimately rests on a confusion of use and mention. He takes the concept of existence to be analyzed in terms of the apparatus of quantification. But if Sellars is correct, then while the concept of existence is a metalinguistic concept, the concepts that are expressed by the quantifiers of logic belong to the object language; and given this contrast between the notions of existence and quantification, the fact that logic and mathematics quantify over variables of higher levels than individual variables turns out to be irrelevant to ontological issues. To determine the extent of our ontic commitment, we must look to the category of names and not to the apparatus of quantification. The apparatus of quantification operates at a logical level below that of existence, so the logician and mathematician can do their work unencumbered by ontological disputes; and that, of course, is as it should be.

NOTES

[1]Perhaps Quine is making this extreme claim in "On What There Is," *From a Logical Point of View* (Cambridge: Harvard University Press, 1953). See especially pp. 9-11.

[2]The notion of a linguistic type is developed in AE.

[3]I intentionally ignore Quine's views about the indeterminary of translation here. The issues raised by Quine's account are simply too complex for an introductory paper of this sort. I think it is fairly clear that the two accounts are incompatible. If Quine is right, then we cannot have the sort of interlinguistic reference that Sellars claims we do employ.

[4]AE, pp. 236-47.

[5]Ibid., pp. 229-36. For additional remarks on the notion, see chapter 2 of *SM*.

[6]Sellars' notion of the distributive singular term is criticized in Nicholas Wolterstorff's "On the Nature of Universals," in my *Universals and Particulars* (Notre Dame, Ind.: University of Notre Dame Press, 1976). While Wolterstorff *may* be right in his claim that the account of distributive singular terms found in AE is not, as it stands, adequate, Wolterstorff's modification of Sellars' scheme is perfectly acceptable to the Sellarsian reduction of talk about the *K* to talk about *K*'s.

[7]AE, pp. 248-57.

[8]See chapter 4 of *SM* for an elaboration of this account.

[9]This use of abstract terms is analyzed in detail in chapter 3 of *SM*. In that context, Sellars is worried about the problem of intentionality. He wants to claim that talk of mental acts representing objects is methodologically derivative from and modeled on talk about language acts standing for or expressing senses. If the latter is ontologically neutral, then so, Sellars argues, is the former. For a detailed account of Sellars' theory of intentionality, see C.F. Delaney's paper on the Theory of Knowledge and my paper on the mind-body problem.

[10]At an earlier stage in my study of Sellars' ontology, I did not think that this objection could be overcome. For an over-hasty formulation of the difficulty, see my "Recent Work in Ontology," *American Philosophical Quarterly,* 1972, pp. 119-38.

[11]This general account of meaning is reiterated in many of Sellars' writings. See, for example, chapters 2, 4, 6-8 and 11 of *SPR*. The issue of meaning as it relates to scientific theories is considered in Gary Gutting's contribution to this volume.

[12]For an account of Sellars' theory of prescriptive language, see William David Solomon's contribution to this volume.

[13]This account is reiterated in Bergmann's writings. See, e.g., chapters 4-5, 11, and 13 of *Meaning and Existence* (Madison: University of Wisconsin Press, 1959).

[14]Sellars' criticism of Bergmann is found in NS.

[15]This principle is never stated explicitly by Sellars; but clearly it is the guiding premise behind his argument. That it needs no justification is, I think, obvious.

[16]Actually, I oversimplify here since Sellars wants to claim that color words are really three words wrapped into one. They can also function as common nouns as in 'chartreuse is a green'.

[17]See, for example, chapter 5 of Strawson's *Individuals* (London: Methuen, 1959).

[18]See, e.g., GE, where Sellars outlines the sort of criticism I present here.

[19]See Geach's contribution to the symposium "On What There Is" in the *Aristotelian Society Supplementary* 1951.

[20]Sellars' criticism of Geach is found in GE.

[21]See NS. See also chapter 4 of *SM* and AE, pp. 258-69.

[22]Sellars' appropriation of this model is intimately connected with his account of picturing, which also derives from the *Tractatus*. For an account of Sellars' doctrine of picturing and its relationship to the concept of truth, see the contributions of Cornelius F. Delaney and Gary Gutting to this volume.

[23]The only place where Sellars confronts this issue is in AE, pp. 258-69.

[24]See chapters 1 and 6 of *From a Logical Point of View* and chapter 4 of *Ontological Relativity and Other Essays* (New York: Columbia University Press, 1969).

[25]An early version of Sellars' theory of quantification is found in GE. A later version is found in NS.

[26]For a more detailed account of the distinction between referential and substitutional theories of quantification, see chapter 4 of Quine's *Ontological Relativity* (New York: Columbia University Press, 1969).

[27]Needless to say, this is a very crude statement of the substitutionalist theory. Since I am concerned with Sellars' version of the account, I shall not bother to clarify the general notion of a substitutionalist account.

[28]Here I benefit from having read some correspondence between Sellars and Gilbert Harman. There, as well as in OPM Sellars makes it clear that he opts for the substitutionalist account.

[29]For this example I am indebted to Christopher Williams. For helpful discussions of these issues, I am also indebted to Charles Davis and Guido Kung.

[30]See RNW. The concept of the language of omniscience is connected with another limit concept in Sellars, the notion of the Peirceian Conceptual Scheme, that scheme that the scientific community will accept in the "long run." For more on these issues, see the contributions to this volume by Cornelius F. Delaney and Gary Gutting.

[31]The expert in these matters will note the absence in my account of any discussion of the inability of substitutional theories to handle talk of a non-denumerably infinite number of objects. One might think that since the language of omniscience is a mere limit concept, its linguistic resources are strong enough to permit such talk. The difficulty here is that the language of omniscience must represent a historical possibility so that its linguistic resources could never be adequate to quantification involving nondenumerably many objects. Perhaps a footnote *SM* (p. 148), where Sellars expresses doubts about the coherence of Cantorian infinities, provides a clue. It may be that Sellars wants to construct mathematics without recourse to nondenumerable infinities. This would seem to require important modifications of classical mathematics; but since Sellars never expands upon the suggestion contained in this footnote, we cannot be certain how he would make such modifications.

[32]I prescind from the issues surrounding the Russell-Strawson debate on referring here. As I state this condition, it holds whether one is a Russellian or a Strawsonian. Sellars' own account of these issues is found in "Presupposing," *Philosophical Review* 63 (1954): 197-215.

[33]The distinction here is that between meaning and truth conditions, 'E' means 'some', so that it falls within the object language; its truth conditions, however, are to be stated in the metalanguage.

[34]This criterion of ontic commitment requires a good bit more commentary than I provide here. Thus, one would have to show that "fictional" names never function as subjects of true subject-predicate propositions.

[35]This account allows for the possibility of shifting senses of 'exists' so that what exists according to the predicate resources of one conceptual scheme may not exist vis-à-vis the predicate resources of another scheme. The concept of an object that really exists is definable in terms of the predicate resources of the Peirceian Conceptual Scheme, where we have, I take it, the instantiation of the language of omniscience.

Philosophy of Science

Gary Gutting

Sellars has remarked that philosophy of science is simply "philosophy that takes science seriously."[1] His own philosophy illustrates this *mot* in the sense that, in its broadest scope, it is an effort to situate science properly in a total view of the human situation (cf. the "synoptic vision" of the two images—manifest and scientific—set up as the goal of philosophy in PSIM). Consequently, his views on topics associated with the academic specialization called "philosophy of science" reflect to an uncommon extent his general epistemological and metaphysical views. Conversely, some of Sellars' specialized philosophy-of-science ideas (e.g., on the nature of theoretical explanation and the role of models) play an integral role in the development of his general philosophical positions. Therefore, an examination of Sellars' philosophy of science is not only valuable in its own right but is also a good approach to the understanding and evaluation of his philosophical system as a whole.

Sellars' point of departure in philosophy of science is the classical work of the logical empiricists. This, of course, does not mean that he accepts the standard logical-empiricist conclusions; indeed, he is one of their most powerful critics. However, his critique can be usefully viewed as a series of modifications (some radical) of the logical-empiricist account of science. In particular, he begins (LT, 106-7) with the standard logical-empiricist division of science into: (1) a theoretical framework, construed as an uninterpreted formal calculus; (2) an observational framework, containing both singular, observation sentences and empirical generalizations; and (3) correspondence rules somehow linking the theoretical and the observational frameworks.

I will begin in Section I with Sellars' discussion of the theoretical framework; this will be primarily concerned with his formulation and defense of the claim that scientific theories have ontological significance. Section II will deal with the observational framework, especially

73

its ontological and methodological relations to the theoretical framework; here the nature of correspondence rules will be a major concern. Section III will focus on Sellars' views on laws and induction.

I. The Theoretical Framework

Amidst the contemporary rejections of logical empiricism, realistic construals of theoretical entities have enjoyed such a resurgence that the view may well be on its way to becoming a new dogmatism. For Sellars, however, realism is not a dogma or a slogan but a carefully analyzed and justified position. His discussions (especially LT and SRI) put equally great emphasis on the reasons for realism and on the precise sense in which realism is true.[2]

Sellars approaches realism through an analysis of theoretical predicates. He begins (LT, 113) with the apparently trivial point that, at the very least, theoretical predicates have *translational* meaning; that is, theories can be translated from one language to another.[3] Thus, it is perfectly correct to say ' "Molekuel" (in German) means *molecule*.' However, in the context of Sellars' theory of meaning, this is not a trivial point, since terms that have translational meaning play roles in a language and, putting it roughly, to play a role in a language is to express a concept (have conceptual meaning).[4] Of course the actual justification of this move must come from Sellars' defense of his version of a meaning-as-use theory.

Granted that theoretical predicates have conceptual meaning (and hence are suitable *candidates* for a connection with extralinguistic facts), the next and most crucial question is, Do they denote? Do they actually refer to anything in reality? According to Sellars (LT, 115-16), a term denotes if two conditions are satisfied: (1) the term must be a *common noun* applicable to particulars; and (2) there must be entities that satisfy the criteria specified by the term.

Condition (1) reflects Sellars' views on the connection between logical quantification and ontological commitment. In opposition to Quine, he denies that "to be is to be the value of a bound variable" and instead defends the much more restrictive condition that to be is to be the value of a bound variable only in an expression of the form (Ex)(Nx), where N is a name (a common noun) and x is a variable which takes singular terms as its values. In terms of our current question of whether theories have any sort of ontological significance, condition (1) is not crucial, since scientific theories clearly do in general have predicates that meet the condition (e.g., 'molecule', 'electron', 'gravitational field' are all common nouns). Therefore, we can move immediately to the question of whether or not there are entities satisfying the criteria specified by these terms. However, if it is a question of the precise ontological commitment of a particular theory, condition (1) will make a crucial difference.[5]

Turning to condition (2), the following preliminary point should be noted: Theoretical expressions have no hope of satisfying it if they are construed (following positivists like Nagel) as predicate *variables*. For Nagel,[6] all predicate constants are observational. Hence theoretical predicate expressions are for him *essentially* variables; that is, there are no constants that can be substituted for them to turn the statement forms in which they occur into singular descriptive statements. (This is so since the predicate constants of the observational language are the only ones available and none of them can satisfy the theoretical postulates; if they did, they would be theoretical and not observational terms.) Thus, this view excludes theoretical expressions from singular descriptive linguistic contexts and hence prevents them from having any denotation.

Sellars' response to this view, which threatens to nip the project of scientific realism in the bud, is that the notion of a term that is a variable in the strong sense intended by Nagel is incoherent. For it amounts to saying that there are variables that admit in principle of *no* substitution instances. In such a case, he maintains, the notion of a variable has itself lost all significance. It is as if, for the case of an individual (rather than a predicate) variable, someone were to maintain that 'Fx' (where 'F' is a consistent predicate constant) is an open sentence although there could (in principle) be no individual constant of which F was true. In either case, the claim that there is a *variable* involved is a sham. To be a variable is to be an expression for which constants can be substituted.[7]

However, this does not mean that theoretical expressions should be straightforwardly construed as predicate constants. An expression does not qualify as a predicate constant until it is connected with extralinguistic objects;[8] and it is this connection that is presently in question. Therefore, we should regard theoretical expressions as *candidate* predicate constants. If our argument for realism succeeds, we will then be justified in regarding them (at least those occurring in theories judged to have ontological significance) as being full-fledged predicate constants.

We are now ready to face head-on the crucial question, Do the terms of scientific theories have a denotation? Or, rephrasing the question in accord with Sellars' understanding of denotation, Are there any entities that satisfy the criteria specified (connoted) by these terms?

Sellars leads us (LT, 117-18) to the answer to this question by a specification of what we need to know in order to answer it affirmatively. Suppose the theoretical entities in question are molecules. Then, in terms of our analysis so far, to know that molecules exist is to know that there are things that satisfy the criteria specified by the common noun 'molecule'—i.e., to know:

(A):   (Ex) x is $P_1 \ldots P_n$,

where $P_1 \ldots P_n$ are the criteria for being a molecule.

But what do we need to know in order to know that (A) is true? (A) is a statement in a theory (e.g., kinetic theory). According to the theory, if we know the truth of certain observation statements (e.g., the statement that there is now a gas exploding in this room), we are entitled to say that certain sorts of theoretical entities (e.g., a set of molecules composing the gas and as a group moving rapidly away from a common center) exist. Accordingly, we know that molecules exist if, first, we know that gases exist and, second, we know that kinetic theory (the theory that tells us gases are composed of molecules) is a *good* theory. More generally, we know that certain theoretical entities exist if: (1) we know that certain existential observational statements are true;[9] (2) we know that there is a theory that says that if these observational statements are true the theoretical entities exist; and (3) we know that the theory in (2) is a "good" theory.

But what is meant by a "good" theory? Sellars provides a seemingly traditional answer: A good theory is one that is adequate for *explaining* the observed phenomena. However, the argument for realism depends crucially on a proper understanding of theoretical explanation, an understanding that is contrary to that of the logical-empiricist tradition.

The crux of the matter is this: A good theory (hence a theory whose theoretical entities can be said to exist) must, Sellars says, explain the observed phenomena. However, there are two competing senses in which a theory might be regarded as explaining observed phenomena (i.e., that which is expressed by the sentences of the observational framework). The first sense is that of the logical empiricists. Particular observable facts are directly explained by deductive subsumption under empiricial generalizations (which are, of course, themselves part of the observational framework). Theoretical explanation is a second-level affair in which the empirical generalizations are themselves explained by deductive subsumption under theoretical laws. From this point of view, the fact that a theory is "good" provides no basis whatever for accepting the existence of entities described by its theoretical predicates; for its goodness consists in an ability to organize the observational framework's empirical generalizations by subsuming them under higher-level premises. The phenomena can, of course, be deductively subsumed under the theory in virtue of the transitivity of logical implication. But the crucial point is that the theory is *not necessary* to explain the phenomena themselves. Whether or not we accept the theory, the phenomena can be explained by the empirical generalizations. In other words, whether there are any theoretical entities or not, we still have an adequate explanation of the phenomena. Therefore, there are no grounds for asserting the existence of theoretical entities.

The second sense of explanation, which is that defended by Sellars (LT, 120-21), has the theory (not empirical generalizations) *directly* explaining the observed phenomena. Sellars rejects the logical empiricists' "levels-picture," in which the theory directly explains only the empirical generalizations, which themselves explain the phenomena. Instead he views the theory as explaining the phenomena by explaining the fact that they conform (to the extent that they do) to the empirical generalizations. Thus, a gas behaves the way it does because it is composed of molecules that obey the laws of kinetic theory; and this is also the reason why, to a certain approximation, it obeys Boyle's law. On this account, knowing that a theory is "good" surely does give us grounds for asserting the existence of its theoretical entities. For if there are no such entities, we have no explanation for the observed phenomena.

How are we to choose between these two views of explanation? Sellars admits, in a striking passage, that "*if* the observation framework permits the formulation of inductive generalizations—statistical or non-statistical," which hold within the limits of observational error, "then the positivistic interpretation of theoretical entities is inescapable" (P, 96). But, he argues, the antecedent of this conditional is false; and, deprived of this premise, the logical empiricist views on explanation and the status of theoretical entities lose their plausibility. Thus, Sellars holds that we must regard theories as directly explaining the phenomena simply because empirical generalizations are not by themselves able to do so. They (as a whole) are always in some respect outstripped by the facts—always, in some empirical details, inaccurate.[10]

Sellars emphasizes (LT, 122) that he does not mean merely that all empirical generalizations are statistical, rather than strict, generalizations. Rather, his claim is that when theoretical entities are postulated this is because the empirical laws of the relevant domain, whether strictly universal or statistical in form, have been found to be incorrect as a description of the observed facts. Granted this, theory is the only source of genuine explanation and hence must be regarded as directly accounting for the observed phenomena. In so doing, it also explains the approximate correctness of the empirical generalizations. That is, it explains why the phenomena obey the empirical generalizations to the extent that they do and, even more importantly, why in some cases the phenomena do not obey the empirical generalizations.

Sellars does not dwell on the reasons for asserting that empirical generalizations are inaccurate. Presumably, there is no logical reason why this must be so. (It is surely logically possible for gases to exactly obey Boyle's law.) Accordingly, it seems that Sellars' appeal must be to the *de facto* situation of science: Theories have been introduced because, as a matter of fact, not all the phenomena can be accounted for on the basis of deductions from empirical generalizations. Even the most sophisticated constructions in the manifest (observational) framework have failed to account for the facts of that framework itself. Consequently, we have had to move to a scientific (i.e., microtheoretical) framework.

Accordingly, there is one sense in which scientific realism is for Sellars a contingent thesis. It could have happened that a complete explanation of the world might have been given solely in terms of the ontology of the manifest image, with no need for a move to postulated theoretical entities. However, in another and more fundamental sense, scientific realism is not a contingent thesis. The general methods of science (which may or may not involve postulation of theoretical entities) are, according to Sellars, the best ways of accounting for what occurs in the world. Hence, in virtue of the connection that Sellars (as we shall see) discerns between explanatory power and ontological significance, it follows that science is the source of the best account of what really exists. As Sellars puts it, "Science is the measure of what there is, that it is, and of what there is not, that it is not". (EPM, 173.) This conceptual point about the ontological significance of science is not a contingent thesis and would remain true whether or not science had to posit entities beyond those of the manifest framework. Hence, if scientific realism is construed as the view that the ontology of the manifest framework must be replaced by a different, postulated scientific ontology (of atoms, waves, etc.), then it is a contingent thesis. But if it is construed more broadly as the view that the explanatory accounts of science—whether or not they move beyond the ontology of the manifest framework—are the touchstone of reality, then it is not a contingent thesis.[11]

II.   The Observational Framework

Although Sellars thinks he has thus established the existence of the theoretical entities of good theories, the full impact of his realism depends on a proper analysis of the relation of these theoretical entities to the entities of the observational framework. Like the positivists, Sellars formulates this question in terms of the role of correspondence rules (i.e., rules somehow correlating the terms and sentences of the theoretical language with those of the observational language): "The crux of the matter concerns the correspondence rules which connect theoretical concepts with observation framework counterparts". (SRI, 193.) However, his view of the nature of correspondence rules is very unpositivistic.

It will be convenient to discuss the role of correspondence rules in terms of how they relate both the *sense* and the *denotation* of observational and theoretical terms. On one common positivist account, the observational language is the source of both the sense and the denotation of the theoretical language, the idea being that theory is just an indirect but convenient way of saying things that could in principle be said in the observational language about observational entities. Thus the role of the correspondence rules is to import sense and reference from the observational level to the theoretical level. However, this construal, which amounts to saying that theoretical terms have no sense or denotation of their own, has been refuted by the above argument for scientific realism.

A second way of looking at correspondence rules would be to regard them as correlating *independent* senses and denotations. On this view, theoretical language would be admitted to have its own sense and denotation quite independent of the observational language. Each language talks in its own way about different sets of entities, and the correspondence rules assert empirical relations between the two different domains.

Sellars does recognize a class of correspondence rules, which he calls *methodological* correspondence rules, that effect this sort of empirical correlation between two apparently independent domains. Such rules "correlate predicates in the theory with predicates which, though empirical, need not pertain to the domain of the objects for which the theory is a theory." (TE, 71.) A typical example of a rule of this type would be one correlating certain observable spectral lines with a particular excitation state of a group of atoms. In such a case, Sellars points out, it is absurd to say that the correspondence rule has *identified* the spectral lines with the atomic state; rather it has singled out the spectral lines as correlated with and *indicative* of the atomic state (TE, 72). Methodological rules express simply an operational correlation between theory and observation.

However, Sellars notes that there is another kind of correspondence rule, which he calls a *substantive* correspondence rule (TE, 71). These are rules that *identify* observational entities and properties with theoretical entities and properties. An example would be the statement that the temperature of a gas *is* the mean kinetic energy of the molecules that compose the gas. Clearly, this kind of rule cannot be regarded as simply correlating two separate domains; for it says that, in some sense, the two domains are identical. The problem, however, is to determine the exact meaning of this identity.

This leads to a third way of construing correspondence rules (limiting ourselves from now on to substantive correspondence rules), namely, as assertions that the denotation (but of course not the sense) of certain observational terms is the same as that of certain theoretical terms. On this view, the two languages talk about the same things but in terms of different senses. We would, for example, say "that gases are identical with populations of molecules, while denying that the empirical properties of gases are identical with the theoretical properties of populations of molecules." (TE, 73.)

For Sellars, this approach involves an important preliminary difficulty (cf. PSIM, 26). There are certain observational entities (e.g., pink ice cubes that are colored through and through) that, if they were identified with the corresponding theoretical entities (e.g., a swarm of molecules with a cubical shape), could no longer be described by some of the observational predicates (e.g., being pink through and through) that in fact apply to them. The reason is that being pink through and through is an *ultimately homogeneous* property (one that pervades in a continuous way the entity that has it). Obviously, no system of *discrete* particles (e.g., a swarm of molecules) could possess such a property. Consequently, identifying observational and theoretical entities requires saying that certain predicates that do in fact apply to the entities *cannot* apply to them.[12]

However, this difficulty is not, for Sellars, an insuperable one (cf. PSIM, 36-37). The argument of the preceding paragraph showed that it is impossible to identify observable entities with *systems of discrete particles,* not with any and every possible theoretical entity. In particular, if science would develop theoretical correlations for pink ice cubes and the like, which were themselves continuous, the above considerations would pose no difficulty.

Consequently, Sellars accepts in principle the idea of identifying observational and theoretical entities. His more basic objection concerns the desire to preserve the observational predicates alongside of the theoretical predicates as essential elements in our description of reality. Essentially, Sellars' view is this: Why insist on keeping the observational predicates when the theoretical predicates, as we saw in the argument for the reality of theoretical entities, have all the explanatory power (and more) of the observational predicates? If a scientific theory can account for the phenomena of the world and the observational framework cannot, surely we should admit that the observational framework should be rejected as incorrect.

Implicit in the above view is one of Sellars' key insights—the parity between explanatory power and descriptive significance. The language that does the best job of explaining the behavior of a domain of entities is, *a fortiori*, the language best suited for describing these entities. Thus Sellars says:

> A descriptive term is one which *in its basic use,* properly replaces one of the variables in the dialogue schema—
> What brought it about that x is Φ?
> The fact that y is Ψ. (EAE, 451.)

The general point being made here is this: Things behave the way they do because of what they are; therefore, the best account (explanation) of how they behave will have to be based on the best description of what they are.

On the basis of this view, Sellars suggests as correct a fourth construal of correspondence rules "as statements to the effect that the objects of the observational framework *do not really exist–there really are no such things*". (LT, 126.) Thus, correspondence rules for Sellars assert that observational terms do not denote (i.e., their senses do not correctly describe the actual world) and that they can be replaced by more adequate theoretical terms.[13]

The major obstacle to such a view of correspondence rules is the belief that the observational framework has a privileged foundational role in knowing, precisely because it is the only possible locus of the experience on which all our knowledge about the world must be based. But, Sellars replies, this belief is just the myth of the given and, as such, simply false.[14] It is just not true that the current observational framework is the only framework in which we could have direct experiential contact with the world. It would be in principle possible for a theoretical scientific framework to take on the observational role of the physical object language that currently plays this role (cf. SRI, 196-99).

Thus the myth of the given appears as the final obstacle to a proper understanding and acceptance of the reality of theoretical entities. Unless we reject it, we can give no account of correspondence rules consistent with the argument establishing the reality of theoretical entities. In this way, a rejection of the myth of the given appears as a basic condition of possibility for Sellars' scientific realism. Without it, realism cannot survive the challenge of giving an adequate account of the relation of the theoretical and the observational frameworks. Thus two of Sellars' most fundamental doctrines, scientific realism and the rejection of the given, are seen to be inextricably interconnected.

So far, our discussion of the observational framework has focused almost exclusively on the *ontological* question, Do the entities of the observational framework exist? As we have seen, Sellars' answer is a decisive no.[15] However, this answer does not by any means settle the question of the overall significance of the observational framework for Sellars. It is typical of his philosophy to insist on a sharp distinction between questions of existence and questions of significance (e.g., the nonexistence of meanings does not reflect on the irreducible importance of the framework of semantical discourse, and the nonexistence of persons does not diminish the ethical significance of that category). In the case of the observational framework, the rejection of the existence of its entities is balanced by an emphasis on its *methodological* significance in science. This significance is elucidated in the course of Sellars' defenses of three characteristic theses: (1) that the observation framework is not a theory; (2) that the observation framework, though to a certain extent *replaceable* by the current theoretical framework, should not now be so replaced; and (3) that the nature of the observational framework exercises a regulative influence on the character of future science. Let us discuss each of these in turn.

(1) Sellars disagrees with Feyerabend's claim[16] that the observational framework of everyday experience and language is a theory in the same sense as any scientific theory. Of course, he admits that the observational framework is in important ways like a theory: it involves a conceptualization of the world, and it is replaceable by a better conceptualization, such as is given in the theoretical frameworks of science (cf. LT, 125). Sellars even is willing to compare the correspondence rules connecting the observational and the theoretical frameworks to the correspondence rules whereby one theory is reduced to another. In both cases, the sense and denotation of one account are rejected in favor of the sense and denotation of another account. Nevertheless, Sellars finds it necessary to emphasize one vital nontheoretical characteristic of the observational framework. This is the fact that it, unlike a theory, has no external subject matter (cf. SRI, 172-73). If we are asked, "What is atomic theory about?" we can not only give the trivial reply, "Atoms" (which gives the internal subject matter of the theory); we can also say, more significantly (in terms of external subject matter), "The microstructure of macroscopic bodies." But in the case of the observational framework, the only correct answer is in terms of internal subject matter: "Observational objects."

This point is much more than a verbal one. Sellars makes it to emphasize the vital truth that there is, *as a matter of fact,* no level of experience more basic than that of the observational framework of everyday discourse. This truth has a dual importance. On the one hand, it blocks any attempt to reintroduce the myth of an unchangeable, foundational given by an appeal to a level of sense-data more basic than that of macroscopic physical objects. On the other hand, it emphasizes that the observational framework, although a replaceable conceptual structure, is the *de facto* starting point (and in this sense a foundational given) of all knowledge. In view of the strong emphasis Sellars gives to his rejection of the given, it is worth emphasizing this last point by citing a text in which he explains the sense in which he has *not* rejected a given:

> To reject the myth of the given is not to commit oneself to the idea that empirical knowledge as it is now constituted has no rock bottom level of observation predicates proper. It is to commit oneself rather to the idea that even if it does have a rock bottom level, it is *still* in principle replaceable by another conceptual framework in which these predicates do not, *strictly speaking*, occur. It is in this sense, and in this sense *only* that I have rejected the dogma of givenness with respect to observation predicates. (SRI, 187, Sellars' emphasis.)

Thus the ontological inadequacy of the observational framework does not affect the methodological truth that it is, as a matter of fact, the starting point for all knowledge.

(2) Sellars likewise disagrees with Feyerabend's claim that the observational framework ought to be here and now replaced by the more adequate theoretical framework. In contrast he holds that although, from an ontological point of view, the observation framework is in principle replaceable by the currently available theoretical framework, it would be a bad move methodologically to so replace it. Sellars defends this view in two ways. First, he makes the obvious point that science for all its success has by no means yet achieved a completely adequate theoretical picture of the world (P, 97). Consequently, it would be premature to throw out the observational framework, which still gives us good service in the pragmatic job of getting around in the world, in favor of a new framework that would itself eventually have to be replaced. Indeed, switching from the observational framework, which has provided such a successful basis for doing science so far, to a better but still inadequate framework might even ultimately hinder the progress of science. Think, for example, simply of the time that would be lost in retraining ourselves (or our children) to make observations in terms of the new framework. In this case, says Sellars, "the better is the enemy of the best."

But Sellars has a more specifically philosophical reason for postponing the actual elimination of the observational framework. Following the tradition of philosophers like Berkeley, Kant, and Whitehead, he believes that physical objects must have essentially qualitative, "content" properties as well as the so-called primary structural and mathematical properties (SRI, 190-91). Indeed, he holds that the latter sort of properties could not exist without a basis in qualitative properties. (The pinkness-through-and-through of an ice cube, which was discussed above, is an instance of such a qualitative property.) Of course, there is no reason to say that the qualitative properties of the objects of the observational framework will have to appear in any ultimately adequate theoretical framework. But such a theoretical framework will (for the reason outlined above in the discussion of the identification of the entities of the observational framework with theoretical particles) have to contain *counterpart* qualitative predicates. Needless to say, current science contains no such predicates. Consequently, to substitute its theoretical framework for the observational framework would eliminate from our world view the crucial realm of the irreducibly qualitative.

(3) This brings us to Sellars' third thesis concerning the observational framework, that the nature of the observational framework has a regulative influence on the character of future science. As we have just seen, what we know about the observational framework (or, equivalently, the manifest image) enables us to say, although in only a very general way, something about what future science will be like. In particular, we can say that future science (Sellars suggests in particular future neurophysiology) will have to refer to basic systems that are nonparticulate and ultimately homogeneous. Space does not permit detailed analysis of the substance and justification of Sellars' position on this point. However, it is necessary to say something here about the significance of this position in Sellars' philosophy of science.

To begin with, it would be a serious mistake to think that Sellars' views about the need for counterparts to qualitative predicates in the science of the future are a peripheral matter, not of major importance in understanding or evaluating his basic philosophical viewpoint. In fact, these views follow immediately from Sellars' central conception of the two images, the manifest and the scientific, and their relations to one another.

To develop this point, we should recall that for Sellars the manifest and the scientific images are not separate, unrelated world views. The scientific image is developed as a more adequate "likeness" of the manifest image (PSIM, 20) that will explain the manifest image better than it can explain itself.[17] Consequently, when Sellars says the scientific image can replace the manifest image (at least as an explanation and description of the world), he does not mean that the latter can be eradicated. Rather, Sellars says, the very project of philosophy as a stereoscopic vision of the two images "implies that as I see it the manifest image is not overwhelmed in the synthesis." (PSIM, 9.)

At this point, two questions become crucial: (a) What kind of continuity is being required in the move from the manifest to the scientific image? (b) How can this demand for continuity avoid the myth of the given? With regard to (a), Sellars says that there must be "sufficient structural similarities between manifest objects and their scientific counterparts to account for" the success we have in "living, thinking, and acting in terms of the manifest framework." (PSIM, 28.) This suggests that Sellars' view is roughly that the precise entities and properties of the two images may be as different as you please, but there must be nonetheless some sort of isomorphism between the ways these entities and properties are related in the two images.

Obviously, this vague appeal to difference in content and similarity in structure needs further clarification. I believe the needed clarification can be found by turning to Sellars' views on the role of models in science. In commenting on Mary Hesse's discussion of models,[18] he criticizes her because, as he sees it, she "construes theoretical concepts pertaining to micro-theoretical entities as *identical with* concepts pertaining to the entities of the model, once these entities have been purged of those features which constitute the known negative analogy." (SRI, 179.) This is a mistake, Sellars says, because by *identifying* theoretical concepts with the concepts of the model, we exclude the possibility of developing genuinely new theoretical frameworks and hence reintroduce the myth of the given. The correct approach, according to Sellars, is to locate the identity not on the level of first-order predicates, which describe the basic entities of the theory, but on the level of the second-order predicates, which express various properties (e.g., transitivity, asymmetry, perceptibility) of the first-order predicates. Thus, in the case of kinetic theory and its billiard-ball model, we should not identify molecular mass, position, and velocity with billiard-ball mass, position, and velocity; these predicates should be regarded as having different meanings. However, the similarity enters in because molecular and billiard-ball predicates have second-order predicates in common (e.g., in both cases mass is an intrinsic, nonrelational property, velocity is expressible as the first derivative of position, position is a continuous variable, etc.). This suggests that we might similarly explicate the "structural similarities" between the manifest and the scientific frameworks as identities of second-order predicates.[19] This seems especially appropriate when we recall that all of Sellars' characterizations of future science are in terms of the properties (qualitative, ultimately homogeneous) that its basic predicates will have to have.

But now we must turn to question (b), Has this way of construing the continuity between the manifest and the scientific frameworks avoided the myth of the given? Isn't Sellars saying that certain second-order predicates of the manifest framework are inviolable and irreplaceable? And doesn't this amount to the reintroduction of a given?

An answer to this question depends on a clear understanding of what Sellars is rejecting when he rejects the given. In a passage quoted above (p. 83), Sellars emphasizes that the *only* sense in which he rejects givenness for observation predicates is that the observational framework is replaceable by another framework in which the observation predicates do not occur. Thus, for Sellars, the predicates of the observational framework play the role of an epistemological given only if it is required that *they themselves* must occur in any theoretical framework. However, this does not exclude the possibility of these predicates' making their influence felt (even if they are not present), via their second-order properties, on the new predicates of the theoretical framework. Rejecting the given only means rejecting immutably true descriptions of the world and immutably appropriate descriptive categories. Immutable *structures* (specified by second-order predicates) of descriptive frameworks are *not* rejected. Such structures are apparently Sellars' equivalent of the Kantian categories.

Even if the above remarks reconcile us to the consistency of Sellars' position, we may well feel that acceptance of immutable structures in the sense specified still amounts to an unfortunate return to the spirit of the myth of the given. However, I think such misgivings are out of place for the following reason: The basic spirit behind the idea of a given (e.g., in empiricist epistemologies) is that of providing an immutable foundation for scientific knowledge by exhibiting a set of statements *describing the world* that are inviolable and hence will have to be asserted by any adequate scientific account. Thus, the essential thrust of the myth of the given is to provide science with a set of true basic statements that are *scientific* in the sense of being directly descriptive of the world but nonetheless not subject to test by the hypothetico-deductive techniques of science. Or, to put it in a slightly different way, the idea of a given is to exhibit truths indistinguishable in type of content from the general run of scientific truths, which nevertheless fall outside the scope of scientific method. Now I think it is clear that nothing Sellars has said implies the existence of any such basic scientific truths. Science is in his view still capable of rejecting any description of the world, no matter how well entrenched. What Sellars adds is the idea that, when a transition is made to a radically new description of the world, there are still some criteria available to guide us in the setting up of a new description. But none of these criteria force the preservation of any particular elements of the old description.

III. Laws and Induction

In both its observational and its theoretical dimension, science exhibits a characteristic concern with the formulation and justification of *laws*. As a result, two central problems of philosophy of science have been (1) the analysis of the significance of lawlike statements and (2) the discussion of how such statements can be justified. Sellars' views on these subjects, which have not attracted the attention they deserve, are well worth examination both for the light they shed on the relevant philosophical problems and as illustrations of the power and unity of his philosophical system. In this section I will discuss in turn his account of the nature of laws and his account of their justification.

(a) The nature of scientific laws

The problem of the nature of scientific laws, like its classical ancestor, the problem of causality,[20] is defined by the opposition of an empiricist and a rationalist pole (CDCM, 267). According to the empiricist view, a law is essentially an assertion of the constant conjunction of two states of affairs, A and B. According to the rationalist view, it is essentially an assertion of a relation of physical implication (P-implication) between A and B. Intelligent defenses of both views involve, of course, refinements and clarifications that bring the views closer together. For example, the empiricist must add qualifications that distinguish lawlike assertions of constant conjunction from "accidental" ones; the rationalist must explain how physical implication differs from formal logical implication in ways that allow for the empirical character of science. But the two viewpoints continue to represent radically different alternatives in our explication of scientific laws.

Typically, Sellars' account of laws effects a mediation and synthesis of what he regards as genuine insights by proponents of these two opposing views (cf. CDCM, 285). Put simply, his view is that the empiricist is right in claiming that the world contains only constant conjunctions of events and hence that a description of reality need not include reference to causal powers or their equivalents. But, on the other hand, the rationalist is right in maintaining that the language of causal necessity is an essential and irreducible element of rational discourse about the world. P-entailments, although they have no descriptive significance, express essential *norms* (*rules*) of rational practice. Thus, Sellars' view of the role of causal necessity in science is similar to his view of the role of the observation basis: It has no *ontological* significance, but has an essential *methodological* place.

Let us give a more detailed exposition of the ideas summarized in the above paragraph. The typical empiricist account of laws presents them as special cases of descriptive 'all'-statements—i.e., as having the basic form, (x) Ax ⊃ Bx, but being distinguished from nonlawlike (accidental) generalizations of the same form by further properties such as being supportable by inductive evidence, and so on. While admitting that it is possible to characterize laws in this way, Sellars argues that such a characterization is basically misleading in regard to the logical role played by laws in scientific language. As Sellars sees it (cf. IM, 322), this role is best represented by regarding laws as *material rules of inference*—i.e., rules for moving from statement X to statement Y that, unlike formal rules of inference, depend on the nonlogical terms of X and Y. Thus, a law like, "Water boils at 212° F" is best rendered by, "From 'x is water' infer 'x boils at 212° F'."

The most immediate motivation for regarding laws as material rules of inference is the desire to implement the idea that the necessity of laws does not correspond to an ontological fact but rather to a methodological directive. If laws are rules of inference, then their direct function is to tell us what we ought to do, not what is the case. (This construal paves the way for Sellars' own version of a pragmatic "vindication" of induction, which I will discuss below.) However, we can find more profound motives—and a significant connection with Sellars' philosophical system—in his theory of meaning and rejection of the epistemological given.

To appreciate this deeper systematic motivation for the rule-of-inference view of laws, consider first the epistemological basis of a positivist account of laws. For the positivist, science is built on the foundation of an ever-growing set of incontrovertible particular facts (e.g., this piece of copper expands when heated). On this factual foundation are built, first of all, empirical generalizations, which summarize an indefinite number of similar particular facts and, secondly, theoretical generalizations, which serve to organize empirical generalizations and statements of particular fact in a deductive system, which is the locus of scientific predictions and explanations. But both types of generalization, empirical and theoretical, derive both their meaning and epistemological authority from the factual basis. Given this viewpoint, treating laws as material rules of inference parallel to formal rules of inference would be misleading because laws, unlike formal rules of inference, have no meaning or authority independent of the facts that they generalize. We could, of course, for convenience introduce material rules corresponding to laws; but in order to justify or even understand such rules we would have to recall that they *really* express generalizations of facts.

By contrast, Sellars rejects a privileged status for particular observed facts with respect to both the meaning and the justification of scientific statements. Regarding the former, Sellars thinks all scientific terms derive their meaning from the role they play in the language of science, not from some sort of semantic relation to observed facts. This implies that the meaning of a term is a function of the contexts in which it is used and hence, for example, that the assertion via a law of a correlation between one property and another makes a difference in the meaning of the terms that express those properties. In other words, a law provides one determinant of the meaning of the terms that occur in it (in contrast to the positivist view for which the meanings of the terms must be independently available before a law can be meaningfully formulated). Accordingly, knowing a scientific law amounts to knowing something about the meaning of (and hence rules of usage for) the terms involved. Construing laws as material rules of inference is a natural way to recognize this basic truth.

With regard to the justification of laws, Sellars' rejection of an unrevisable factual given makes it just as respectable to reinterpret a purported fact in the light of an accepted law as to revise the law to accommodate the fact. (Which choice we make—revision of the law or revision of the fact—will depend on our criteria of simplicity, explanatory power, and so forth.) The potentially regulative role of a scientific law with respect to the facts subsumed under it is recognized by regarding the law as a material rule of inference.

At this point a major objection must be faced. Sellars' construal of laws as rules of inference admittedly guarantees their necessity; but it seems to do so by giving up their empirical character. After all, material rules of inference govern the *meanings* of terms; and truths about meanings are not empirical. But laws of nature are obviously based on experience, not on the analysis of meanings. Hence Sellars' account of laws is inadequate.

The above objection is, of course, much less persuasive today than it would have been when a sharp analytic/synthetic distinction was accepted. However, the objection cannot be overcome merely by gesturing in the direction of contemporary dissatisfaction with the positivists' distinction of truths of meaning from truths of experience. An adequate reply requires some positive remarks on the relation between meanings and experience in science.

In Sellars' view (cf. CDCM, 287), there are two different ways of arriving at assertions about meanings. On the one hand, we can reflect on meanings that are antecedently given to us and, while remaining in our armchairs, unpack truths implicit in these meanings. Mathematics is a common source of this kind of assertion about meaning. On the other hand, we can reach decisions to use words in new ways (hence to modify their meanings) and, on the basis of these decisions, make assertions about meanings. In the latter case, unlike the former, there may be an experiential basis for a decision to use a term in a new way. For example, the discovery of a new species could prompt us to revise the meaning of 'mammal'; the discovery of a new form of radiation to revise the meaning of 'energy'. In fact, Sellars suggests that it is precisely the switch from the first, merely ampliative, approach to meaning to the second, innovative, approach that characterizes science:

> The motto of the age of science might well be: *Natural philosophers have hitherto sought to understand 'meanings'; the task is to change them.* (CDCM, 288; Sellars' emphasis.)

The decision to change a term's meaning is implemented by adopting a new material rule of inference—i.e., a new law of nature.[21]

This emphasis on the scientist as a changer of meanings—as opposed, for example, to the positivist's conception of him as a gatherer of facts—is of course a direct corollary of Sellars' rejection of a privileged status for any conceptual framework as a foundation for scientific explanation. The positivist could regard science as securely tied to the network of meanings defined by the observation framework and hence primarily concerned with gathering, on this basis, more and more "facts" (both general and particular). But for Sellars the idea of a privileged pregiven observation framework and its unproblematic facts is unacceptable. Consequently, the scientist, having had the observational rug pulled out from under him, must take as his primary task the construction (and criticism and modification) of conceptual frameworks adequate for dealing with the world. Since a conceptual framework is essentially a system of meanings, the scientist for Sellars is primarily an arbiter of meanings. However—and this is the crucial point in response to the objection we are considering—this preoccupation with meanings obviously does not have a nonempirical character. For the systems of meanings the scientist tries to construct are explicitly designed to describe the world of our experience.

Given this emphasis on the scientist's concern with changing meanings, a Sellarsian account of science must pay some attention to the problem of conceptual change that has been so much discussed in recent philosophy of science. Let us look briefly at two important aspects of this problem: the question of meaning variance and the question of the truth of scientific theories. (Sellars' treatment of these issues is found in CC and in *SM*, 13 ff.)

In the positivist account of science, the simply given facts of experience provided the basis for continuity of both meaning and truth through successive scientific theories. Although Einstein's relativity theory might differ radically from Newton's mechanics, the facts they explained were, to a great extent,[22] the same; and this common factual core provided a set of invariant meanings that made the two theories empirically comparable and a body of empirical truths that remained stable in spite of theoretical changes. But once we reject the positivist's factual given and recognize that factual meaning and truth are functions of theoretical meaning and truth, it seems that the continuity of science has been lost. Radically different theories will provide radically different interpretations of the "facts" and hence will not have a common observation basis upon which they can be compared. And, in place of a progressive accumulation of scientific truths, we will have only a discontinuous succession of different scientific world-views. Further, this lack of continuity seems to correspond to a lack of rationality in transitions from one scientific theory to another. For if two successive theories cannot agree on a common body of factual truths, how can there be an empirical basis for accepting one rather than the other? It would seem that decisions between scientific theories will have to be matters of subjective taste or ideological prejudice.

Although some philosophers of science, especially Feyerabend, have seemed willing to accept this conclusion, most have tried to find some way of maintaining a rational continuity throughout the development of science without returning to the invariant observation basis of the positivists. As we shall see in the following paragraphs, Sellars' theory of meaning is an invaluable aid to doing just this.

Those who, like Kuhn and Feyerabend, have emphasized the radical differences between successive scientific theories (e.g., between Newtonian and Einsteinian mechanics) pay special attention to the different world-pictures provided by the theories.[23] Thus, the world of Newtonian mechanics is one of discrete mass-points in three-dimensional Euclidean space, whereas the world of general relativity is one of gravitational and electromagnetic fields in four-dimensional Riemannian space. Even if the two theories use some of the same terms ('mass', 'velocity', 'energy'), these terms refer to very different entities. However, for Sellars, meaning is not defined in terms of reference but in terms of linguistic role. Consequently, for him, although two terms that differ in reference will differ in meaning, the extent of the difference will depend not on the dissimilarity in the objects they refer to but on the different roles they play. Further, these roles can be compared in detail by exhibiting the rules for the use of each term in its linguistic system. Terms will differ precisely to the extent that they are governed by different rules of use. Thus, for example, classical and relativistic 'mass', for all the differences in their referents, share a common core of use, in both theoretical and experimental contexts, that justify our regarding them as two species of the same generic concept (cf. *SM*, 130-31; CC, 184-86). (In Sellars' dot notation, both 'mass$_c$' and 'mass$_r$' are •mass•s.) In this way, Sellars' theory of meaning provides a way of expressing the continuity of science, even when there are radical changes in its world view.

Sellars takes a similar approach to the question of truth in science (*SM*, 133-34). Here the problem is that regarding science as a succession of different conceptual frameworks (which, as we have noted, may well have radically different views of the world's ontology) seems to exclude the view that science comes progressively closer and closer to the truth about the world. Kuhn, for example, while admitting that successive scientific theories represent a continuing increase in problem-solving ability, denies that there is any parallel progress toward a true picture of reality.[24] For successive frameworks present alternative views of the world (e.g., a particle picture, a wave picture) and do not seem to be converging to any final view to which all earlier views approximate.

For Sellars, however, truth is not defined in terms of picturing (although, of course, true theories do correctly picture reality). Rather, truth is defined, first of all, as semantic assertibility within a given linguistic system. Given this definition and his theory of meaning, Sellars is easily able to extend the concept of truth to cases in which we want to say that a statement s in a framework F is true with respect to another framework F'. Roughly, this will be the case when there is a parallel sentence s' in F' which plays a role in F' similar to that played by s in F and is true (semantically assertible) in F'.[25] For example, the principle of conservation of energy is true in the framework of classical physics (where it was discovered) as well as in the successor frameworks of special relativity and quantum mechanics. This is not because there is a single statement about energy conservation common to these three frameworks (this is not possible because the term 'energy' has different meanings in the three frameworks) but because the classical principle of energy conservation has true analogues in the other two frameworks. Accordingly, Sellars is able to give sense to the idea that science progressively accumulates more and more truths about the world throughout its historical development.

The above brief discussion does little more than touch the surface of the profound issues raised by the problem of scientific change. However, it should suggest the significant degree of illumination that the Sellarsian system can bring to this problem.

(b)   The problem of induction

Many recent discussions of induction (e.g., by Goodman and by Strawson) have attempted to "dissolve" the classical problem by showing that the demand for a justification of induction is misplaced. Strawson,[26] for example, argues that following inductive procedures is part of what is meant by "being rational," so it makes no sense to ask whether it is rational to accept the conclusions of inductive arguments. It is typical of Sellars' attitude toward traditional philosophical puzzles that he does not accept the dissolution approach to the problem of induction. Whereas many philosophers have regarded the revolutions of twentieth-century philosophy as eliminating classical problems by showing them to be ill-formed, Sellars uses twentieth-century developments to fashion new and more fruitful solutions to the classical problems. This combination of problematic continuity with revolutionary methods of solution is one of the most exciting and powerful aspects of the Sellarsian system.

In the case of induction, classical solutions have generally been based either on appeals to metaphysical relations of productive causality or on Kantian appeals to necessary categories of the mind and/or language. Since, as we have seen, Sellars accepts Hume's view that in the world there are only constant conjunctions, the first kind of appeal is not open to him. The second, Kantian, approach is much more congenial. On the basis of his account of meaning as use and of his construal of laws as material rules of inference, Sellars is able to argue that our very possession of a set of concepts that are applicable to the world requires our acceptance of a set of corresponding material rules of inference (which expresses the concepts' meanings) and hence of a set of laws of nature. As he puts it in SRLG, p. 355:

> There is no such thing as a problem of induction if one means by this a problem of how to justify the leap from the safe ground of the mere description of particular situations, to the problematical heights of asserting lawlike sentences and offering explanations. . . . The role of material moves in the working of a language . . . can be characterized both as constituting the concepts of the language and as providing for inferences, explanations, and reasons relating to statements formulated in terms of these concepts, [therefore] it is clear that to be in a position to ask the question, "Is it ever reasonable to assert one matter of fact on the basis of another matter of fact?" is to be in a position to answer with an unequivocal "yes!"

Hence Sellars is able to conclude immediately that it is reasonable to accept laws of nature. The very idea of a language about the world requires such laws.

However, this Kantian line of thought is not sufficient to dispose of the problem of induction. For even after we have recognized that *some* system of laws is necessary if we are to say anything at all about the world, we must still face the problem of *which* particular system of laws should be accepted. "The problem is not 'Is it reasonable to include material moves in our language?' but rather '*Which* material moves is it reasonable to include?' " (SRLG, 355-56.)

An approach to solving this problem can be found by reflecting further on the significance of Sellars' construal of laws as material rules of inference rather than empirical generalizations. Unlike empirical generalizations, rules are not ordinarily characterized as true or false. But we can, nonetheless, have good reason for accepting or not accepting rules; that is, given the goals of a certain kind of activity, we can show that these goals will be either furthered or not by adoption of a given rule. Accordingly, in his discussion of induction, Sellars does not follow the classical line of trying to show directly that there are reasons for thinking that inductive methods lead to correct (true) results; rather, like Reichenbach and Salmon, he tries to show that, quite apart from the question of truth, it is reasonable to accept the results of applying inductive methods.[27] Thus, Sellars' approach takes the form of what Feigl has called a "vindication" rather than a "justification" of induction. The basic strategy of such an approach is to show that, as scientists, we have certain goals (ends-in-view) that can be achieved only by accepting inductively supported conclusions. Reichenbach, for example, tried to show that induction is the only sure way to attain the scientist's goal of discovering the actual relative frequency of a property B in a total population of objects A (provided that there is any such relative frequency at all).[28] Sellars follows the same basic "pragmatic" strategy, but tries to avoid the difficulties that arose for Reichenbach and his followers by giving a more careful account of the relevant goals of science.

Sellars develops his account of the goals of science (and the vindication of induction based on them) in the context of a very original and powerful explication of the concept of probability.[29] He begins by noting (IV, 367) that the concept of probability is applicable in three different scientific contexts: (1) to theories (theoretical probability); (2) to laws (nomological probability); and (3) to assertions about the relative frequency of a given property in a given domain (statistical probability). However, as we will see, these three different senses of 'probability' are not independent. The explication of the probability of theories will make essential reference to the probability of laws, and the explication of the probability of laws will make essential reference to statistical probability. Further, Sellars regards each type of probability as a particular instance of a single general concept of probability. Therefore, although our main concern will be with assertions of nomological probability, we will also discuss the other two types of probability.

Before turning to a discussion of the particular types of probability, let us make a few comments about the general concept that Sellars thinks they all instantiate. First of all, he insists (IV, 373) that to say a statement is probable is *not* to say that it is the conclusion of an inductive argument that "implies" its conclusion with something less than deductive force. (This theme is elaborated in NDL.) Like Popper, Sellars rejects the positivist view that scientific statements are justified by a special sort of nondemonstrative inference. However, he does think that the locution "Hypothesis H is probable" can be satisfactorily explicated by reference to an appropriate *deductive* argument.

Obviously the "appropriate deductive argument" in question cannot (in general) be one that has H as its conclusion; this would confer deductive certitude on scientific hypotheses and be inconsistent with their inductive character.[30] Rather, Sellars suggests that the appropriate deductive argument is a *practical* one that has as its conclusion the *intention,* "I shall accept hypothesis H." Thus he proposes that the proper analysis of the locution, "It is probable that-h" is "There is a good deductive argument for accepting that-h". (Cf. IV, 374.) More specifically, Sellars suggests that to say that H is probable is to say that there exists a good deductive argument of the following form:

> I shall bring about E (where E is some end-in-view).
> Bringing about E implies accepting H if it satisfies condition C.
> H satisfies condition C.
> Therefore, I shall accept H.

From this it should be clear how Sellars' account of probability provides him with a locus for his pragmatic vindication of induction. If a scientific hypothesis is probable, then there is a sound practical argument, based on our goals as scientists, for accepting the hypothesis. The vindication of induction will be carried out by finding for each case (theories, laws, assertions of relative frequencies) an appropriate scientific goal that, when substituted for E in the above general form, will yield a sound argument for accepting the H in question.

The first and most straightforward case is that of theories (IV, 383). As scientists we want theories that have a certain complex of desirable properties (e.g., theories that are simple, generate testable lawlike statements, generate acceptable approximations of probable lawlike statements, generate no falsified lawlike statements). If a theory has all of these properties, let us say that it is ϕ. Then we can construct the following practical argument for accepting a theory T if it is ϕ:

> I shall bring it about that I accept theories that are ϕ.
> Bringing this about means accepting theory T if it is ϕ.
> Theory T is ϕ.
> Therefore, I shall accept T.

(Here T corresponds to H in the general schema given above, ϕ to the condition C, and E is "the state of accepting theories that are ϕ.") To say that T is probable is precisely to say that the above practical argument exists.

Notice that in order to be ϕ a theory has to "generate acceptable approximations of *probable* lawlike statements." Since this condition is essential—i.e., since a theory is probable only if it subsumes under it probable laws (or approximations to such laws)—theoretical probability is dependent on nomological probability. Accordingly, we next turn to this latter concept of probability.

Sellars proposes (CDCM, 291; IV, 387) the following as a general schema for a lawlike statement: 'K is an unexamined class of A's' P-implies 'm/n of the members of K are B's'. (A is a *finite* class—cf. note 28.) Typically, the empirical grounds for accepting a statement of this form will be the fact that (approximately) m/n examined A's have been found to be B's—that is, the fact that the proposed law "accords with the observed facts." Consequently, the practical argument for accepting a lawlike statement L will have to have the following form:

> I shall bring about E.
> Bringing about E implies accepting L if it accords with the
>   observed facts.
> L accords with the observed facts.
> Therefore, I shall accept L.

The key question, of course, is whether we can find an appropriate E to put into this argument—that is, an end-in-view that is shared by the scientific community and that implies accepting lawlike statements that accord with the observed facts. Sellars suggests (IV, 392) that the following E will do the job: E = the state of being able to draw inferences about the composition of unexamined classes of A's with respect to the property B in a way which also provides an *explanatory* account of the composition with respect to B of *examined* A's. It is obvious that this is an end-in-view shared by the scientific community: Scientists do want to be able to make predictions and give explanations regarding the correlation of various properties. But why does this end logically entail accepting L if it accords with the observed facts (i.e., if L asserts that the composition of unexamined classes of A's with respect to B is approximately the same as this composition for observed classes)?

The crucial problem here can be stated as follows: granted that the goal of doing science requires that we make some sort of projection as to the composition with respect to B of unexamined classes of A's, why should this projection be the one that accords with the composition of examined classes? (This problem is similar to that encountered by Reichenbach in his attempt to vindicate his "straight rule.") Sellars' solution hinges on the key fact that the goal of the scientist is not only to predict the future but also, at the same time, to *explain* the past. It is the latter goal that requires a projection in accordance with what has been observed.

> To give an explanatory account of the composition of the class K of *examined* Xs one must, logically, assert that the composition is the most statistically probable composition on the basis of the finite population (P) of Xs which are known to exist but of which only the members of K have been examined. (IV, 393.)

Sellars' point seems to be this: in addition to *predicting* the composition of unexamined classes of A's, the scientist also wants to *explain* why examined classes of A's had the composition they did—e.g., why were 95 percent of the philosophers we observed neurotic? This fact can be explained if we can assert that 95 percent of *all* philosophers are neurotic and hence that we should expect a random sample[31] of philosophers to contain a 95 percent proportion of neurotics. An explanation of this sort can be given if our sample of *examined* philosophers is adequate (e.g., large and diverse enough) to warrant the claim that, in all probability, the total population of philosophers has (approximately) the same proportion of neurotics as it does.[32] Hence, we can use the scientist's goal of explanation as a justification for projecting the observed proportion of neurotics in the population of philosophers, provided we know that our observed sample is (probably) representative of the total population.

At this point it becomes clear that the analysis and justification of nomological probability is dependent on an analysis and justification of statistical probability. A law is probable if there is a good argument for accepting it. There will be such an argument provided (1) the law accords with the observed facts and (2) it is (statistically) probable that the total population approximately matches the observed sample in its proportional composition. Hence we must analyze statistical probability and show how statements involving it can be justified.

We are interested in the probability of statements S of the form "The total population of A's (and hence any random sample of A's) has (approximately) the same proportion of B's as does K (an observed sample of A's)." Typically, this probability is said to be established by the observation that in a (large enough) random sample of A's, m/n of the

A's were B's—i.e., by the observation that S accords with the observed facts. As before, we interpret this probability as expressing the claim that there is a good practical argument for accepting the statement. This argument will have the following general form:

> I shall bring about E.
> Bringing about E entails accepting S if it accords with the observed facts.
> S accords with the observed facts.
> Therefore, I shall accept S.

Once again, the crucial point is the discovery of an appropriate E.

The discovery of the appropriate E turns on noting a relevant mathematical fact (IV, 405): that, for samples of a given size (out of a finite population), an exactly calculable percentage of these samples will match, within a specifiable range of deviation, the proportion of A's that are B's in the total population. For example, for samples of 1,500 A's, it can be mathematically proven that 95 percent of these samples will differ by no more than 3 percent from the total population in the proportion of B's that they contain. And for larger samples, the percentage of "matching" samples will be progressively larger.[33] Hence, if, whenever I am presented with a specific sample of A's, I assert that it matches (within a specified range), the total population of A's, I can mathematically calculate the percentage of times that I will be right as a result of following this policy. Further, if I follow this policy with regard to sufficiently large samples, the percentage of times that I am right will be greater than 50 percent. In view of all this, it seems that the appropriate E is the following (cf. IV, 405): The state of knowing how often we are right in answering questions as to whether or not a given sample of A's matches (within a certain range) the total population in proportion of B's. This end-in-view can be achieved by asserting that each sample of a given size does match the total population.[34]

We have of course no way at all of knowing that the assertion we make about any particular sample of A's matching the total population will be correct. All that we know is that following our policy of always giving an affirmative answer will eventually result in our being correct a specifiable percentage of times. But if our goal is precisely to know how often we are right, then the policy in question is justified.

In summary, we can give the following Sellarsian account of science as an inductive enterprise: We find (given a particular scientific framework) that a particular relative frequency of a given property holds for observed members of a particular population—i.e., that m/n of observed A's are B's. If the number of observed A's is (statistically) large enough, then, in view of our intention of making projections about the future in such a way that we know how often we will be right, it is reasonable to make the general statistical assertion: m/n (approximately) of all A's are B's. Further, in view of our intention of making projections about the future that will at the same time provide explanations for facts discovered in the past, it is reasonable to accept the following law (construed as a material rule of inference or P-implication): 'K is a finite unobserved class of A's' P-implies 'm/n elements of K are B's'. Finally, if T is a theory that yields a large number of acceptable laws (or close approximations of them) and has other desirable theoretical attributes (simplicity, etc), then, in view of our intention of possessing such theories, it is reasonable to accept T.

In conclusion, let us note a few points about the relation of Sellars' vindication of induction to other themes in his philosophy. (1) The vindication provides a "foundation" for scientific knowledge but without appealing to any epistemological given. Rather, the ultimate foundation of scientific knowledge turns out to be the *intentions* of the scientific community. This reflects Sellars' general tendency to ground the unique and irreducible character of a given conceptual framework (e.g., that of semantics, that of ethics) not in facts about special kinds of entities but in rules expressing the intentions of the community that uses the framework. In this sense, Sellars' account of induction—as well as much of the rest of his philosophy—can be quite properly characterized as "pragmatic."

(2) Sellars' approach to induction fits in neatly with his approach to the truth and the ontological significance of scientific theories. As we noted earlier, the general strategy of a vindication of induction, as originally conceived by Reichenbach and Feigl, is to circumvent Hume's problem by focusing on arguments for asserting statements (whether or not they are true) rather than on arguments for the truth (or probable truth) of the statements. Sellars adopts this basic strategy. But once he has established that a statement ought to be *accepted* by scientists (i.e., that it *can be asserted* within the conceptual framework of science), his account of truth as semantic assertibility allows him to move directly to the further claim that the statement is true (i.e., true in the relevant scientific framework). Finally, Sellars can, as we saw in the first sections of this chapter, move from the explanatory power of the scientific framework to its ontological significance. In this way, the true statements of science can be shown to provide an accurate *picture* of reality. Accordingly the pragmatic vindication approach to induction—which at first sight might seem to imply an instrumentalist view of science as a mere art of prediction—seems to mesh perfectly with Sellars' scientific realism.

(3) The vindication of induction connects with Sellars' ethical theory

in the following way: The ends that provide the ultimate premises in the arguments for accepting theories, laws, etc. express a commitment to promoting the truth. However, if this commitment were simply a matter of my *happening to like* promoting the truth, I would not be justified in asserting the *categorical* conclusion, 'I ought to accept S.' Like any other merely idiosyncratic desire, my wanting the truth could only generate a "hypothetical imperative," viz., 'If I have end E, then I ought to accept S'. If the commitment to truth expressed in the ends of science are to generate "categorical imperatives," they must derive from "the intention *as a member of a community* to promote the total welfare of that community." It is "because truth is a necessary condition of securing the common good that the search for it presents itself to us, on reflection, as categorically reasonable—in the truest sense a moral obligation." (NDL 437-38; Sellars' emphasis.)

Conclusion

We began this chapter by noting that Sellars' philosophy is one that takes science seriously; and our discussion has provided ample illustration of this point. However, it is important to note another theme that has become apparent in the course of our exposition. Time and again we have encountered an equally characteristic emphasis on the continuity of science with the world of concrete human activities and concerns. For example, we have seen Sellars insist—in a way not generally characteristic of scientific realists—that science emerges from and maintains an irrevocable methodological connection with the manifest image—the realm, as Sellars says, in which man encounters himself as man (PSIM, 6). Similarly, in his treatments of law and induction, Sellars gives a vital "foundational" role to the intentions of the human community of scientists. This shows that for Sellars a proper understanding of science requires construing it not only as a system of impersonal conceptual structures (although this sort of construal is invaluable) but also as a human activity. In this way, the philosophical project of taking science seriously merges with the broader project—which in fact defines Sellars' entire enterprise as a philosopher—of taking both science and man seriously.

NOTES

[1]He made this comment in his introduction to a series of lectures given at the Carnegie Institute on the Philosophy of Science at the University of Notre Dame in July, 1971.

[2]Compare Sellars' comments on the dangers involved in the contemporary "stampede" away from classical phenomenalism (P, 60).

[3]Although Sellars is aware that there are many and diverse types of theories in science, his discussions focus almost exclusively on "postulational" theories— i.e., those that posit unobserved entities to explain observed phenomena (LT, 106). It is such theories that constitute the scientific, as opposed to the manifest, framework (PSIM, 7).

[4]The reason it is not exactly accurate to say that to play a role in a language is to express a concept is that there are terms (Sellars cites exclamations like 'alas') that play a role in languages and yet do not seem to express any concept—what would fill the blank in ' "alas" expresses the concept _____' parallel to ' "round" expresses the concept Circularity' or ' "not" expresses the concept Negation'? Sellars suggests that, essentially, the terms that play roles but do not express concepts are those that play no role in *inferences* (formal or material) in the system. Thus, to use his example "All men are mortal, alas" has no more implications (except pragmatic ones) than does "All men are mortal" (cf. LT., 115, n. 1). This idea ties in with Sellars' doctrine that to express a concept is to be essentially involved in a network of laws (rules of inference). In any case, the refinement discussed here does not affect the claim that theoretical predicates have conceptual meaning, since they obviously do make a difference in the inferences that can be drawn from sentences in which they occur.

[5]For a concrete example of the complexities that can arise when we try to determine the precise ontological import of a particular scientific theory, see Sellars' discussion of special relativity in TWO, 567ff.

[6]Sellars makes reference to Nagel's discussion in *The Structure of Science* (New York: Harcourt, Brace and World, 1961), pp. 90ff. Sellars' critique is found in SRI, 174ff.

[7]The ideas of this paragraph are the basis for Sellars' critique of the Ramsey-sentence elimination method as a support for instrumentalism. Cf. SRI, 177, and LT, 117.

[8]Sellars expresses the fact that a predicate is connected with extralinguistic objects by saying that it is "extra-linguistically meaningful" (SRI, 176). However, it is essential to realize that this is an entirely different sense of 'meaning-ful' than the sense involved in Sellars' semantics, where the crucial point is that meaning is *not* a relation between words and objects.

[9]'True' here means true (semantically assertible) *within* the observational conceptual framework. As we shall see, Sellars rejects this framework as a locus of knowledge about what there is, and in this sense he denies the existence of observational entities. But this does not alter the fact that within the observational framework it is correct to assert the existence of observational entities. Cf. notes 13 and 15.

[10]For example, Boyle's law is merely a rough approximation that must be corrected when we take account of the size of the molecules that make up gases. Likewise, Kepler's laws do not describe the actual orbits of the planets because they ignore the gravitational influence that the planets exert on one another. For

many more instances of the inaccuracy of physical laws, cf. Michael Scriven, "The Key Property of Physical Laws—Inaccuracy." in *Current Issues in the Philosophy of Science,* ed. H. Feigel and B. Maxwell (New York: Holt, Rinehart, and Winston, 1961), pp. 91-101.

[11]A further question, which we will not discuss here, is whether—contrary to Quine's thesis of ontological relativity—science could ultimately arrive at a *unique* account of what there is.

[12]For a clear exposition of this argument, see C. F. Delaney, "Sellars' Grain Argument," *Australasian Journal of Philosophy* 50 (1972): 14-16.

[13]However, there is a more general sense in which observational terms refer—although under a false description—to the actual world. Thus, for example, the observational term 'rock' refers to what is actually (supposing the correctness of current theories) a certain kind of molecular structure. Because of this, there is a sense in which observational statements like "this is a rock" are true; cf. note 15.

[14]On Sellars' critique of the myth of the given, see C. F. Delaney's paper on the theory of knowledge.

[15]It is important, however, to note that this denial of the existence of observational entities is not a statement made within the observational framework (where it would be absurd) but a statement about the explanatory and descriptive inadequacy of that framework itself (cf. PSIM, 27). Also, Sellars' theory of truth provides a way of defining the 'truth' (in a derivative sense) of statements in rejected conceptual frameworks. (See *SM,* 133-34.)

[16]Sellars' criticism focuses on the views developed by Feyerabend in "Explanation, Reduction, and Empiricism," in ed. H. Feigl and G. Maxwell, *Minnesota Studies in The Philosophy of Science,* (Minneapolis: University of Minnesota Press, 1962), vol. 3.

[17]It is very important to note that the scientific image is "scientific" in the rather special sense of employing *postulational* theories to explain observed facts. A great deal of what would be generally accounted science (e.g., the formulation of empirical generalizations) goes on in the manifest image. Cf. PSIM, 6-7.

[18]Hesse's views are found in her book, *Models and Analogies in Science* (Notre Dame, Indiana: University of Notre Dame Press, 1966). For her reply to Sellars' criticisms, see "An Inductive Logic of Theories," in *Minnesota Studies in the Philosophy of Science,* ed. M. Radner and S. Winokur (Minneapolis: University of Minnesota Press, 1970), 4:176-80.

[19]There are two further analogies between the role of models and the role of the manifest framework. First, Sellars' emphasizes that, at the current stage of scientific development, models are necessary because "by virtue of their visualizable character," they "provide a surrogate for the 'qualitative' predicates which must, in the last analysis, be the underpinning of theoretical magnitudes if they are to be the sort of things that could 'really exist'." (TE, 70.) Second, Sellars makes it clear that in principle (though not in any currently attainable practice) the model as an independent support of a theory could be eliminated by expressing everything it adds "by the explicit working of a logistically contrived deductive system". (SRI, 179.) Thus, like the manifest framework, models are currently essential, especially as a locus for the qualitative dimension that science now lacks; but, also like the manifest framework, the model is in principle capable of being eliminated in favor of a fully adequate ultimate scientific theory. All these similarities suggest that for Sellars the most basic function of a model is to serve as an expression of the relevant aspects of

the manifest framework that are omitted in the current stage of a given theory's development.

[20] I will concentrate here only on those aspects of Sellars' views on causality that are immediately relevant for the analysis of scientific laws.

[21] Sellars notes (CDCM, 288) that such a change in meaning need not involve a change in the explicit definition of the term in question. I suppose this is because the explicit definition expresses a *core* of a term's meaning that is deemed essential to its application. However, since a new use of the term has been introduced, its meaning (in a broader but still precise sense) has changed.

[22] The positivist would, of course, emphasize that the scope of the two theories was different in that Einstein's theory explained facts (e.g., the behavior of particles moving near the speed of light) that Newton's theory did not.

[23] Cf., for example, Feyerabend's "How To Be a Good Empiricist," in *The Delaware Seminar*, ed. Baumrin (New York: John Wiley & Sons, 1963), 2:14.

[24] Cf. T. Kuhn, *The Structure of Scientific Revolutions* (Chicago: University of Chicago Press, 1962).

[25] For more on Sellars' account of truth, see C. F. Delaney's article on the theory of knowledge.

[26] Cf. his *Introduction to Logical Theory* (London: Methuen, 1952), chap. 9.

[27] However, as we shall note below, Sellars' view of truth as semantic assertibility allows him to move from a result's acceptability within a scientific framework to its truth.

[28] The reason Reichenbach must add the qualification "provided there is any such relative frequency of all" is that he regards the scientist as dealing with *infinite* populations, for which it is possible that the relative frequency of a given property will not converge to any limit and hence not be definable. Sellars avoids this difficulty and some other related ones by regarding the scientist as dealing only with *finite* populations.

[29] The exposition that follows is based on Sellars' important but little discussed article, "Induction as Vindication."

[30] In some cases we might say that a given hypothesis was probable because it could be deduced from some other well-established hypotheses. But this would be a probability derivative from that of the well-established hypotheses; and, to avoid an infinite regress, we would have to eventually find hypotheses that had a nonderivative probability.

[31] By a "random sample" Sellars means simply a sample which we have no reason to think differs significantly in composition from the total population. A sample of A's is random with respect to the property B if we know nothing relevant to the proportion of B's it contains except the fact that it is a sample of A's.

[32] There may of course be other explanations of why the property in question had the frequency it did in the sample we observed. For example, all the philosophers we observed may have been undergoing psychoanalysis; and it may be true that 95 percent of people undergoing psychoanalysis are neurotic. But it is obvious that such explanations in terms of further relevant characteristics of the observed sample must eventually be based on an appeal to the fact that the members of our sample belong to *some* population for which the same relative frequency holds as for our sample.

[33] For a good exposition of the mathematical statistics being employed here, cf. D. C. Williams, *The Ground of Induction*, (Cambridge, Mass.: Harvard University Press, 1947), chap. 4. It should be emphasized that Sellars' use of this mathematical information in his vindication of induction differs significantly

from the use of it by Williams, who is attempting an a priori justification of induction.

[34]The only other way of being sure of how often we will be right would be to say that each sample does *not* match the total population. But if we specify that the samples in question are to be large enough that over 50 percent of them match the total population and add the goal of being right more often than we are wrong, the policy of asserting the sample to be a good match is the only one suited to achieve our goal.

Philosophy of Mind
The Mind-Body Problem

Michael J. Loux

The doctrine of scientific realism plays a central role in all of Sellars' work; his writings on the mind-body problem are no exception. Indeed, it would not be inaccurate to say that in Sellars' hands the mind-body problem just is the problem of formulating a philosophically adequate account of the various mental phenomena within the context of the ontology provided by science. And for Sellars this task has two sides, for he wants to insist that the phenomena of thinking and sensation present the scientific realist with two quite different sets of philosophical issues. In this paper, I want to consider both sides of this task. In the first two sections, I examine Sellars' account of thinking; and although the topic takes me in a number of different directions, the ultimate aim of these sections is to exhibit Sellars' attempt to construct an account of conceptual phenomena that is consistent with the basic insights of scientific realism. In the last section, I address the issue of sensation; here, I explain why Sellars takes what he calls sense impressions to present theoretical difficulties for the scientific realist, and I try to indicate what Sellars thinks would be required for the resolution of those difficulties.

I

Philosophers have frequently contended that when we speak of persons as deliberating, wondering, calculating, deciding, forming intentions, and the like, we are pointing to the occurrence of mental episodes of various sorts. These episodes (usually called *mental acts*) are said to be inner or private. The point of such characterizations is to deny the public observability of mental acts and to point to the privileged access a person has to those mental acts that he himself undergoes. Their defenders have further insisted on the irreducible conceptuality of these episodes and have resisted attempts to assimilate mental acts to the category of raw feels—things like bodily sensations and sensory images. Mental acts, we are told, differ from raw feels in being intentional—in being of, for, or about objects, properties, and states of affairs.

Now defenders of mental acts have regularly thought that the framework of inner conceptual episodes commits us to a radical form of mind-body dualism. Thus, they have maintained that intentionality is a property that cannot be exemplified by anything physical and have concluded that the subjects of mental acts must be immaterial substances. They have also claimed that an individual is immediately aware of his own mental acts, that he is acquainted with them in their intrinsic nature. Then, toward convincing us of the immateriality of the subject that undergoes these acts, they have asked us to consult the data of introspection, insisting that since what we experience when we are aware of our deliberatings, inferrings, and the like is not any kind of material or physical process, those mental episodes require a nonphysical subject.

But since he insists upon embedding the framework of mental acts in a dualistic ontology, the defender of mental acts owes us an account of how the immaterial substance that undergoes mental acts is related to the physical organism that is a living human body. It is, however, notorious that all of the available accounts of this relationship (interactionism, parallelism, occasionalism, epiphenomenalism) have serious difficulties. Furthermore, he has to provide an account of our ability to *know* about inferrings, wonderings, and deliberatings other than our own. He has to explain how we can have knowledge of the mental acts of substances that are, by his own admission, inaccessible to us. Typically the appeal here is to some version of the argument from analogy; but that line of reasoning has been shown to have obvious and crippling defects.

Confronted with these all too familiar epistemological and ontological puzzles, one is inclined to deny that conceptual phenomena like those listed earlier either are or presuppose mental acts. The temptation is to embrace a form of philosophical behaviorism and to insist that concepts like deliberating, wondering, and inferring can be analyzed in terms of actual and possible patterns of overt human behavior. The advantages of such a strategy are obvious. In the case of conceptual phenomena at least, it eliminates puzzles about mind-body relations; and since it identifies conceptual phenomena with patterns of publicly observable behavior, philosophical behaviorism has a ready explanation of our knowledge about things like the deliberatings and calculatings of other human beings. But despite its obvious strengths, the philosophical behaviorist's account of conceptual phenomena has few defenders on the contemporary scene. Part of the resistance to behaviorism stems from the belief that careful phenomenology does, in fact, reveal the kind of inner episode the behaviorist is unwilling to countenance; but more commonly behaviorism is dismissed on the grounds that the connection between conceptual phenomena and overt behavior is simply not analytic. Thus, it is possible for me to behave in all the relevant ways and (as far as can be behaviorally determined) to be disposed to behave in those ways while not, say, inferring that Socrates is a man. Likewise, I can infer this proposition and be both firm and successful in my resolution never to let on.

But if a behaviorist analysis of conceptual phenomena is inadequate, then we seem forced to adopt an ontology of inner conceptual episodes after all. Nonetheless, our initial confrontation with the framework of mental acts should make it clear that a theory of the conceptual can be acceptable only if it avoids the ontological and epistemological perplexities of dualism. What seems to be called for, then, is a theory of conceptual phenomena that preserves the essential features of the framework of mental acts without embracing dualism. More precisely, we want a theory of thinking that (1) recognizes the existence of mental acts, (2) attributes to them the property of intentionality, and (3) explains the privileged access an individual has to his own mental acts but that (4) provides a satisfactory account of how we can genuinely be said to have knowledge of the mental acts of others and (5) does not commit us to a dualistic ontology. In general terms, we can characterize Sellars' theory of thinking as an account of conceptual phenomena that is formulated to satisfy all of (1) through (5).

The central theme of Sellars' account is the view that the framework of inner conceptual episodes is to be thought of as something like a theoretical framework designed to explain overt human behavior. To see why Sellars would think that an account of this sort holds out the promise of satisfying the criteria laid out in my (1) through (5), we have to recall some general themes from his account of theories. The first point to recall is Sellars' strongly realistic interpretation of theoretical frameworks. According to Sellars, a theory postulates the existence of unobservable entities as a means of explaining certain observable phenomena; and he insists that to have good reasons for adopting a theoretical framework is to have good reasons for thinking that the entities postulated by the theory really exist (LT, 118). Given this sort of interpretation of theories, the claim that our framework of conceptual episodes is to be construed as a postulational or theoretical framework is bound to result in an account of thinking that satisfies my (1).

Furthermore, Sellars wants to claim that while the relationship between the postulated entities of a theory and the observable phenomena they are invoked to explain is logically synthetic, a theory so correlates its postulated entities with the relevant domain of observable phenomena that the relationship between them is noncontingent. Given the molecular theory, for example, it is a *synthetic yet conceptual* truth that macro-objects behave in certain ways because they are composed of micro-objects of certain kinds. Thus, while the connection between macro-objects and micro-objects is not analytic, the theory licenses the inference from the observable states and processes of macro-objects to the unobservable states and processes of micro-objects. Given the theory, then, one can *know* that certain unobservable swarms of molecules are behaving in ways that perception itself does not make manifest (*SM*, 68-69).

But if a theory does, in fact, license the inference from the observable to the unobservable, the interpretation of mental acts as postulated entities would seem to yield an account that could satisfy my (4) without embracing any version of logical behaviorism. If inner conceptual episodes are to be thought of as entities postulated to explain certain forms of observable behavior, then we can explain our ability to know about the mental acts of others merely on the basis of overt behavior by construing it as the ability to use a theory to infer the existence of unobservable processes from observational premises (*SM*, 68-69).

A third theme from Sellars' account of theoretical frameworks is the view that the construction of a theory always involves the appeal to a model. According to Sellars, the scientist takes a set of familiar objects and argues that if we think of the entities to be postulated on analogy with the familiar objects we can understand why the observable phenomena the theoretical entities are meant to explain occur as they do. Thus, in constructing the molecular theory, the model was perhaps swarms of tiny commonsense objects (e.g., swarms of dust-motes) and the suggestion was that if we take macro-objects to be composed of things thought of on analogy with the tiny objects of the swarms we can understand the occurrence of certain problematic forms of behavior on the part of macro-objects. Sellars wants to deny, however, that models function merely as aids to scientific imagination. He insists that the scientist's very characterization of the entities to be postulated is parasitic on the characterization appropriate to the familiar objects of the model; for in laying down principles for the description of the entities he means to postulate, the scientist takes the predicates applicable to the objects of the model and analogically extends them to apply to the postulated entities. Thus, the expressions used in identifying and describing the properties, states, and processes of the objects in the model are given a new sense and in that sense serve as the parameters for understanding the domain of postulated entities.[2]

The use of analogy in the construction of theoretical frameworks bears directly on the issue of intentionality outlined in my (2); for as the theoreticity of mental acts is presented in Sellars' writings, the contention is that overt speech is to be thought of as the model for mental acts. Thus, Sellars takes thinking to be a kind of "inner speech," and he argues that the language of intentionality that applies to inner conceptual episodes can be thought of as an analogical extension of the language in terms of which we characterize the semantical properties of overt speech. According to Sellars, then, talk of thoughts as *of, about,* or *for* objects, properties, and states of affairs is simply an extension of the discourse in which we specify what words mean, refer to, denote, and the like (EPM, 186-89).

The final theme from Sellars' analysis of theories that is relevant to his account of mental acts is his rejection of the view that the statements of a theory can function exclusively as conclusions of inference from the observable to the unobservable. Although Sellars agrees that when a theory is first presented its statements function only in this way, he wants to insist that, given practice in employing a theory inferentially, individuals can be trained to use its statements noninferentially as perceptual and introspective reports. To think otherwise, he claims, is to be caught in the grips of "the myth of the given" and to suppose that the commonsense statements that constitute the observation base of a theory have an unchallengeable right to serve as the vehicles for reporting our experiences.[3]

But because he believes that theoretical claims can come to function in contexts that are not inferential, Sellars maintains that his account of conceptual phenomena can satisfy the condition laid down in my (3). Central to the theme of privileged access is the notion that the position of a person P with respect to his own mental acts is different from that of other people. As the point is usually put, persons other than P have to rely on overt behavior in ascribing mental acts to P, whereas P can ascribe them to himself without any appeal to behavioral evidence. Sellars suggests that we think of an individual's noninferential self-ascription of mental acts to be a case where theoretical statements have taken on a reporting role; we can characterize the individual's ability to engage in self-ascription by saying that he has been trained to respond immediately in ways that originally required inference (EPM, 189).

That leaves us with condition (5); and here Sellars argues that as it is explained in his account the concept of a mental act turns out to be ontologically neutral. The central point is Sellars' contention that the phenomenon of intentionality lacks the ontological consequences traditionally attributed to it by dualists. As I have indicated, he takes the intentionality of mental acts to be modeled on talk about the meaning and reference of overt speech; and according to Sellars, to engage in semantical discourse is merely to provide a functional classification of overt linguistic episodes. But, then, to say what a mental act is of or for is not to make any claim about what it is in its intrinsic nature; it is merely to classify that act according to its function or role in inner speech. Thus, Sellars can conclude that the intentionality of mental acts fails to commit their defenders to even the weakest version of mind-body dualism.

Now, Sellars wants to argue that, since the intentionality of the conceptual is ontologically neutral, facts about our introspective awareness of mental acts will also fail to establish the dualism of the framework of mental acts; for according to Sellars, our knowledge of our own mental acts proceeds in terms of the concepts the "theory" ascribes to them. But if those concepts are merely functional and specify nothing whatever about the intrinsic nature of mental acts, then the fact that introspection fails to reveal mental acts as physical or material processes can hardly be expected to show that they are processes of some immaterial substance. (PSIM, 32-34; BBK, 57-59.)

II

This brief sketch of Sellars' account needs to be expanded. In particular, the central theme of the account—the theoreticity of the mental—needs to be elaborated. Sellars wants to deny that the theme is as puzzling as it initially appears. As he repeatedly tells us, he does not mean to say that the notion of an inner conceptualizing arose "as a self-conscious scientific hypothesis" or that it is "the sort of thing we would normally classify with 'highly confirmed theories.' " (SM, 155.) The point is rather that it is fruitful to think of inner episodes as though they were part of a theory, that the framework of mental acts has the kind of logic it would have if it had been introduced as a consciously developed theory.

In arguing for the theoreticity of mental acts, then, Sellars is not committed to the view that at some moment in history an individual or group of individuals actually postulated mental acts in the attempt to explain certain features of human behavior. He is, however, committed to the view that the concept of a mental act could have been introduced in this way; and this, in turn, commits him to the view that it is at least in principle possible for human beings (or something sufficiently like human beings) to employ a conceptual scheme that, while lacking the notion of a mental act, incorporates the resources for introducing this notion. And, of course, since Sellars wants to avoid skepticism about the objective validity of the framework of mental acts, he is committed to the further claim that individuals operating with this scheme would be rationally justified in enriching it by the postulation of mental acts (*SM*, 155).

Thus, to establish the coherence of his interpretation of thinking, Sellars has to convince us not only of the possibility of a conceptual scheme of this sort but also of the rationality of enriching it in the way described. The strategy he employs here is one borrowed from the work of contract theorists in political philosophy who defend their account of political authority by way of a piece of logical fiction. In the same way, Sellars appeals to a myth in his attempt to convince us of the intelligibility of taking mental acts to exhibit the logic of theoretical entities. For reasons that will emerge shortly, Sellars' piece of logical fiction has come to be known as the Jonesian myth. Its central characters are members of what Sellars calls a Rylean community, where the expression 'Rylean' is meant to bring out the fact that the concept of thinking employed by these individuals is one that can be analyzed in terms of what Sellars takes to be the essentially behavioristic framework of Ryle's *The Concept of Mind*. Thus, for Sellars' Ryleans, to think that p (where 'to think' has the *episodic* sense of 'to have a thought occur to one') is, in the primary sense, simply to say 'p' and, in the secondary sense, to have what Sellars calls a short-term, proximate propensity to say 'p'.[4]

By Sellars' own admission, the concept of saying invoked in this formula is fairly specialized. He insists that it is richer than the notion of saying that applies to the mere parroting of words. According to Sellars, a Rylean thinks that-p only when he says (or is disposed to say) 'p' as one who understands the language in which 'p' is embedded. Furthermore, as Sellars uses the term 'say' in this formula, only sincere or candid utterances count as sayings of 'p'. Consequently, the utterance of a sentence within the context of a play or as a means to deceive someone would not count as a thinking in the Rylean sense. But while the concept at work here is richer than some notions of saying with which we are familiar, Sellars wants to insist that it is weaker than the generic concept of saying that takes as its species notions like warning, telling, and informing. This very rich concept of saying applies only to utterances as they function within the social context of linguistic communication; but according to Sellars, Rylean thinking, even in its primary sense, requires no audience at all. It is a kind of saying that is utterly spontaneous, the sort of thing done by the child who utters "Yuck! That tastes like spinach!" or "That man is really fat!" It is, Sellars tells us, what we are accustomed to call thinking out loud.[5]

For the Ryleans of Sellars' myth, then, to think that something is the case is either to think it out loud or to have a short-term, proximate propensity to think it out loud. But while all Rylean thinking can be analyzed in terms of overt linguistic behavior, Sellars wants to insist that it can take a variety of forms. As he puts it, Ryleans can deliberate out loud, infer out loud, form intentions out loud, make decisions out loud, and so on. Nor are all instances of these different forms of thinking out loud confined to the object language. Sellars tells us that his Ryleans can engage in metalinguistic thinking; and he wants to insist that some of their metalinguistic thinkings out loud involve the application of semantical concepts to overt linguistic episodes. Thus, Ryleans think out loud that linguistic expressions have this or that meaning, refer to this or that object, or denote this or that class of things.

Underlying the claim that Ryleans can engage in semantical discourse is the contention that talk about meaning is not even implicitly mentalistic. Sellars wants to deny, that is, that the application of the semantical categories presupposes a familiarity with the framework of mental acts.[6] In a similar vein, he insists that individuals who employ only the behavioristic concept of thinking current in his Rylean community could engage in theory construction. (EPM, 183-86.)

Now, Sellars asks us to focus on a stage in Rylean history where the members of his mythical community have in fact mastered the techniques involved in the postulation of unobservable entities; and within this historical context, he introduces us to a remarkable Rylean he calls Jones. Jones has a philosophical temperament and is given to frequent periods of reflecting out loud on the framework of thinking that is his heritage. It turns out that in the midst of one of his reflective periods, Jones stumbles across a phenomenon that strikes him as anomalous. The phenomenon in question concerns the short-term, proximate propensities that Ryleans, in the secondary sense at least, call thinkings. Jones notes that individuals are subject to shifts in these propensities, that one such propensity can be replaced by another. He further notes that within the Rylean framework one can explain these shifts only in terms of the occurrence of thinkings out loud. On the Rylean account, verbal propensities culminate in the appropriate thinkings out loud; and when they so culminate, they are discharged and replaced by different propensities. What Jones notices, however, is that a short-term, proximate propensity to think out loud can be replaced by another such propensity even when it has not culminated in the appropriate thinking out loud. Thus, he notes that while his propensity to think out loud "There are deer at the watering hole" typically gives way to some other such propensity upon his thinking out loud "There are deer at the watering hole," that propensity can be replaced by another even during a period of extended silence. Jones has, of course, caught on to the techniques involved in theory building. He is familiar with the pattern that leads from exceptions to empirical generalizations to the postulation of unobservable entities; and since he recognizes the first stage of this pattern in his anomaly, Jones is inclined to suppose that human beings are the subjects of imperceptible episodes whose occurrence makes possible an explanation of the problematic propensity-shifts.

But Jones realizes that before this intuition of his can be developed into a full-fledged hypothesis he has to provide a characterization of the episodes he wants to postulate. In this context, Jones reflects once again on the anomalous propensity-shifts; and it occurs to him that since his imperceptible episodes are to provide an account of what the Rylean framework takes overt linguistic episodes to explain—shifts in verbal propensity—we could readily understand how their occurrence gives rise to the occurrence of the phenomena to be explained if we were to construe them as something analogous to overt linguistic episodes.

Thus, Jones takes his episodes to constitute a kind of "inner speech"; and giving a new sense to the Rylean term, he speaks of them as thoughts. He recognizes there is a variety of dimensions within which we characterize linguistic episodes—the phonetic, the syntactic, the semantic, and the pragmatic; but not too much reflection convinces him that the linguistic interpretation of his imperceptible episodes receives its most coherent expression when those episodes are taken to be characterized in terms of concepts modeled on the various semantical categories of meaning, reference, denotation, and the like.

Jones realizes, however, that the development of this picture presupposes detailed analyses of the various semantical concepts as they apply to overt speech; and his intuitions tell him that the best course here is to start with the concept of meaning. Initially he finds himself inclined to analyze this notion in relational terms. He assumes that he has no option but to take statements like:

(1) 'Socrates' refers to the teacher of Plato

and

(2) 'Man' denotes (is true of) featherless bipeds

to be correlating linguistic expressions and nonlinguistic objects; and since he recognizes (1) and (2) to be near relatives of meaning statements like

(3) 'Bachelor' means unmarried male,
(4) 'Hombre' (in Spanish) means man,

and

(5) 'Deux et deux font quatre' (in French) means two plus two equals four,

he is prepared to conclude that meaning talk asserts the existence of word-world relations. However, Jones is reminded of the variety of expressions that can be the subject matter of meaning talk. He is reminded, for example, of

> (6) 'Non' (in French) means no,
> (7) 'Der' (in German) means the,

and

> (8) 'O' (in Spanish) means or,

where a relational account is totally out of the question; and since he holds 'means' to be univocal over (3) through (8), he finally concludes that a relational account of meaning statements is mistaken.

Convinced now that the surface grammar of meaning statements is misleading, Jones toys with the suggestion that what follows the subject term in statements like (3) and (4) is, appearances to the contrary, a one-place predicate. Coupling this suggestion with what he takes to be the truism that meaning statements identify the use (in the sense of linguistic role) of the expressions whose meaning they elucidate, Jones comes up with the view that meaning statements serve to *classify* linguistic expressions functionally or in terms of their linguistic roles.[7]

Toward clarifying this interpretation of meaning talk, Jones introduces a form of quotation as yet unknown in his Rylean community, which he calls dot quotation.[8] Very generally, the application of Jones's new quoting device to a term N has the effect of creating a metalinguistic common noun •N• that is true of all those linguistic expressions that, in their own language, play the role that N plays in the base language. Thus, we who speak English could employ dot quotation to construct metalinguistic sortal terms like •man•, •blue•, and •two plus two equals four• by means of which we could provide, for our fellow speakers of English, functional classifications of expressions from the whole range of human languages. Now, what Jones wants to claim is that the appeal to dot quotation makes explicit the logical form of meaning statements. As he analyzes them, (3) through (8) become

> (3') 'Bachelor' is an •unmarried male•.
> (4') 'Hombre' is a Spanish, •man•,
> (5') 'Deux et deux font quatre' is a French •two plus two equals four•,
> (6') 'Non' is a French •no•,
> (7') 'Der' is a German •the•,

and

> (8') 'O' is a Spanish •or•.[9]

Having analyzed meaning talk, Jones turns to the task of explicating
semantical notions like references and denotation. He remains steadfast
in his conviction that talk about reference and denotation is intimately
related to talk about meaning. Only now, his success in providing a
nonrelational account of meaning suggests a parallel treatment of reference and denotation. In the end, Jones concludes that statements in
which we apply the concepts of reference and denotation involve the
existential (or, as he prefers to call it, the particular) quantification of a
special kind of variable. He represents this variable by the symbol S and
stipulates that it range over dot-quoted terms. On Jones' reading, our (1)
and (2) become

> (1′)   For some S, 'Socrates' is an S and S is materially equivalent
>   to •the teacher of Plato•

and

> (2′)   For some S, 'man' is an S and S is materially equivalent to
>   •featherless biped•,

where the notion of material equivalence, invoked to bring out the
extensional dimension of referential concepts, is so understood that to
speak of the material equivalence of dot-quoted terms is to point to the
coextensionality of the expressions of which they are true.[10]

Jones takes (1′) and (2′) to show that the only relations relevant to the
analysis of statements like (1) and (2) are relations between words, and
he concludes that what is fundamental in semantical discourse is not a
set of correlations tying language to objects in the world but rather the
kind of functional classification that is perspicuously represented by the
device of dot quotation. Against the background of this intralinguistic
interpretation of semantical discourse, Jones reformulates his claim that
the episodes of inner speech are to be characterized in semantical terms.
He tells us that what he calls thoughts are to be understood in terms of
concepts analogous to those at work in the functional classification of
overt speech; and toward providing the linguistic resources for the
expression of these concepts, Jones takes the familiar dot-quoted expressions and gives them new senses. In their new senses, Jones stipulates, dot-quoted terms are to provide a framework for classifying inner
episodes according to their various "linguistic" or conceptual roles.[11]

This framework for characterizing his inner episodes provides Jones
with the resources for developing his original sketchy intuitions into a
full-blown theory. As Sellars describes it, what Jones finally comes up
with is the hypothesis that

> people's propensities to think out loud, now this, now that, change during
> periods of silence as they would have changed if they had, during the interval,

been engaged in a steady stream of thinkings-out-loud of various kinds, because they are the subject of imperceptible episodes which are:

(a)   analogous to thinkings-out-loud;
(b)   culminate, in candid speech, in thinkings-out-loud of the kind to which they are specifically analogous;
(c)   are correlated with the verbal propensities which, when actualized, are actualized in such thinkings-out-loud;
(d)   occur, that is, not only when one is silent but in candid speech, as the initial stage of a process which comes "into the open", so to speak, as overt speech (or as sub-vocal speech), but which can occur without this culmination, and do so when we acquire the ability to keep our thoughts to ourselves. (*SM*, 159.)

Jones is anxious to teach his new theory to his Rylean colleagues, but as he thinks it through one last time, it dawns on him that the unfamiliarity of dot quotation will make it difficult for the "plain man" to learn his theory. In his search for a less forbidding system of labels, Jones is reminded of the surface structure of semantical statements, according to which words mean this or that, refer to this or that, and are true of this or that. Although misleading, that structure is familiar. Consequently, while he is conscious of appealing to a grammar that misleadingly suggests a relational theory of thinking, Jones invokes a system of labels that is modeled on the familiar structure at work in the application of semantical notions. Thus he replaces labels like:

the •Socrates• thought,
the •man• thought,

and

the •two plus two equals four• thought

with labels like

the thought of Socrates
the thought about men

and

the thought that two plus two equals four. (*SM* 87-88, 165-66.)

In this more teachable (but philosophically misleading) form, Jones presents the theory to his Rylean colleagues, teaching them to employ it in interpreting and explaining overt human behavior. Initially, he teaches them "to use the theory as a theory, i.e. to infer the existence of mental acts of various kinds from behavioral evidence." (*SM*, 166.) Then, exploiting their ability to employ the theory in inferential contexts, he teaches his colleagues to use the statements of the theory as vehicles for responding noninferentially to their own mental acts. As Sellars puts it:

> Jones brings this about, roughly, by applauding utterances by Dick of 'I am thinking that p' when the behavioral evidence strongly supports the theoretical statement 'Dick is thinking that p' and by frowning on utterances of 'I am thinking that p' when the evidence does not support this theoretical statement. Our ancestors begin to speak of the privileged access each of us has to his own thoughts. *What began as a language with a purely theoretical use has gained a reporting role.* (EPM, 189; Sellars' emphasis.)

It turns out, of course, that Jones is successful in his enterprise. People learn the rudiments of his theory; they see its superiority to the Rylean framework; and in time the Jonesian framework of mental acts displaces its Rylean predecessor.

There is more to the Jonesian myth; for as we shall see in III, Sellars employs an extension of this piece of logical fiction in presenting his account of sense impressions. Nonetheless, what I have so far presented of the myth exhibits its role in demonstrating, first, that the framework of mental acts *could* have arisen "as a self-conscious scientific hypothesis" and, second, that its development would have proceeded "by a series of steps none of which violates accepted standards of rationality." (*SM*, 155.) The myth also highlights the resources in Sellars' account for satisfying the conditions outlined in my (1) through (5) from section I. Indeed, after stating the myth, it is unnecessary to comment further on Sellars' ability to accommodate the features of conceptual phenomena specified in my (1) through (4); but given the subtlety of his use of the myth in confronting the issues involved in my (5), I want to conclude my account of Sellars' position on thinking by indicating how the myth exhibits the ontological neutrality of his account of conceptual phenomena.

As I indicated in section I, two features of conceptual episodes have traditionally been taken to entail the inherent dualism of the framework of mental acts—our immediate awareness of mental acts and the intentionality of those acts. Now, the Jonesian myth attempts to show that it is a mistake to take these two features of mental acts to provide grounds for logically independent arguments for dualism. According to the myth, an individual's awareness of his own mental acts proceeds by way of concepts belonging to the intentionality family. Thus, Jones teaches his colleagues to respond noninferentially to their own mental acts in terms of the same concepts that they employ in the inferential ascription of mental acts. He teaches them to say, "I'm having a *thought of Socrates*" and "I'm having a *thought that two plus two equals four*." But if we grasp our own mental acts only in terms of concepts like these, then the phenomenon of immediate awareness provides no grounds for dualism separate from those associated with the intentionality of mental acts.

One important source of the belief that the intentionality of mental acts entails the immateriality of their subject is the assumption that this feature of mental acts is to be understood in relational terms. This assumption has given rise to the picture of mental acts as episodes entering into a unique relation with a unique domain of objects (a domain populated by entities with exotic titles like 'intentional object', 'subsistent', and 'intentional inexistent'). Now, the Jonesian myth is so formulated as to show that proponents of this assumption about the relational structure of intentionality have been misled by the surface grammar of talk about thinking. We do speak of the thought *of* Socrates, the thought *about* men, and the thought *that* two plus two equals four; but, according to the myth, a reconstruction of such idioms shows them to invoke not a system of concept-world relations but the apparatus of functional classification.

Now, Sellars wants to insist that once we understand the "object-directedness" of mental acts in the functional terms of the myth we can come to appreciate the ontological neutrality of the framework of conceptual episodes. On that interpretation, our concepts of mental episodes do not characterize them intrinsically; they classify them in terms of their roles in inner speech without specifying what kind of thing plays the various conceptual roles.[12] Thus, our concept of a mental act as this or that intentional item (e.g., as the thought of Socrates or the thought that two plus two equals four) is simply the notion of an episode *of some kind or other* that plays a particular role in inner speech. What is central to the concept, then, is the conceptual role it points to; it specifies neither explicitly nor implicitly what kind of "stuff" that role or function is to be embedded in.

But if, as Sellars argues, our framework of conceptual phenomena commits us to a merely functional concept of mental acts, then it carries no commitment whatever about what thoughts will turn out to be in their "real nature." Mental acts could turn out to be processes or episodes involving an immaterial substance; but they could also turn out to be the neuron firings of contemporary neurophysiology. Thus, our framework of conceptual phenomena presents no special problem for the scientific realist, the philosopher (like Sellars) who takes science to be "the measure of all things, of what is that it is, and of what is not that it is not." (EPM, 173.) He can accept that framework along with all of the themes to which it has given rise—the episodic character of thoughts, their privacy, their intentionality—while insisting that, in the final analysis, it is the ontology of science that provides us with the conceptual resources for specifying the kinds of things mental acts really are.

III

But the ontological neutrality of mental acts is only half of what Sellars takes the scientific realist to need; for according to Sellars, a philosophy of mind is consistent with the rigors of scientific realism only if it can accommodate (within the ontology of science) what he calls sense impressions. As Sellars describes them, sense impressions are the various sensory states of perceivers—visual sensations, tactile sensations, and the like—and although he is aware that philosophers have been suspicious about such things, Sellars insists that sense impressions are as much a part of our commonsense picture of the world as mental acts.

But while he takes the category of sense impressions to play a central role in nonphilosophical thinking, Sellars holds that it is easy to be confused about their precise nature. Classical sense-datum philosophers, for example, recognized the importance of sensory states; but according to Sellars, their account of those states was mistaken in two crucial respects. First, they took them to be epistemic in nature. Indeed, they typically thought of the having of what they called a sense-datum as the paradigmatic instance of empirical knowledge. Sellars, however, insists that the sensory states of our conceptual framework are not properly epistemic; having a sense impression may be a necessary condition of perceptual knowledge, but sense impressions do not themselves constitute knowledge, perceptual or otherwise. Second, sense-datum theorists generally took the framework of sensory states to be a discovered framework, claiming that careful phenomenology is sufficient to establish its objective validity. Sellars, on the other hand, wants to claim that sense impressions, like mental acts, exhibit the logic of theoretical entities.[13]

In developing this interpretation of sense impressions, Sellars appeals to an extension of the Jonesian myth. In the extension of the myth,[14] Jones enriches the framework of mental acts with sense impressions in the attempt to explain the occurrence of those conceptual representations that are central to perceptual experience. Part of what Jones tries to explain is central in the account of sense-datum theorists—the conceptual representations ingredient in illusory perception—but as Sellars presents his story, Jones is also concerned to explain the occurrence of conceptual representations in veridical perception. Jones notes that in veridical perception there is a correlation between the content of our conceptual representations and the various features of the perceptual environment they represent; and he concludes that this correlation, no less than the occurrence of conceptual representations in illusory perception, stands in need of explanation (*SM*, 17-18).

Toward providing the required explanation, Jones comes up with the hypothesis that we are the subjects of imperceptible states that, while not conceptual themselves, are causally responsible for the occurrence of the conceptual representations that are central to perception. In developing this hypothesis, Jones takes as his model the domain of physical objects and their perceptible properties. Thus, his sensory states turn out to be something like inner replicas of physical objects with properties that are the analogues of the primary and secondary qualities of the model (EPM, 191). Toward characterizing these states, Jones coins expressions like 'sense impression of a red rectangle' and 'sense impression of a blue triangle'. However, as he uses these labels, the phrases 'of a red rectangle' and 'of a blue triangle' do not serve to characterize the postulated states merely extrinsically in terms of their standard causes. Nor, as Jones interprets them, do they carry their familiar senses. Rather, they serve to give an intrinsic but analogical characterization of Jones' postulated states in accord with the procedures for the analogical development of theories (SM, 9-23). His characterization of his sensory states complete, Jones suggests, first, that the correlation between a conceptual representation and the perceptual environment in veridical perception results from the fact that the conceptual representation is caused by a sensory state of the perceiver, which has properties that systematically correspond with those of the perceptual environment, and, second, that the conceptual representation in an illusory perception results from a sensory state of the perceiver with properties that are not the analogues of those exhibited by the immediate perceptual environment.

The earlier discussion of Sellars' account of mental acts should make it clear how this extension of the Jonesian myth is to be filled in. As with the framework of mental acts, Jones teaches his colleagues how to employ the theory of sense impressions, first, as a tool for inferring the existence of sense impressions—both their own and those of others—and, second, as a system of statements for responding noninferentially to their own sense impressions. Finally, just as Jones' colleagues ultimately adopt the framework of mental acts, they come to accept Jones' theory of perception; and sense impressions become part of our conceptual heritage.

The parallels between this account of sense impressions and the earlier account of mental acts are striking, so striking that one is prepared to conclude that the framework of sense impressions presents no special problems for the scientific realist. It turns out, however, that the ontological neutrality of mental acts is not shared by sense impressions, for while our concept of a mental act is a purely *functional* notion, Sellars wants to insist that our concept of a sense impression incorporates a *qualitative* dimension. As we have already seen, Sellars construes our concept of a mental act as the notion of an episode *of some sort or other* that plays a particular role or function. On Sellars' account, then, the concept picks out the act in terms of its role without specifying the qualitative features of the matter embedding that role. On the other hand, Sellars takes our concepts of sense impressions to involve intrinsic characterizations of sensory states in terms of qualitative properties. When we identify a sensory state as the sense impression of a red triangle, for example, we are pointing to qualitative features of the impression that are essential to it in its "real" nature and that, consequently, must be exhibited by anything with which we want to identify that impression. Thus, the scientific realist has to find a place within the ontological framework of science for the qualitative dimension of sense impressions; it is Sellars' contention that the realist faces serious difficulties in this enterprise. To appreciate these difficulties, we have to get clear on the more basic difficulties that Sellars takes the framework of perceptible physical objects to pose for scientific realism.

We can sum up these difficulties by saying that physical objects have perceptible properties incompatible with the scientific realist's account of them as systems of imperceptible particles. Thus, Sellars' famous ice cube is pink;[15] but it is unclear how it could be pink if it were a system of particles none of which can even intelligibly be characterized as colored. Sellars, of course, does not mean to deny that systems can have properties exhibited by none of their components. A collection of pieces of wood, nails, and so forth, has the property of being a ladder; but none of the objects entering into its constitution does. In this connection, Sellars presents us with a principle specifying in just which cases it is possible for a system of objects to have properties shared by none of its components. This principle (Sellars frequently calls it the *Principle of Reducibility*) is meant to exclude purely emergent properties, that is, properties of systems that cannot be defined in terms of properties of and relations between the objects that make up the systems. We can state the principle as follows:

> It is impossible for a system, S, of objects to exhibit a property, P, which none of the constitutents ($a, \ldots, n$) of S exhibit, unless S's exhibiting P consists in the fact that $a, \ldots, n$ exhibit properties other than P or enter into relations of various kinds. (*SM*, 27.)

Now it should be obvious that this principle permits the collection of wood, nails, and so forth, to be a ladder; for the collection's being a ladder results from the fact that its component parts bear various kinds of relations to each other. Sellars, however, wants to deny that his Principle of Reducibility allows the scientific realist an account of the pinkness of the ice cube; for he denies that there are any properties of or relations between the imperceptible particles of the ice cube to which we could coherently reduce its pinkness. On the contrary, the pinkness of the ice cube has what Sellars calls an *ultimate homogeneity*. The ice cube is pink through and through; it presents itself to us as a whole every part of which is pink. Consequently, the suggestion that it is made up of imperceptible particles—particles that logically cannot be pink—would seem to be incoherent (*SM*, 26).

Of course, the difficulties pointed to in the case of the pink ice cube can be generalized into an argument to show that physical objects cannot be systems of imperceptible particles.[16] The argument would convince some philosophers that the claims of the scientist cannot be taken at face value; but being a scientific realist, Sellars draws a quite different moral from these reflections. He takes the incompatibility between the framework of perceptible objects and the ontology of science to establish that the framework of physical objects is ultimately false, that pink ice cubes, physical objects generally, do not exist. Toward dispelling the puzzlement that a claim of this sort is likely to occasion, Sellars provides a Kantian account of the unreality of physical objects. The perceptual world, he tells us, is merely phenomenal; it is the way in which the noumenal world that is adequately characterized by physics appears to or is conceptually represented by human beings (P, 97).

Sellars, of course, realizes that the scientific realist owes us an account of the existence of the framework of physical objects. If the world is as the physicist tells us, then why does it appear to human beings to have properties that are inconsistent with those specified by the physicist? The answer, of course, is to be found in the appeal to sense impressions. But while Sellars agrees that it is sense impressions that cause human beings to represent systems of imperceptible particles as things that are, for example, pink through and through, he wants to deny that the appeal to sense impressions is nonproblematic (SSI, 408-9).

The difficulty is that sense impressions are states of persons. It is persons who have sense impressions, pink and red; or as Sellars likes to put it, it is persons who sense pinkly and redly. Now, on the scientific realist's account persons as well as physical objects turn out to be systems of imperceptible particles; but none of the scientific objects that the realist tells us make up persons are the kinds of things of which we can say "this senses pinkly" or "this senses redly." Thus, we have another case where a property is exhibited by a system but not by any of its components. Given Sellars' Principle of Reducibility, then, it must be possible to specify other properties of or relations between the scientific objects making up human beings to which we can reduce system properties like sensing-pinkly and sensing-redly. Sellars, however, denies that there are any such properties or relations. Sense impressions, he contends, "inherit the ultimate homogeneity" of the sensible properties on which we are to think of them as modeled (SSI, 408). As Sellars puts it:

> Sensing-redly as conceived in the Manifest Image does not consist in a relationship of objects in states other than sensings. A sensing can *include other sensings,* as when we sense a-red-circle-in-a-green-square, but it cannot consist of non-sensings. (SSI, 409.)

Now, it is not as though the realist could escape this difficulty by seeking his account of the perceptible qualities of physical objects in other quarters; for it is only because sense impressions are as much a part of the framework of common sense as perceptible physical objects that they present themselves as candidates for this explanatory role. Thus, even if the realist were to invoke some other explanatory hypothesis here, he would still have to accommodate sense impressions within the ontological framework of science. If, however, he were to declare the framework of sense impressions unreal, the realist would have one more merely phenomenal framework to account for. And however the account would go, it would require the existence of entities capable of explaining the ultimate homogeneity that has been plaguing the realist. But if the above discussion is not off track, the ontology of science is simply lacking in such entities.

What all of this seems to suggest is that the scientific realist is incapable of formulating an adequate philosophy of mind; for while mental acts present him with no difficulties, the ontology of science lacks the resources for accommodating the ultimate homogeneity of perceptible qualities and sense impressions. Sellars, however, is unwilling to draw such far-reaching conclusions from these difficulties. Although he agrees that the issue of ultimate homogeneity rules out that naive form of scientific realism that takes *present-day* science to be "the measure of all things," he wants to deny that it should lead us to reject the basic insights of scientific realism. What we have to recognize, Sellars insists, is that what he calls the scientific image is not yet complete, that while the science of today provides the main outlines of an ideal picture of the world, there are many details it has not yet filled in. Perhaps, Sellars suggests, when the scientific image is complete, the ontology of science will have the resources for accommodating sense impressions.

Toward filling in these very general suggestions, Sellars engages in a bit of proto-science and tries to sketch out the way in which the complete scientific image will accommodate sense impressions. The contention here is that in the complete image toward which present-day science is moving, certain neurophysiological states will play the role that in our commonsense framework is played by sense impressions. As Sellars puts it, these states will be the successors or counterparts of the sense impressions of our framework (SSI, 405-6). They will not, however, be states of basic individuals but states of systems of basic objects. However, unlike their predecessors—sense impressions—these neurophysiological states will be reducible in the completed image; for according to Sellars, science will take a system's exhibiting one of these states to consist in the fact that the constituents of that system exhibit other, more basic properties (SSI, 409-10, 415, 417). But for this reduction to succeed, the systems in question will have to include constituents whose properties will enable us to explain, once and for all, the ultimate homogeneity that characterizes the framework of common sense. Sellars insists that they will, telling us that among the constituents of the relevant neurological systems will be particulars (he calls them *sensa*) whose properties will be analogues of the perceptible qualities of the physical object framework. Thus, giving the familiar predicates new senses, the complete scientific image will characterize sensa as red, pink, and so forth, and will contend that it is because sensa are in their own way pink, red, and the like that systems of imperceptible objects appear to human perceivers to have the various perceptible qualities they do. Sellars says:

> Thus, at the end as at the beginning of our journey, our image of man-in-the-world would include color with its ultimate homogeneity as an occurrent attribute of actually existing particulars. Indeed, in the Scientific Image, as yet dimly discerned, the successor concept to sensing-a-red-triangle would be the concept of a neurophysiological state which includes the actual existence of a red triangle—where the concept of a red triangle would be the successor concept to the "manifest" concept of a physical object which is red and triangular on the facing surface. (SSI, 411.)

Over the years Sellars' speculations on the precise terms in which science will characterize sensa have gone in a number of directions; but he has always denied that they will be characterized in terms appropriate to particles. He has also consistently held to the view that sensa will be incapable of appearing in any contexts but those provided by the neurophysiological states in question. Thus, the appeal to sensa will represent the appeal to objects that are not physical in the sense that they are not objects that are either "necessary to and sufficient for the scientific description and explanation of non-living matter" or definable in terms of objects that are. Sellars calls this sense of physical *physical*$_2$. But while he takes the appeal to sensa to involve an enrichment of the ontology required for the account of inorganic matter, Sellars wants to deny that the postulation of sensa will involve embracing anything like the bizarre ontologies of, say, epiphenomenalism or Cartesian dualism.

While they would differ from the ontological primitives of present-day science in not being *physical₂*, sensa would be *physical₁*; i.e., they would be part of the spatio-temporal order, and, so, unlike the phantasms of Hobbesian epiphenomenalism and the spiritual substances of the Cartesian tradition, they could be intelligibly thought of as entering into causal interaction with other scientific objects, both those that are and those that are not *physical₂* (SSI, 401).

But, of course, the complete image is not yet before us, so while Sellars' proto-science may seem plausible, it is impossible to be certain that the scientist's picture of the world will, in the final analysis, contain Sellars' sensa or anything like them. Consequently, as Sellars himself recognizes, we cannot now be certain that even a sophisticated version of scientific realism that makes the complete scientific image "the measure of all things" provides an adequate account of sense impressions. Now, at first sight this may appear to be a relatively parochial issue with ramifications only in fairly circumscribed regions of the philosophy of mind and the philosophy of science. In fact, the implications of this issue are much broader than that. What is involved here is the relationship between the manifest and scientific images of man-in-the-world; and for Sellars, the fusion of these two images into a single vision is the goal of philosophy itself (PSIM, 4). Thus, our doubts about the scientific realist's ability to accommodate the ultimate homogeneity of sense impressions are, for Sellars at least, doubts about the success of the philosophical enterprise as a whole.

NOTES

[1] I do not mean to suggest that all of these items are on a par. Sellars wants to insist upon a distinction between mental acts and mental actions, where the latter but not the former are things we can decide to do, do intentionally, do on purpose. Clearly, some of the things I list here are mental actions and not mental acts. Sellars, however, holds that mental actions are "composed" of mental acts; thus, even the performance of mental actions proceeds in terms of occurrences of mental acts.

[2] EPM, 181-83. In this brief account, I am forced to skip over points that are essential to an understanding of Sellars' analysis of theories. Thus, I have had to suppress the fact that, for Sellars, a model is always accompanied by both a positive commentary, which points out just how the objects in the model and the postulated objects agree, *and* a negative commentary, which indicates how they differ. For an extended discussion of Sellars' account of theories, see Gary Gutting's paper on Sellars' philosophy of science (included in this volume).

[3] This theme runs throughout Sellars' writings in epistemology. See, e.g., the

attack on the "myth of the given" that is found in EPM. See also C. F. Delaney's paper on Sellars' theory of knowledge (included in this volume).

[4]This formula is frequently repeated in Sellars' work. See, e.g., LTC, 101-14 for a discussion of the thinking central to the Rylean community. For a look at the Jonesian from a different perspective, see C. F. Delaney's paper on Sellars' theory of knowledge.

[5]In this context, Sellars insists that Rylean thinking cannot be handled within the context of an Austinian theory of speech acts inasmuch as such a theory construes all utterances as actions. Sellars, however, wants to insist that some Rylean utterances are acts (actualities) but not actions (things done intentionally, on purpose, and so on). He is, of course, committed to insisting this, since he wants to make overt speech the model for thinking. The point here is that some conceptual episodes are acts without being actions; but, then, if all linguistic episodes were necessarily actions, it would be impossible to interpret all conceptual episodes as linguistic episodes.

[6]This issue was central in the Chisholm-Sellars correspondence published in *Minnesota Studies in the Philosophy of Science,* vol. 2, ed. Herbert Feigl (Minneapolis: University of Minnesota Press, 1958). Obviously Sellars' contention has to be supported by detailed analyses of the various semantical notions. Those analyses come a bit later in my presentation of the Jonesian myth.

[7]This account of meaning runs throughout Sellars' work. For early versions of the account, see LT, 109-18, and EPM, 161-64. For a later version, see, e.g., *SM,* 77-82. For additional insights into Sellars' theory of meaning, see once again C. F. Delaney's paper on Sellars' theory of knowledge and my paper on his ontology (also included in this volume).

[8]The convention of dot quotation is systematically presented in AE and is employed throughout subsequent writings. For a detailed account of the convention, see once again my paper on Sellars' ontology.

[9]Actually the reconstruction of meaning statements is more complicated than my (3′) through (8′) suggest. One has to invoke the strategy of distributive singular terms to convert (3′) through (8′) into general statements. See once again my paper on Sellars' ontology for an account of these issues.

[10]See *SM,* 82-87, where Sellars develops this sort of account. Here too one has to invoke the strategy of distributive singular terms to complete these reconstitutions.

[11]Here, again, one should remember the way in which negative commentary is relevant to the use of a model. Jones will insist, for example, that inner speech does not proceed by the wagging of an inner tongue.

[12]One sees the ontic neutrality of functional classification even in the case of our semantical characterizations of overt language. Thus, our concept of, say, an overt •Socrates• permits a great deal of latitude in what vocal utterances and written inscriptions can count as •Socrates•s; and as we move from one language to another, the material differences among •Socrates•s are compounded.

[13]These points recur in all of Sellars' writings in epistemology and the philosophy of mind. See, e.g., the extended treatment of sense impressions in *SM,* 9-30.

[14]See EPM, 190-95. For a more detailed account of sense impressions, see Delaney's paper on Sellars' theory of knowledge.

[15]This famous example first occurs in PSIM, 26.

[16]Sellars usually discusses the issue of ultimate homogeneity in terms of colors; but he seems inclined to think that the other secondary qualities of physical objects yield parallel problems.

Philosophy of Mind
Action and Freedom

Gary Gutting

Sellars' fundamental philosophical project is the attempt to delineate the mutual relations of the manifest and the scientific images of man.[1] In spite of his insistence on the ontological primacy of the scientific image, Sellars does not follow the simplistic course of rejecting the manifest image as false and enthroning the scientific image as "The Truth." Rather, he emphasizes the need for synthesis, for seeing how the two images form a single unified vision ("fall together in one stereoscopic view" [PSIM, 5]). The central focus of this project of synthesis is the concept of a *person*. Persons are the "primary objects of the manifest image" (PSIM, 9); and it is on their construal vis-à-vis the scientific image that the success or failure of the Sellarsian synthesis hinges.

In what sense does Sellars hope to unify the conceptual framework of persons with that of science? In the final paragraph of PSIM, he makes an important but potentially misleading comment on this question:

> The conceptual framework of persons is not something that needs to be *reconciled* with the scientific image, but rather something to be *joined* to it. (40; Sellars' emphasis.)

This comment is perfectly appropriate if we interpret it (in accord with Sellars' following sentence) as saying that the synthesis is not to be effected by developing scientific language to the point where we can translate into it, without remainder, all the truths of the framework of persons. In such a case *reconciling* the frameworks would actually be a matter of *reducing* one to the other, a move that Sellars firmly rejects. But the comment will mislead us if we take it to mean that the synthesis is merely a matter of making conceptual room (e.g., via a distinction of reasons and causes) for a *juxtaposition* of two independently articulated frameworks. The irreducibility of the manifest framework to the scientific framework must not be allowed to overshadow the fact that the

127

objects of the manifest framework, including persons, really *are* collections of scientific objects.

This point is preeminently illustrated by Sellars' treatment of freedom, the primary property of persons in the manifest framework. He eschews the "instant compatibilism" of the early action theorists, based on an unbridgeable conceptual gap between actions and events, and instead embarks on the much more difficult classical route of reconciling the freedom of our actions with their causal explainability. This route is necessary for Sellars because persons are systems of theoretical scientific entities and hence their actions can be explained by scientific (and hence perhaps deterministic) laws.

Philosophical problems about freedom have of course traditionally arisen from attempts to unite the manifest framework with other frameworks (religious or scientific) that seem to pose a threat to our manifest freedom. In Sellars' case, it is the prospect of an ultimately deterministic science that poses the threat. The central question is, Can our idea of ourselves as free agents be maintained in the face of a scientific causal explanation of all events? I will discuss this question and Sellars' affirmative answer to it by presenting: (I) His construal of the meaning of scientific determinism; (II) His analysis of freedom as a manifest concept, with special emphasis on the conditions for the applicability of the concept; and (III) His argument for the compatibility of freedom and determinism as he construes them.

I. The Thesis of Scientific Determinism

Sellars construes the general thesis of scientific determinism in the classic Laplacean sense—i.e., as the claim that a complete description of the universe at a given time can be logically derived, via scientific laws, from complete descriptions of earlier states of the universe. When a complete description of Q can be logically derived via scientific laws from a complete description of P, then Sellars says that P causally (or physically) necessitates Q.[2] Accordingly, the general thesis of scientific determinism is that the state of the universe at a given time is causally necessitated by antecedent states of the universe. As applied to human actions, this thesis entails that

> When X does A at t, this means there was an antecedent partial cross-section of the universe such that, relatively to that cross-section, it is physically necessary that X do A at t; or, equivalently, such that it is physically impossible, relatively to that cross-section, that X do something other than A at t. (FD, 161-62.)

To adequately understand Sellars' view of freedom and determinism, we must appreciate three major interpretative points about the thesis of scientific determinism. The purpose of this section is to explicate these points.

The first point concerns the thesis' implications regarding the predictability of events. Claims of universal determinism have been rejected by some because of alleged inconsistencies in the idea that members of a system could predict all future states of the system, including their own.[3] Sellars acknowledges the probable validity of these "Gödelian" difficulties, but maintains that they impugn only the idea of *epistemic* predictability—that is, "predictability by a predictor *in the system*". (FD, 145; Sellars' emphasis.) But, he notes, the thesis of scientific determinism does not entail epistemic predictability; rather, it entails only *logical* predictability—i.e., the logical derivability of descriptions of later states of the universe from descriptions of earlier states, quite apart from the question of whether any member of the universe could have access to the relevant descriptions and hence be able to carry out the derivations.[4]

The second point concerns the status of the determinist thesis vis-à-vis the scientific enterprise. Given the essentially indeterministic form of current quantum theory (not to mention the lack of a deterministic social science), there can be no question of presenting—as incautious philosophers and scientists alike are wont to do—the thesis as an accomplished result of science. Nor does it seem that Sellars regards the thesis as an essential regulative principle of science, since he does not appear to regard the indeterminism of quantum mechanics as an in-principle objection to it. Rather, Sellars seems to regard the thesis as an important but not essential explanatory ideal (to use Toulmin's phrase) of science, an ideal that may well, but need not, be achieved by the ultimately adequate explanatory theory of science. The point of Sellars' compatibilist argument will be to show the irrelevance of the future development of science (in either a deterministic or indeterministic direction) to the issue of human freedom.

The third, and most important, point concerns the precise meaning of 'scientific' in the phrase 'scientific determinism'. Sellars' use here is essentially the same as his use of the term when he speaks of the 'scientific image': the science referred to is the result of the postulation of nonmanifest (theoretical) entities in order to obtain explanatory theories. Thus understood, scientific determinism contrasts with what Sellars calls 'vulgar determinism', a determinism "formulated in terms of the concepts and categories of common sense psychological explanation". (RD, 156.) According to this view, which Sellars regards as "a snare and a delusion" (RD, 169), the laws and antecedent conditions that causally necessitate X's action A can be formulated exclusively in terms of such manifest-image categories as 'habit', 'character', 'desire', and so forth. More specifically, vulgar determinism is the view that all human actions can be causally explained as expressions of the agent's *character* (RD, 157), which is to say that they can be predicted "with respect to evidence pertaining to what the person in question has done in the past and the circumstances as he saw them in which he did [them]." (PSIM, 12.) This type of determinism *does* exclude human freedom, since it regards persons as caused (e.g., by their habits) to do what they do. But, Sellars says, vulgar determinism is based on a conceptual confusion between habits and causal properties (RD, 157). Although all our actions may well be caused, this cannot (logically) be because they are all habitual or "in character."[5] For habits and character are themselves formed by our actions; it is contradictory to say that we *begin* by acting in character or out of habit.

Another way to view the error of the vulgar determinist is as a confusion of the *character* and the *nature* of a person. As defined above, the former corresponds to a person's actions insofar as they can be predicted solely on the basis of his observed past behavior. The latter corresponds to the person's actions insofar as they can be predicted *no holds barred*—that is, predictable not just on the basis of past behavior but also on the basis of the most adequate theoretical redescription of the person (e.g., as a system of elementary particles). Defined in this way, the nature of a person is a concept of the scientific, not the manifest, image (FD, 146). If scientific determinism is correct, all of a person's actions are predictable on the basis of his nature. But the vulgar determinist confuses this possible truth with the incoherent claim that all actions of a person can be predicted on the basis of his character.

As Sellars defines it, vulgar determinism is essentially the view that all actions are habitual (or in character) and so is refutable on purely conceptual grounds. We might, however, devise a modified version of vulgar determinism that, while not characterizing all actions as habitual, nonetheless held that all actions are explainable on the basis of laws formulated in terms of manifest-framework concepts. A crude example of such laws is given by the form "Whenever an agent in psychological state P (e.g., hunger) encounters a stimulus S (e.g., sees a platter of food), he will perform an action A (e.g., eat the food)." The existence of such laws for all human action seems to be a conceptual possibility; and, if they do exist, there are no free human actions, since for any action we could show how the agent was caused to perform it by such things as his inherited desires, conditioned dispositions, and so forth. However, Sellars can rightly reject this modified form of vulgar determinism on empirical grounds: We do not have and have no reason to expect complete causal explanations of human actions without recourse to a redescription of persons and their properties in terms of postulated theoretical entities. Modified vulgar determinism, though not absurd, is still false.[6]

Scientific determinism, however, remains as a conceptual and an empirical possibility and requires reconciliation with human freedom. But before we can discuss Sellars' effort of reconciliation, we must look at his analysis of the meaning of freedom.

II.   The Meaning of Freedom

We are, of course, interested here in freedom as a moral concept, not a political or religious one. Morally speaking, it is persons who are deemed free (morally responsible) and this in virtue of the freedom of their actions. So our primary concern will be with the sense in which our actions can be free.

According to Sellars, the primary requirement for a free action is that it be *voluntary*. An action A is voluntary just in case "if, just before doing A, the agent had willed not to do A, he would not have done A". (FD, 159.) In this sense of 'voluntary', anything that is an action in the strict sense (e.g., anything that I truly *do* as opposed to have happen to me) is voluntary. A paradigm case of involuntary "action" is my being thrown out of a window by a team of professional wrestlers (FD, 160); and here, of course, I am a patient rather than an agent.

At the heart of the concept of a voluntary action A is the idea that, even though the agent did A, he was able to do something other than A (FD, 162). And since, as Sellars' definition of 'voluntary' indicates, what the agent does depends on what he *wills* to do, his acting voluntarily also entails that the agent was able to will other than he did. Consequently, we can set up as the first (and most fundamental) necessary condition for a free action the requirement that the agent be able to do and will other than he did.

Of course this condition is not alone sufficient. An action may be an action strictly speaking (voluntary in the broad sense defined above) and still not be free. Consider, for example, my reluctant decision, after being suitably threatened, to accompany the team of professional wrestlers to visit their boss. Even here I would not have acted as I did if I had not willed to do so; but my action was nonetheless not free but *compelled*. Although compulsion initially refers to an external force (like the wrestlers), it is extended to cover other cases in which our actions are morally excusable—e.g., when we are influenced by an "inner compulsion" such as drug addiction or mental derangement.

There are various degrees of compulsion (consider the difference between a threat to disconnect my cable TV and a threat to initiate a nuclear war), which correspond—in different ways for different people and situations—to various degrees of diminution of freedom and moral responsibility. Therefore, an action cannot be judged unfree just because it occurred under some sort of compulsion. On the other hand, an entirely free action (if such there be) would require the absence of all compulsion. In this sense, we can say that a second necessary condition of a free action is that the agent not be compelled to do it.

The two necessary conditions of freedom we have enunciated appear to be jointly sufficient. At any rate, it is with respect to these two conditions that the thesis of scientific determinism poses a challenge to our freedom. If science can causally explain everything, it seems that either we do not act at all (i.e., are not able to will and do other than we do), or, at best, we are compelled to act as we do. Sellars, however, argues that scientific determinism, properly construed, is consistent with both these necessary conditions of freedom.

Since, as we have seen, scientific determinism is a claim about the existence of causes, the attempt to reconcile freedom and determinism will crucially depend on a proper understanding of the sense in which the presence of causes is and is not inconsistent with the two necessary conditions of freedom. A major feature of Sellars' treatment of freedom is the care and nuance with which he analyzes the role of causality.

Actions, we have said, are the specific locus of freedom. There are three possible general views regarding the relation of free actions to causes, each with important philosophical supporters. The most recent view—put forward by early action theorists—is that it is a category mistake to describe actions as either caused or uncaused. Actions are explained by *reasons,* not causes; causality is a category applicable to events, not to actions. The other two views allow the application of the category of causality to actions. One—that of the classical libertarian—holds that free actions are precisely those that are uncaused. The other—that of the classical compatibilist among others—holds that free actions are caused, but in a particular way that sets them off from unfree actions.

Sellars implicitly rejects the first two of these views in his action theory, which is characterized by the following two central theses:[7] (1) the reasons that explain actions are causes of the action, and (2) the immediate cause of any action is a volition. With regard to (1), Sellars endorses Davidson's argument[8] that, even though an agent has a reason to do A, we cannot specify this reason as *the* reason why he does A unless we can say that it causes A (AE, 202-3). In a typical case, someone with a good knowledge of my character and circumstances could suggest several reasons for my performing a given action. Suppose, for example, I make a point of walking the two-and-one-half miles to my office each day. Those who know me may rightly point out that I am (a) concerned about my weight; (b) like to impress my friends with my good physical condition; (c) enjoy being outdoors; and so forth. Given my character and circumstances, any one of these could be the reason for my action. But surely the one that *is* the reason is the one that in fact *causes* my action.

But although Sellars endorses Davidson's defense of the classic construal of reasons as causes, he does not think that Davidson has given an adequate account of the precise mode of causation that is involved (AE, 202). In particular, Davidson does not bring to light the role, emphasized in Sellars' thesis (2), of volitions.

In order to arrive at the central role of volitions, Sellars raises the basic question, unanswered by Davidson, How is it that reasons are causes? Or how does it come about that a given reason is the cause of a given action? Consider my walking to my office each day in order to impress my friends. Here the reason for my action is *impressing my friends*. Its being the reason implies, first of all, that I have the intention of impressing my friends—i.e., that I have the thought "I shall impress my friends."[9] But this rather general intention will not lead to the specific action in question unless I have beliefs that provide a logical connection between my intention and the action to which it gives rise. Thus, I must have beliefs that support the proposition, "If I want to impress my friends, I should walk to my office in the morning." Given this proposition and my intention to impress my friends, I engage in a simple process of practical reasoning which has as its conclusion the intention, "I shall walk to my office in the morning." If circumstances remain relevantly the same, this intention will develop, come morning, into the intention, "I shall walk to my office *now*." And it is this intention that is the proximate cause of my walking to my office. Such an intention (viz., an intention to act *now*) is what Sellars calls a *volition*. Hence, volitions appear as the proximate causes of actions. Thus volitions are, as Sellars says, "the point at which the conceptual order evokes its image in the real order, as, in observation and self-knowledge, the real order evokes its image in the conceptual order." (SM, 177.)[10] A reason causes an action by being expressed in an intention that is a causal antecedent of the volition that is itself the immediate cause of the action.

The above account will, of course, be acceptable only if the classical view that every action is caused by a volition is defensible. Sellars is well aware that this view of volitions does not enjoy its former repute and defends it primarily by replying to the main contemporary objections. A discussion of these objections will both clarify and support the plausibility of Sellars' view of volitions.

(a) Some philosophers—e.g., Ryle—have rejected volitions as part of their general rejection of all mental episodes in favor of a behaviorist construal of mind as a set of dispositions. Sellars' judgment that such a construal, for all its methodological value, can only "end in absurdity" (FD, 156) is grounded in his detailed analysis of the mental and is discussed in the preceding paper on intentionality and the mind-body problem.

(b) But even if we countenance mental episodes in general, it may still seem that volitions cannot be included among them. For, it has been urged (e.g., by Richard Taylor in his *Action and Purpose*), the idea of volitions as the source of all actions leads to a vicious regress since a given act of volition will itself require a preceding volition as its source, *ad infinitum*. To this objection Sellars gives the straightforward reply that volitions are not themselves actions but merely mental occurrences.

> Volitions are not to be construed as pieces of conduct. They are "actions" only in that broadest sense in which anything expressed by a verb in the active voice (e.g., sleeping) is an action. They are actualities, indeed episodes, but not actions in any more interesting sense. (MCP, 233.)

What lies behind this reply is, of course, Sellars' construal of volitions as a species of *thoughts* and his conviction that "it is a logical fact about thoughts that they are not directly brought about" (FD, 157)—i.e., that they are not actions. To appreciate the force of this latter point, we need only note with Sellars the fact that an action is the sort of thing that we can—even if we in fact do not—reflectively decide to do. Thus, even an action on impulse could, if it is truly an action, be done reflectively. But it is clearly conceptual nonsense to say that I reflectively decided to have a particular thought. (For one thing, the reflective process would itself involve having the thought.) We can decide to dwell on a thought once it has occurred or even take steps to insure that we will have or not have thoughts of a given kind (thus, *indirectly* bringing about or avoiding the thought). But the thought itself *occurs to us*; we do not *do* it (Cf. *SM*, 74).[11]

The reply then to Taylor's regress objection is that volitions are not actions and hence not the product of a preceding volition.

(c) Even if we accept mental episodes and volitions as a species of mental episode, it may seem that it is wrong to regard volitions as the *causes* of actions, since they are *logically* tied to the corresponding actions. The point can be put most effectively as follows: In any case of causality—e.g., my slamming the door's causing the soufflé to collapse—there is, as Hume points out, no contradiction in saying that the cause occurred, but the effect (even though there were no intervening factors) did not. But not so for the case of a volition and the action corresponding to it; it *is* a contradiction to say that I had the volition "I shall slam the door *now*" but (though there were no intervening factors) did not slam the door. If there were no intervening factors (e.g., someone grabbing my arm, sudden paralysis) and I did not slam the door, then it follows logically that I did not will to slam the door. Hence there is a logical tie of volitions and actions that precludes them from being in the (contingent) relation of cause and effect. Sellars' response to this objection (cf. FD, 157-59; AE, 203-4; MCP, 234) is based on the fact that, since it is a thought, a volition has an intentional as well as a causal status. The physical event E that is the volition could indeed be causally connected with any sort of behavior. (For example, the neural occurrence that is the volition 'I shall slam the door' could be the cause of the physical movements of opening rather than closing a door.) But then, of course, we could not properly give E the kind of *intentional* characterization we do (i.e., we could not characterize it as an "I-shall-slam-the-door" volition). In short, the logical connection of volitions and actions that the objection discerns is in the intentional, not the real, order and so does not exclude a real causal relation of volitions and actions. Sellars drives this point home by noting the analogous case of perception: If the above objection were valid, it would also follow that a red book could not be the cause of my perceptual belief that I am seeing a red book (MCP, 234). For it is a conceptual truth that, in standard conditions, the belief that I am seeing a red book is caused by a red book.

With regard to the problem of freedom, the upshot of the above action-theoretical considerations is that, since all actions are caused by volitions, free actions cannot be construed as either uncaused or beyond the categorical application of causality. We must take the third option of regarding free actions as caused in a particular way. The question that now arises is about the precise nature of the causation of free actions. How exactly are we to formulate the two necessary conditions of freedom in causal terms? With regard to the second necessary condition (an action is free only if the agent is not compelled to do it), there is little difficulty. Compulsion must be understood in terms of what Sellars calls the "interventionist" model of causality (FD, 142). This model views causation in terms of the following general pattern:

> One thing (or a group of things) by changing in a certain way causing a different thing (or a group of things) to change in a certain way. (AE, 195.)

Typically, an interventionist causal relation is one expressed by locutions of the form, 'X caused Y to Z by doing A' (MCP, 229); e.g., 'Jones caused the pawn to move by pushing it'.

This model corresponds to the ordinary sense of causation and derives, Sellars suggests, from an "original"[12] usage in which causal power was exercised only by persons (FD, 142). Vis-à-vis the second necessary condition of freedom, the essential feature of this model is its conception of a cause as a thing separate from that which it causally affects. Construed in terms of interventionist causality, this condition specifies that an action is free only if the agent is not caused to do it by an intervening (outside) cause.

Formulating the first necessary condition of freedom (an action is free only if the agent could have willed and done otherwise) in causal terms is a much more difficult enterprise, one that will take us to the heart of Sellars' defense of compatibilism.

One major contemporary suggestion as to how to construe this condition is advanced by philosophers (e.g., R. Taylor, Chisholm, Donagan) who defend the model of agent (or nonoccurrent) causation. Donagan, citing Broad, gives the following clear formulation of this model:

> Acts of volition are events, but their causes are not prior events to which they are related according to laws of nature. . . . On the contrary acts of volition are caused "*by the agent or self*, considered as a substance or continuant, and not by a total cause which contains as factors *events* in and *dispositions* of the agent."[13]

A typical purported instance of agent causation would be 'Jones caused his finger to move', where the moving of Jones' finger is a basic (minimal) action.[14] The distinctive character of this mode of causation can be brought out by comparing it with the interventionist mode, 'X caused Y to Z by doing A'. If we try to fit our example of agency causation to this model, we can take 'Jones' as X, 'his finger' as Y, and 'move' as Z; but there is no possible replacement for A. Jones does not move his finger by doing anything else. Thus, in agent causation, as opposed to interventionist causation, the cause does not exercise causal efficacy by *doing anything*.[15] As Chisholm puts it, in agent causation the agent has the divine attribute of being an unmoved mover.[16]

From the viewpoint of agent causation, the first necessary condition of freedom is interpreted as follows: The autonomous (nonoccurrent) agent, who (at time t and in circumstances C) caused volition V (and hence action A), could have caused at exactly the same time and in exactly the same circumstances,[17] a volition V' incompatible with V (and hence an action A' incompatible with A). It seems clear that such an interpretation makes freedom incompatible with the thesis of scientific determinism. For there is, according to this interpretation, no causal explanation of the occurrence of volition V at time t in terms of antecedent states of the universe as is required by the determinist thesis. V can be explained only by reference to the agent that caused it. And the causality of this agent cannot be included in a scientific account, since there is no action or state of the agent that could be invoked as the state of the universe that gave rise to V rather than V'. Perhaps the point can be best put as follows: A scientific explanation of V would have to refer to a *law* that specified the circumstances that are sufficient for the occurrence of V. But on the agency account, there are no such circumstances, since, for any given specification of circumstances, the agent could have caused V' rather than V.

The agency account poses a major threat to Sellars' compatibilism, and he has accordingly paid it significant attention. His discussion of the account focuses on its central claim that persons (agents) are the causes of their volitions and actions. Initially, he argued that this claim was simply false or, at the very best, just a misleading way of making the trivial point that persons will and act (MCP, 232). But further reflection, stimulated by Donagan's valuable discussion of Sellars' views on freedom, has led him to a more refined position.[18] According to this position, it can be correct and nontrivial to say that a person causes his actions and volitions; but what is then being said can ultimately be completely explicated in terms of "occurrent" causation, i.e., in terms of causes that are events, not nonoccurring agents (cf. RD, 167). If this is so, the fact that persons can sometimes be said to cause their actions and volitions does not support the view that agents are the subjects of a special sort of causation.

Consider first the causing of actions. Sellars notes that if a cow's kicking the lantern caused the fire then we are entitled to say that the cow caused the fire. By parity of reasoning, he acknowledges, if the arsonist's willing to set the fire caused his action of setting the fire, we are entitled to say that the arsonist caused his action of setting the fire. In both cases, the principle is that the subject "in" which an event occurs can be said to be the cause of whatever is caused by the event. But, as this formulation of the principle makes clear, it is the event that is the real cause, not the agent. The same principle can be applied to the case of volitions. If my itching is the cause of my volition to scratch, we can say that I am the cause of this volition. But again, it is the event (the itching) that is the real cause. Further, particularly in the case of volitions, there is little point to saying that X is the cause of his Y-ing unless there is reason to emphasize that the Y-ing is not (to any relevant extent) explainable by factors outside of X but is rather explainable by antecedent states of the agent himself. Apart from a context of this sort, the claim that a person caused his volition (or action) is indeed little more than a misleading way of saying that he willed (or acted) (cf. RD, 169-70).

So, in sum, Sellars' view is that the language of agent causation can indeed have a point, but in every instance that point has to do with the locus of the nonagent (occurrent) cause of an action or volition.

But if we reject the agency-causation account, how are we to construe, in causal language, the first necessary condition of freedom? What sort of causal conditions exclude our acting in the strict sense? The answer to this question is the central theme of Sellars' defense of compatibilism, to which we now turn.

III.   The Defense of Compatibilism

It would be a mistake to regard Sellars' defense of compatibilism as essentially a repetition, in contemporary terminology, of the classical argument of Hume, Mill, and Schlick. As he notes (FD, 141), this argument is primarily designed to show that actions can be caused without being compelled. This is a valid and important point, and it reconciles the thesis of scientific determinism with what I have called the second necessary condition of freedom. (In Sellarsian terms, the nub of the classical argument is that the causes posited by scientific determinism need not be causes in the interventionist sense that defines compulsion. For example, the scientific cause of a thing's changing in a certain way may well be an antecedent state of the thing itself.)

But the classical distinction of causality and compulsion does nothing to effect a reconciliation of determinism with the first necessary condition of freedom. Accordingly, it does not adequately respond to the sophisticated libertarian who, while acknowledging that my action can be caused without being compelled, nonetheless urges that determinism is inconsistent with my being able to act (will) other than I do—i.e., with the existence of actions in the strict sense. Sellars, therefore, does not focus his defense of compatibilism on the causation/compulsion distinction (RD, 149-50). Rather, content with the classical argument on this point, he concentrates on the first necessary condition of freedom, our being able to do and will otherwise. To signal this change in focus, we might call Sellars' compatibilism not classical but *neoclassical*.

As the preceding section made clear, Sellars' argument must be based on a careful characterization in causal terms of the condition of being able to act and will other than one did. He first discusses the case of acting and then the case of willing.[19]

When we claim that a person is able to act in a certain way (e.g., is able to make a Dobos torte), we must specify both the time period (P) and the circumstances (C) with respect to which the claim is made. Thus, my wife is able to make a Dobos torte this afternoon, but she was not so able on the afternoon of her first birthday; likewise, she is able to make one in her own (adequately stocked and equipped) kitchen but not in a weather-observation hut in the Antarctic. For a given time period P and set of circumstances C, a first condition for being able to do A is that the circumstances C not *prevent* the agent from doing A during P. Circumstances C prevent me from doing A during P, when although (i) C does not entail[20] that I not *will* A during P, nevertheless (ii) C does entail that I not *do* A during P.[21] When I am not prevented from doing A, Sellars says that I am *in a position* to do A.[22] But being in a position to do A is not alone sufficient for being able to do A. My six-year-old daughter may well will to make a Dobos torte (having eaten one last week) and be in circumstances (e.g., her mother's kitchen) that do not entail her not making one. Nonetheless, she is not able to make a Dobos torte because she does not have the skills (for example, manual dexterity) requisite for this difficult action. We would say that, though circumstances do not prevent her from making the torte, she does not *have the ability* to make one. So having the ability to do A is another necessary condition of being able to do A. Put more precisely, *having the ability to do A* means that if I am in a position to do A then my willing to do A entails that I do A. (If I am in a position to do A—i.e., nothing prevents me from doing A—and I have the ability to do A but do not do A, that can only be because I do not will to do A.)

The two necessary conditions formulated in the above paragraph are jointly sufficient for being able to do A. So we can give the following definition:

(Throughout period P and in circumstances C) x is able to do A
= def (Throughout P and in C) (i) x is in a position to do A and (ii) x has the ability to do A.

Thus, Sellars presents x's being able to do A as a function of both external circumstances (clause i) and internal ability (clause ii).

Consider now the case in which, at time t (during period P) and in circumstances C, I in fact do A', an action incompatible with A. Then, according to scientific determinism, there is an antecedent state of the universe (S) that entails my doing A' and hence my not doing A. Can I nonetheless be said to be able to do A—i.e., to be able to do other than I did? I can if the determinist thesis can be shown to be consistent with the two conditions of being able to do A.

The consistency of condition (ii) with determinism is straightforwardly shown. According to determinism, S entails my not doing A, whereas, according to condition (ii), my willing A entails (given that I am in a position to do A) my doing A. These two propositions lead to a contradiction only if their antecedents are both true. But in fact they are not both true. Since by hypothesis I did A', I did not will A; for willing A would have caused my doing A.

What about condition (i), that x be in a position to do A? This means that the circumstances (C) of x's action do not prevent x from doing A; and it might appear that S, the antecedent state of the universe which, according to determinism, entails x's not doing A, is a circumstance preventing x's doing A. But Sellars urges that this is a mere appearance and that careful reflection will show the necessity of distinguishing *antecedent states of the universe* that are causally relevant to x's doing or not doing A from the *circumstances* (properly speaking) of A that are referred to in the definition of 'is able to do A'. This crucial distinction lies at the very heart of Sellars' neoclassical compatibilism. I will, however, postpone discussion of it until we have seen how Sellars' defense of the claim that determinism is compatible with our being able to *will* other than we do likewise depends on this distinction.[23] Let us turn then to the compatibility of determinism with being able to will otherwise.

Anticompatibilists, of course, urge that proof, on the assumption of determinism, of our ability to do other than we did does not establish compatibilism. It must, they insist, also be shown that we are able to *will* other than we did. Sellars agrees with this point since, on his view, actions are caused by volitions and so, if we are not able to will otherwise, we are able to do otherwise in only a superficial sense. The point can be put this way: being able to act otherwise may be merely a *relative* matter of being able to act otherwise if one so wills; but freedom requires an *absolute* sense of being able to do otherwise based on an unconditional ability to will otherwise (cf. RD, 175).

How are we to understand 'being able to will'? As in the case of action, Sellars formulates a definition in terms of prevention. Of course the definition of prevention for the case of being able to *act* is not appropriate here, since willing is not a species of acting. However, the new sense of prevention is not hard to find. Since willing is not acting, the key difference is that it makes no sense to speak of directly willing to will.[24] So the first clause in the definition of 'preventing from acting' is inappropriate for the case of willing, and the condition expressed in the second clause is alone decisive. Thus, Sellars proposes the following definition:

> (Throughout time P and in circumstances C) x is
>   prevented from willing to do A
> $=_{\text{def}}$ (Throughout P and in C) C entails that x does not will to do
>   A.

Given this, he defines 'able to will':

(Throughout time P and in circumstances C) x is able to will A
$=_{def}$ (Throughout P and in C) x is not prevented by C from
willing A.

We can now come very quickly to the heart of the matter. Suppose I in
fact will to do A', which is incompatible with A. Then, as before, if
determinism is true, the antecedent state of the universe (S) entails that I
will A' and hence that I do not will A. If S is regarded as a set of
circumstances in the sense involved in our definitions, then determinism
is clearly inconsistent with being able to will otherwise. But, as we noted
above, Sellars denies that S can be construed as a set of circumstances in
the appropriate sense. Let us see why.[25]

We can begin by recalling that a claim that x is able to do or will A is
made with regard to a particular period of time P throughout which x is
said to be so able. It appears then that a necessary condition on the
circumstances of an action is that they obtain throughout this time
period. Thus, it seems that a state of the universe antecedent to the time t
(which falls within the period P) of an action would fail to be a circumstance of the action simply because it does not obtain *throughout* this
period. However, matters are not this simple. For one thing, we can
always satisfy the temporal requirement by a little verbal maneuvering.
Thus, if S is a state of the universe before t, we can define another state
of the universe S', which consists in *having been in state S before t*. S'
will entail anything relevant to our being able to act or will at t that S
does, and it meets the condition of obtaining at t.

We might be inclined to reject as merely "pseudocircumstances"
states of the universe that meet the temporal condition only in virtue of
such verbal maneuvering. But this would be a mistake. Consider, for
example, the state of affairs of x's having heard an explosion at t', a time
prior to the period P with regard to which we are considering x's abilities
to act and will. As Sellars points out, such a state of affairs

> defines a physically relevant circumstance which obtains with respect to x
> during a *subsequent* period of time. There are various things which he may not
> be capable of during that period—e.g., feeling peaceful and unafraid. (FD,
> 174; my emphasis.)

So clearly some states of the universe that do not obtain at t should be
admitted as circumstances of an action or willing at t.

What then does distinguish real circumstances (ones that can prevent
an action or willing) from states-of-affairs that are merely pseudocircumstances? Sellars suggests that we can discern the essential difference by reflection on the above example of hearing an explosion. He
summarizes the difference in the following rather cryptic passage:

The law which relates hearing explosions at t to not being in certain states during the subsequent period is a *specific* [kind of][26] law of nature, an "historical law" which is paralleled at the physical level by historical laws pertaining, for example, to elastic substances. (FD, 174.)

In a later commentary on this passage (RD, 153), Sellars notes that the "operative phrase" here is "historical law" and that what he had in mind was that

whether or not we are in a position to give a *theoretical* explanation of this fact, it is a matter of inductive fact at the empirical level that hearing an explosion affects the abilities of people to act and will for a certain period of time and hence 'having heard an explosion at t' satisfies the criteria for being a circumstance of action during the subsequent period. (Sellars' emphasis.)

Apparently, the crucial point with regard to this historical law governing the explosion is that it correlates the explosion with the *abilities* of agents. It is precisely this nomological relevance of a state-of-affairs to an agent's *ability* to will (and act) that makes it a real circumstance of an action.

Thus I meant by a *real* circumstance, which *prevents* one from willing otherwise, one which is by virtue of *specific* laws (which need not be historical) physically incompatible with *having the ability to will otherwise*. (RD, 155; Sellars' emphasis.)

So real circumstances are states-of-affairs that causally affect an agent's ability to will (or act); pseudocircumstances do not affect this ability, even though they may entail that the agent *does* will (or act) in a given way.

To avoid confusion, it is essential to be clear about the meaning 'ability to will' in this context. First of all, it is of course not a species of *ability to act,* which was discussed above (p. 139), since willing is not acting. Further, 'ability to will' must not be taken to be a synonym for 'being able to will', which was defined above. Since 'ability to will' has been introduced as part of an explication of the meaning of the term 'circumstances' in the definition of 'being able to will', such synonymy would render Sellars' definition circular. What then does Sellars mean by 'ability to will'? As I understand him, it is a species of the general metaphysical concept of *capacity* (*potentiality*), the correlate of the metaphysical concept of act. Capacities (and the actualities [acts] that underlie them) provide the metaphysical foundation for the practical realm of action.

As Sellars points out (RD, 154), it is a conceptual truth about capacities that a system does not lose its capacity (ability) to ϕ just because it is not in fact ϕ-ing. Thus, a car does not lose its capacity to go

10 m.p.h. just because it is going 100 m.p.h. Similarly, the fact that (as determinism maintains) the antecedent state of the universe entails that I will as I do at t is consistent with my having at t the ability to will otherwise. Only a state of the universe that entails that I do not have this ability is a *real circumstance,* preventing my willing otherwise and hence inconsistent with my freedom.

Putting Sellars' construal of real circumstances into the definition of 'being able to will', we obtain:

> x is able to will A at t =$_{def}$ There is no state-of-affairs that entails that x does not have the ability to will A at t.

Given this sense of 'is able to will', Sellars has surely established that we are able to will other than we do, even if our willings are (in accord with determinism) entailed by antecedent states of the universe. Thus Sellars' defense of compatibilism is successful provided the explication of 'is able to will A' in terms of 'ability to will A' is correct. Is it? The anticompatibilist may well suggest the following alternative definition, which would defeat compatibilism:

> x is able to will A at t =$_{def}$ There is no state-of-affairs that entails that x does not will to do A at t.

According to this definition, it is x's being caused not to will A rather than his being caused not to have the ability to will A that is taken as crucial for his being able to will A. And if this is done, the defense of compatibilism collapses. Further, the alternative definition has an apparent plausibility: is not someone who is caused, say by events before his birth, to will as he does unable to will otherwise?

In fact however the alternative definition is wholly unwarranted. To see this, it is essential to recall that we are discussing 'being able to will otherwise' as a necessary condition of acting in the strict sense. The first condition of freedom requires that a free agent be able to will otherwise in the sense that, if he is not so able, he will not act at all. So the issue is whether the alternative definition is correct in its implication that, if there is a cause for my willing to do A, then my "doing" of A is not strictly speaking an action. To take a concrete example, suppose I will to play and do play Mendelssohn's First Piano Concerto and that a neurophysiologist subsequently demonstrates that the neural event that was my volition was caused by an antecedent neural event. Is my playing the concerto an action or not? To see that it is, we need only recall that A's being caused by my volition is a sufficient (as well as a necessary) condition for A's being my action. Hence, since I willed to play the Mendelssohn, my playing it was an action. But if we adopted the alternative definition of 'is able to will A', it would follow that my playing the Mendelssohn was not an action. Therefore, the alternative definition must be rejected.[27]

Sellars' construal of the first—and basic—necessary condition of freedom in terms of the metaphysical concept of capacity (ability) is an instance of his general (essentially Aristotelian[28]) view that a person, as conceived in the manifest image, is basically a "system of capacities pertaining to the various modes of thinking". (MCP, 239.) Freedom at root is a person's capacity for 'volitional thoughts' and hence for the actions that such thoughts entail. The alternative definition of 'being able to will', on the other hand, locates freedom not in a capacity but in an actuality—i.e., the actual occurrence of particular volitions. This definition corresponds to the (essentially Cartesian) view of the person (or mind) as nothing beyond its acts. The argument in the preceding paragraph against this definition—an argument in the spirit if not the text of Sellars—is a demonstration that this Cartesian view of mind is not consistent with the fact that my volition causes my action (in the strict sense). (Sellars' espousal of an Aristotelian as opposed to Cartesian view of mind also sheds light on the deeper reasons behind his rejection of the agency view of causation. The agency view is implicitly Cartesian, since—as Aristotle realized—an agent that is an "unmoved mover" must be "pure act" and hence not partake of any capacities.)

To summarize Sellars' defense of compatibilism: Freedom is characterized by two central necessary conditions, that we act in the strict sense (and hence be able to do otherwise) and that we act without compulsion. The defense of compatibilism is based on two central distinctions. The first, between causality and compulsion, shows the consistency of determinism with the second necessary condition and has been adequately developed by classical compatibilists like Hume and Mill. The second, between the genuine circumstances of an action and mere antecedent conditions, shows the consistency of determinism with the first necessary condition and is Sellars' own primary contribution to the compatibilist argument. As we saw, this distinction expresses the difference between states of affairs that are causally relevant to our capacity to will and act and those that are not (although perhaps they are causes of our actual willing and acting). And the importance of this distinction is due to Sellars' Aristotelian construal of freedom—like all the basic manifest properties of human beings—as a capacity.

NOTES

[1]For a discussion of the distinction of these two images, cf. my paper in this volume on Sellars' philosophy of science.

[2]On Sellars' understanding of causal necessitation, cf. my paper in this volume on his philosophy of science.

[3]Cf. Karl Popper, "Indeterminism in Classical and in Quantum Physics," *British Journal for the Philosophy of Science* 1 (1950).

[4]As Sellars notes, the use of the term 'predictability' is probably inappropriate in this logical context, although proponents of scientific determinism have in fact frequently used the expression.

[5]In PSIM, Sellars distinguishes between actions that are habitual and actions that are in character: "To be *habitual* is to be 'in character' but the converse is not true." (12; Sellars' emphasis.) But in later papers he seems to ignore this distinction. Thus: "To be predictable . . . means that a person's actions are habitual, inferable by inductive reasoning based on observation of his past behavior. For an action to be predictable is for it to be an expression of character." (FD, 146; cf. also RD, 157.)

[6]This sort of reply to modified vulgar determinism is suggested by Sellars' comments about inclination in RD, 157.

[7]My discussion here does not purport to be a full-scale exposition of Sellars' action theory. I will focus only on aspects of his action theory that are especially relevant to the problem of freedom.

[8]Cf. Donald Davidson, "Actions, Reasons, and Causes," *Journal of Philosophy* 60 (1963).

[9]For a discussion of the nature and logic of intentions, cf. David Solomon's paper in this volume on Sellars' ethics.

[10]As this passage suggests, Sellars' philosophy has the resources to exploit (via a general theory of representation) the parallels that Danto has emphasized between epistemology and action theory.

[11]Sellars does not, of course, deny that there are mental acts that are also actions (e.g., deliberations). But he does urge that all such actions are grounded in nonperformative acts (*SM*, 74).

[12]'Original' here refers to what Sellars calls (in PSIM) the 'original image' of man, a primitive image in which all entities are regarded as persons and from which the manifest image has been derived.

[13]Alan Donagan, "Determinism and Freedom: Sellars and the Reconciliationist Thesis," in *Action, Knowledge, and Reality*, ed. H.-N. Castañeda (Indianapolis: Bobbs-Merrill, 1975). It is to this article that Sellars' "Reply to Donagan" is a reply. The passage quoted is on p. 74; and the material quoted within the passage is from C. D. Broad, *Ethics and the History of Philosophy* (London: Routledge and Kegan Paul, 1952), pp. 214-15. Donagan's formulation of agent causation is atypical to the extent that it speaks of the agent causing both his volitions and his actions. Most proponents of agent causation—e.g., Richard Taylor—reject the role of volitions and speak only of the agent causing his actions. I prefer Donagan's version because it allows us to focus solely on the agent causation issue without having to simultaneously fight the battle over volitions.

[14]A basic action is one that is not done by the agent's doing anything else.

[15]There may be a temptation to say that the agent causes his action by willing to do it—i.e., by his volition. But we must remember that a volition is not an action.

[16]R. Chisholm, "Freedom and Action," in *Freedom and Determinism*, ed. K. Lehrer New York: Random House, 1966, p. 23.

[17]Here I am using 'circumstances' in the most general sense, including any state-of-affairs causally relevant to the action in question. As we shall see later, Sellars introduces a stricter technical use of 'circumstances'.

[18]The article by Donagan is the one cited in n. 13 above. Sellars' "more refined position" is developed in RD, 167-71.

[19]What follows is a very simplified summary of the technical definitions Sellars gives in FD, 164ff. I have been greatly assisted by Donagan's admirable reconstruction of these definitions (*op. cit.*, 62ff).

[20]Here and subsequently I shall use 'entails' to mean 'causally entails' (i.e., 'causally necessitates').

[21]Although Sellars does not argue for his inclusion of clause (i) in this definition, I think we can see the reasonableness of the condition by reflecting on cases where it would not hold. Suppose for example that the exigencies of my life to date have left me ignorant of the existence of the Burgundy wine, Romanée-Conti. The causes that have produced this state of ignorance entail that I do not will to drink a bottle of Romanée-Conti. Now further suppose that Romanée-Conti, exhorbitantly priced as it is, is is far beyond my financial means. Can we rightly say that the wine's high price prevents me from drinking it? It seems clear that we should rather say that the high price would prevent me from drinking the wine if I knew about it. Similarly, if I am a person of sufficient means but nonetheless ignorant of Romanée-Conti, we should not say that its high price does not prevent me from drinking it but rather that, if I knew of the wine, I would not be prevented from drinking it. Thus, the point that justifies (i) is that talk of being prevented or not prevented from doing A is inappropriate (perhaps a category mistake) with regard to someone who is caused not to will A.

[22]We must not, however, think of 'is in a position to' (= 'is not prevented from') as the *contradictory* of 'prevents'; i.e., we must not think that (in circumstances C) x is in a position to do A if *either* clause (i) *or* clause (ii) of the definition of 'prevents' is not satisfied. Such a construal is incorrect since, as the rationale for clause (i) given above (n. 21) showed, (i) is a necessary condition for 'not being prevented from' as well as for 'being prevented from'. Hence, 'in a position to' should be defined not as the contradictory but as the *contrary* of 'prevents', viz., as:

> (In C and throughout P) x is in a position to do A
> =$_{def}$ (i) C does not entail that x does not will A;
> and (ii) C does not entail that x does not do A.

[23]For the case of being able to act otherwise, Sellars finds support for his distinction of circumstances and antecedent states of affairs in the following considerations. According to the first clause of the definition of 'prevents', S could be a circumstance preventing my doing A only if it did not entail my not *willing* A. But S (the antecedent state of affairs that entails that I not do A) *does* entail my not willing to do A, since my willing to do A entails that I do A and S entails that I do not do A. Consequently, S cannot be said to prevent my doing A. (Nor, of course, in the light of n. 21, is S a circumstance which does *not* prevent me from doing A—i.e., a circumstance that puts x in a position to do A.) Thus, if

we regard as genuine circumstances only those states of affairs that can properly be said to prevent or not prevent an action, then S is not a genuine circumstance. However, this argument cannot be extended to the case of being able to will otherwise since, as we shall see, the definition of 'prevents from willing' contains no parallel to clause (i).

[24]We can, if course, speak of *indirectly* willing to will in the sense of willing to take steps that will bring it about that in the future I will A.

[25]Although I will discuss this question of the meaning of 'circumstances' primarily for the case of being able to will otherwise, the points made are also directly applicable to the case of being able to act otherwise.

[26]I insert "kind of" in accord with Sellars' own emendation (RD, 153).

[27]The diehard anticompatibilist may still protest that, even if the alternative definition does not provide a necessary condition for A's being an action, it does provide a necessary condition for A's being a *free* action. But to make such a reply is just to say that although the existence of causes for my willing and acting does not mean that the first necessary condition of freedom (that I act strictly speaking) fails it does mean that the second necessary condition (that my action not be compelled) fails. Hence, such a reply simply falls back into the old confusion of causation and compulsion.

[28]To a rough approximation, Sellars tends to be Aristotelian on matters concerning the manifest image and Kantian on matters concerning the relations of the two images.

Ethical Theory

W. David Solomon

Wilfrid Sellars' writings on ethical theory have received less attention than any other aspect of his work. This is doubly unfortunate since these views are an essential part of the comprehensive philosophical system Sellars has been developing for the last twenty-five years and an understanding of them is required for an understanding of that system. But, also, these views are interesting and important in their own right. At least I will argue in this essay that Sellars' views on ethical theory are both profound and original; whether they are "true" is, of course, another question.

Having lamented the neglect Sellars' ethical views have encountered, however, one must also admit that Sellars is not altogether blameless in the affair. There are a number of reasons, I suspect, why moral philosophers have not given Sellars the attention he deserves. First, his ethical writings are, of all of his writings, the most painfully dialectical in form. He almost always develops his own positions in opposition to various views that he draws from the writings of other moral philosophers, both classical and modern. In trying to spin truth from many-stranded error, however, Sellars frequently leaves the reader unclear about the exact nature of the issues under discussion. A second reason for the neglect of his work derives from his tendency to integrate his ethical theory with his broader views in philosophy of mind and philosophy of language *as he goes along*. Sellars, perhaps more than any other recent philosopher who has written on ethical theory, has tried to develop an ethical theory while drawing out its full implications for other areas of philosophical inquiry. Indeed, some might argue (and not without plausibility) that Sellars is at least as interested in showing how moral discourse and moral thought might fit within his broadly empiricist philosophy of mind as he is in developing positions within ethical theory for their own sake. Be this as it may, the reader who is unwilling to follow Sellars down various side paths (as it may seem) into issues that may appear to belong more properly to philosophy of mind, action theory, or metaphysics will be unlikely to persevere long in the study of his ethical writings.

The comprehensiveness of Sellars' aims in his ethical writings, while doubtless creating difficulties for the reader, also provides much of the interest that his writings have. While in much of recent ethical theory one has the impression that views in philosophy of mind, metaphysics, and philosophy of language are invoked in an *ad hoc* fashion to suit the ethical-theoretical purposes of the writer, one never has that feeling in reading Sellars. Indeed, for Sellars, the tendency of an ethical theory to fit within the constraints of an adequate philosophical "system" seems as important a criterion for its acceptability as others more purely "ethical" criteria.

These difficulties in approaching Sellars' ethical writings have largely dictated the strategy I adopt in this essay. I attempt here to give an exposition of Sellars' ethical views that will make them available to a larger audience and tempt others to the critical work that I must leave largely undone. This general strategy involves two tactical devices: first, I have tried, insofar as is possible, to set out Sellars' main arguments and conclusions freed from the dialectical garb in which he clothes them; second, I have downplayed, again insofar as is possible, the dependence of Sellars' ethical views on his views in other areas of philosophical inquiry. There is a danger in each of these maneuvers, since neither the *dialectical* nor *systematic* aspect of Sellars' philosophical enterprise is an *accidental* feature of it. For this reason I present my exposition below as merely a way into Sellars ethical thought; I present it frankly as a reconstruction and not as a substitute for grappling with Sellars on his own terrain.

Sellars' work in ethical theory moves largely within two distinguishable contexts of discussion. At one level, he works within the classic metaethical tradition in attempting to give an account of the logical structure of moral judgments, in particular ought-judgments. His conclusions here constitute an account of the logic of 'ought', which, he alleges, combines the strengths of the three classical metaethical views: naturalism, intuitionism, and noncognitivism. At another (partly overlapping) level, however, Sellars deals with the set of issues that have classically divided deontological and teleological (or Kantian and utilitarian) ethical theories. Here he concludes that deontologists were largely correct in their account of the *motivational* base of morals while teleologists were more nearly correct in their account of the ultimate *justification* of moral principles.

In the discussion below I try to separate, insofar as this is possible, these two contexts of discussion. In section I I suggest a model for understanding the general problematic of classical metaethics and locate Sellars' own views on metaethics within this model. In the following four sections I discuss various strands of his metaethical view as follows: in III I discuss his arguments against emotivist and imperativist views of the Harean variety; in IV I discuss his general account of practical reason and the role that expressions of intention play within that account; in V I show how his analysis of ought-judgments as complicated expressions of intention can be reconciled with the universalizability of moral judgments; and in VI I explore his account of the intersubjectivity of moral judgments. In VII, I turn to the second context of discussion mentioned above and locate Sellars' views on the justification of moral judgments as a "compromise" between deontological and teleological views.

As the discussion proceeds, it will become evident that the distinction between what I have called the two contexts of discussion is more than a little artificial. Even if this distinction must be transcended at the end of this essay, however, I hope that it will serve, at least for a while, as a device for helping us to see some things in Sellars more clearly than would be possible without it.

II

Sellars' views on ethics, like his other philosophical views, grow out of a profound grasp of the positions and controversies within twentieth-century analytic philosophy. For this reason, I want to locate his general stance within a picture of metaethics painted with fairly broad strokes. While it may seem that we are moving quite far from Sellars in this section, I think that some such characterization of his place in the larger disputes of twentieth-century ethics is essential for understanding him. Indeed, the difficulty in locating Sellars within the standard taxonomy of ethical views is one more reason why his work has attracted so little attention from other moral philosophers.

There is a certain common view of the problematic of ethical theory which is largely shared by Anglo-American moral philosophers from Moore to Hare. I will call the tradition that embodies this view classical metaethics (CM) and those philosophers who work within this tradition classical metaethicists (CMists). CM is continuous with earlier ethical theory in that it conceives of the two fundamental problems in ethics as what I shall call the problem of justification and the problem of motivation. The *problem of justification* can be broadly characterized as the problem of determining the nature of the evidence that is relevant to the truth or falsity of moral judgment and of explaining the relation between this evidence and a moral judgment when the moral judgment is justified. (Of course, a possible view here is that there is *no* evidence relevant to the truth or falsity of moral judgments for the very good reason that there is no significant sense in which moral judgment can be true or false.) The *problem of motivation* can be broadly characterized as the problem of determining how assent to moral judgments, or commitment to moral principles or ideals, or the susceptibility to moral feelings (possession of a moral sense, in an earlier tradition) "relates to" one's behavior or dispositions to behavior.

If the recognition of these two problems as fundamental problems in ethics shows the continuity of CM with earlier ethical theory, the particular way in which these problems were construed within the tradition points to its distinctive character. Both problems were construed with reference to the following trileveled model:[1]

L1) statements of fact,
      ↓
L2) moral judgments,
      ↓
L3) actions.

The problem of justification and the problem of motivation are seen respectively in CM as the problem of the nature of the arrow that connects (L1) to (L2) and the nature of the arrow that connects (L2) to (L3). That there is some sort of connection, however weak, at both levels has seemed obvious to almost everyone; even the most perfunctory reflection on the place of moral thought and talk in our everyday life shows both that we *normally* appeal to facts in support of our moral claims and that we *normally* feel moved to act in accord with moral judgments.

If there has been broad agreement that there is *some* connection between the factual beliefs a man holds, the moral views he espouses, and his actions, however, there has been constant and deep-seated disagreement among CMists about the nature of these connections. At the most general level the disagreement has been over whether the transitions at either point have the character of necessity or whether they are merely contingent. One might hold, for example, that certain facts entail certain moral judgments and that *real* assent to a moral judgment logically guarantees that one will act (or be moved to act) in accord with the judgment, thus making the connections at both points matters of logical necessity. One might hold to the contrary, however, that the connections between both facts and moral judgments and between moral judgments and actions can vary from person to person and that they depend not on some feature of moral judgments that can be grasped by logical or semantical principles but rather on the peculiar psychological makeup of individual moral agents. Thus one might hold that whether a certain set of facts stands in an evidentiary relation to a moral judgment *for some person* depends upon that person's particular aims, goals, or aspirations. In the same way, one might hold that whether some person's assent to a moral judgment "moves" him to action will depend on that person's attitude toward morality—i.e., it will depend on whether he is "for" or "against" morality.

What has been most characteristic of CM has been its adherence to two not unrelated methodological points with respect to this debate. First, CMists have presupposed that the nature of the two points of transition is to be determined by an analysis of the meaning of so-called ethical terms—usually 'good', 'right', and 'ought'. Second, they have presupposed that the crucial question about the nature of the points of transition has been whether these transitions involve entailment relations.

With this broad characterization of the problematic of CM before us, it is relatively simple to set out the positions of the standard metaethical views. Naturalists have argued that the meaning of ethical terms is exhausted by the empirical criteria of their application and, hence, that there is an entailment relation tying (L1) to (L2). They denied, however, that any strong logical tie holds between (L2) and (L3).[2] Noncognitivists, on the other hand, have rejected such an entailment relation between (L1) and (L2); in searching for their reasons for rejecting such an entailment, we have to turn to their treatment of the transition from (L2) to (L3). It was at this point that noncognitivists found the strong logical connection that they had failed to find between (L1) and (L2). They were struck by the close connection between the assertion of moral judgments and actions, and this provided them with a reason, they supposed, for rejecting the entailment relation between (L1) and (L2).[3] The precise explanation of why a strong logical relation between (L2) and (L3) should be thought to preclude such a relation between (L1) and (L2) is a complicated and lengthy matter, but the fundamental reason was that it was felt that there could not be entailment relations both between (L1) and (L2) and between (L2) and (L3). It seems clear that such an entailment cannot hold, however, since if it did, two persons who shared identical factual beliefs could not, without some logical fault, disagree about what actions to perform in similar situations. Most philosophers have accepted as a datum of moral philosophy, however, the view that agreement on factual beliefs need not entail agreement on ideals, aspirations, or choice of lifestyle.

The battle lines between naturalists and noncognitivists are drawn, then, between those ethical theorists who claim that there is an entailment relation between (L1) and (L2) and deny that such a relation holds between (L2) and (L3) and those who claim that there is an entailment relation between (L2) and (L3) but deny that there is one between (L1) and (L2). Each view is in the unhappy position of having to deny what seems from the point of view of the opposing position obvious: naturalists have to deny that moral judgments unqualifiedly commit their users to action, while noncognitivists have to deny that intersubjective standards of factual evidence for moral judgments can be found.

Fitting the intuitionists into this debate is a complicated matter in that it is not at all clear whether intuitionism was determined to have it both ways or whether it was content to have it neither. Seen in one way, intuitionism seems to render mysterious both the connection between facts and moral judgments and the connection between moral judgments and actions. In trying to hold onto the intersubjective character of moral discourse while emphasizing its uniqueness and nonreducibility, intuitionists were forced to postulate special moral (nonnatural) facts in virtue of which moral judgments are true and cognitively meaningful. But intuitionists were never able to clarify the relation between "ordinary" facts and nonnatural facts, thus rendering the move from (L1) to (L2) mysterious; nor were they able to make perspicuous the connection between the apprehension of their peculiar moral facts and action in accord with them, thus rendering the move from (L2) to (L3) mysterious.

If in one sense, however, intuitionism must be considered a failure, there is another sense in which some have thought that it succeeded at least insofar as it managed to keep its heart in the right place. When intuitionism was propounded and defended by its most sophisticated proponent, Prichard, it seemed to have at least a sound grasp of the weakness of opposing metaethical views and a dogged determination to avoid *all* of these weaknesses. Thus, Prichard was determined to fashion an account of the logic of 'ought' that would account for (1) the unique and irreducible character of moral discourse (pace naturalism); (2) the intersubjective character of moral discourse (pace noncognitivism); and (3) the action-guiding character of moral discourse (pace naturalism and certain other forms of intuitionism).[4]

If we now return to Sellars from this excursion through the intricacies of CM, we can best characterize his position within this tradition as one that attempts to retain Prichard's fundamental commitment to the uniqueness, intersubjectivity, and action-guidingness of moral discourse while removing some of the mystery about how these features of moral discourse can cohabit. Sellars says of Prichard's attempt to defend an account of moral judgments that emphasizes both their "fact-stating" character *and* their motivational force.

My difficulty with Prichard on this point (as with the many philosophers who have insisted that moral thinking qua thinking is "conative", no "mere blend" of thinking and "emotion") is that he offers not even the beginning of a satisfactory analysis of this phenomenological insight, an analysis which would account for the fact that moral thinking differs from, but resembles, other forms of thinking by relating both to the fundamental categories of an adequate philosophy of mind. Prichard's grasp of the distinctive traits of moral thinking exhibits the combination of thinness and acuteness which is characteristic of his philosophy. (IIO, 161.)

Sellars' attempt to put flesh on the bare bones of Prichard's insights leads him to construct a comprehensive model for practical reasoning within which he locates moral thought and talk. Sellars is concerned, that is, to identify moral judgments as one form of practical judgment and to explore the relationship between them and other practical judgments. By locating moral judgments within the context of practical reasoning, Sellars assures that these judgments will have practical force. In order to assure the uniqueness and intersubjectivity of moral judgment, Sellars has to characterize the special form that practical thinking has when it is *moral* thinking. I will explore the special character that Sellars attributes to moral thinking toward the end of this essay; in the next few sections I will concentrate on his attempt to integrate moral thinking into a comprehensive view of practical reason.

III

Sellars, as we have seen, wants an account of moral judgments that will do justice to their intimate relation to action. The contingent connection to action that naturalistic and certain intuitionistic views (e.g., Ross') allow is too weak, he thinks.[5] In searching for an account of moral judgments that does justice to their practical character, it is only natural that Sellars should turn first to the noncognitivist views developed by emotivists like Ayer and Stevenson and to the imperativist analysis of moral judgments defended in recent years by R. M. Hare. Each of these varieties of noncognitivism has as its leading idea the view that the primary role of moral language (and of evaluative language generally) is to "influence" behavior and dispositions to behavior. Emotivists have argued broadly that moral judgments are best seen as primarily expressions of attitude that, from the point of view of the speaker, appear as symptoms of the presence of certain attitudes and, from the point of view of the audience, appear as stimuli eliciting or reinforcing certain attitudes in others. If moral judgments are thus tied intimately to the attitudes of their users, the necessary connection between the uses of these judgments and action seems assured, since attitudes are just, in one sense, dispositions to act in certain ways.

While emotivism is attractive in doing justice to the link between moral judgment and action, however, Sellars feels that in this case the price for justice is set too high.[6] Emotivism preserves the practical force of moral judgments by removing moral discourse from the conceptual realm altogether. The constant recourse of emotivists to grunts and groans, boos and yeas, and expletives and interjections as the primary analogues of moral judgment signals their commitment to the broadly nonconceptual character of moral discourse.

But how do we show that moral discourse does belong within the conceptual order? Perhaps the emotivists were right in treating moral discourse as though it had a completely different character—i.e., a nonconceptual one—from fact-stating discourse. In response to this query, Sellars invokes a criterion that he has used in other places to mark off those bits of language, broadly conceived, that are conceptual from those that are not. "The criterion I propose is that a word stands for a concept when there are good arguments in which it is essentially involved." (SE, 408.) One might be inclined to think at first that this criterion as used against the emotivists is question-begging, since one of their central claims was that there really are no good arguments in ethics in the same sense as there are good arguments in, say, science and mathematics. But when emotivists denigrated (or reinterpreted) the role of inference and argument in ethics, they had in mind arguments of this form:

(1)   O is P_1,P_2,P_3 (where P_1-P_3 are empirical properties).
(2)   Therefore, O is E (where E is an ethical "property").

And if Sellars needs to suppose that arguments of this sort are good ones in order to use his criterion, he would indeed be begging the question. There are many arguments, however, that involve moral terms but are not of this character. Consider the following two arguments:

(1)   Jones ought to do A and B.
(2)   Therefore, Jones ought to do A.

or

(1)   All objects of kind K are good.
(2)   This is an object of kind K.
(3)   Therefore, this is good.

Each of these arguments involves essential *uses* of moral terms and only someone determined to hold onto emotivism at all costs would deny that they are good ones. More important, they do not violate the basic strictures of emotivism against "fact-value" arguments and hence are not question-begging in the way the first argument mentioned above is. If we accept Sellars' criterion of membership in the conceptual order (and it certainly seems plausible), emotivism must be rejected on the grounds that it cannot do justice to the conceptual character of moral terms and moral discourse generally.

Of course, this line of criticism as developed by Sellars against emotivism is not original with him. From its inception, emotivism was confronted with the charge that it could not do justice to the role argument and inference play in ordinary moral thought and talk. The evermore complicated recipes that emotivists concocted for integrating the "descriptive" and "emotive" meaning of moral judgments testifies to the extent to which even they were moved by this objection. This general line of argument was developed in an especially powerful way by R. M. Hare, who wanted to preserve what seemed right in emotivism while exorcising its antirationalist tendencies. Sellars, indeed, has been strongly influenced by Hare, and he says in one place:

> The neo-imperativist approach of R. M. Hare is, in my opinion, sufficiently close to the truth to be a useful point of departure for the ideas I wish to develop. While I think that something *like* his account of the concept of ought is true, I do not think that it will do as it stands. Indeed, I think that its very closeness to the truth has enabled it to obscure essential points about the concept of obligation. (IIO, 162.)

By setting out Hare's approach to the action-guidingness of moral judgments and then examining Sellars' objections to Hare's account, we are led quickly to the heart of his theory.

Hare argued in *The Language of Morals* that while the emotivists were right in taking the action-guiding force of moral language to be its central feature, they went wrong in confusing the notion of "getting someone to do something" with "telling someone to do something". As he says there, "The process of *telling* someone to do something, and *getting* him to do it, are quite distinct, logically, from each other".[7] More generally, Hare thought that the emphasis emotivists placed on the tendency of moral judgments to affect causally the behavior of hearers distracted attention from the complicated nexus of logical relations in which they were caught up.

Hare's own view of the proper analysis of moral judgments involved an attempt to retain the action-guidingness of moral judgments in a fairly strong sense but also to preserve the logical connections among moral judgments and between moral judgments and nonmoral judgments. The key notion in his analysis is that of the imperative, and his central claim is that all properly evaluative judgments (including, of course, moral judgments) either are imperative or entail them.

If Hare's account is to handle both the action-guiding character of moral discourse and its conceptual (inference-allowing) character, he must show (1) that imperatives are action-guiding and (2) that there are patterns of inference involving imperatives. The first task is fairly straightforward; if there are *any* action-guiding pieces of discourse, surely imperatives must belong to that class. Hare makes this clear beyond any question by characterizing the assent conditions for an imperative in such a way that to assent candidly to an imperative is (physical and psychological impediments aside) to act in accord with it.[8] The second task above is not so straightforward, however. In particular, since imperatives are neither true nor false, it has seemed to many persons that it is improper to talk of inference here at all. Hare develops a sophisticated apparatus for understanding the deep structure of imperatives, however, which makes his claim that imperatives can play the role of either premise or conclusion in inferences a good deal more plausible than it might at first seem.

I do not have the space here to set out Hare's full defense of the notion of imperative inference, but I can briefly note its leading idea. Hare construed both imperatives and indicatives as having a structure that divides roughly into two parts: a content part and an operator that signals what the speaker is "doing" with the content. Thus, the two sentences

(1)   Jones shut the door. (said *of* Jones)
(2)   Jones, shut the door. (said *to* Jones)

have the depth structures respectively of

(1')   (Jones shutting the door), yes.
(2')   (Jones shutting the door), please.

where the 'yes' in (1') signals that the content is being *asserted* while the 'please' in (2') signals that the content is being *commanded*. Hare argued that inference involves relations among the phrastics (as he called the content) of sentences and that an imperative neustic (as he called the operator) does not absolve its phrastic from its logical relations.

Whatever one may think ultimately of Hare's particular explanation of *how* imperative inference is possible, however, one can hardly fail to be impressed by the examples that he proposes as embodying such inferences. Thus, one of his examples goes as follows:[9]

(1)   Take all of the boxes to the station.
(2)   This is one of the boxes.
(3)   Therefore, take this to the station.

The conclusion of this argument surely seems to follow from the premises in as straightforwardly a logical way as the conclusion of the following purely indicative argument:

    (1)   All of the boxes are at the station.
    (2)   This is one of the boxes.
    (3)   Therefore, this is at the station.

But if these two arguments equally involve *inference,* then Hare has made good his claim that there is imperative inference.

It is at this point, however that Sellars parts company with Hare. He objects, that is, to the central role Hare assigns to imperatives in his account of the logic of moral judgments. He develops two distinguishable but intertwined arguments against Hare's position. He argues first that if the imperatives that Hare places at the center of his account are construed as *commands,* the account fails because commanding as a performance presupposes principles of obligation. If Hare avoids this objection by construing the use of imperatives in a narrower way that does not involve the explicit invocation of the performance of commanding, Sellars argues that the imperatives so construed can play no role in inference.[10]

Let us look first at the argument against commanding as the primary analogue of moral judgments. This argument involves the following three claims:

    (1)   Commands are performances that can only ''come off'' in certain circumstances.
    (2)   Included among the circumstances that are the necessary conditions of a command's coming off are certain relationships between the person who issues the command and the person to whom it is addressed.
    (3)   These special relationships are defined by principles that involve 'ought'-talk.

The thought behind this argument is the Austinian one that commands as performances can only be successfully carried off if the commander in some sense appropriately (by *right*) issues the command. Looking at the same situation from the other end, we can see that the person to whom the command is addressed is really *commanded* to do something only if, again in some sense to be specified, he *ought* to do whatever he is commanded to do. But if the performance of commanding is to shed any light on the logic of ought-judgments in particular and normative language generally, it is necessary that an understanding of commanding performances not involve the use of normative language. Since commanding performances do ''depend on'' norms that are acknowledged by the performers in the commanding situation, it would be a mistake to construe the use of moral judgments as just a "special kind" of commanding.

Even if one agrees with this argument, however, one might claim that it really does not touch Hare's position, since Hare need not understand imperatives as full-blown commands. There are many uses of sentences in the imperative mood, after all, that do not constitute commands. Directions in cookbooks, for example, are frequently couched in the imperative mood, but it would be absurd to suppose that for this reason we must think of the author of the book as issuing commands.

In order to counter this "thin" interpretation of the imperativist position, Sellars develops the second argument that we mentioned above. This argument depends on a distinction that he draws between three ways in which a speaker's intentions relative to the actions of another person might become known to that person (Cf. IIO, 166). Thus, in order of strengthening involvement with one's audience, we have:

(1)   Merely intending out loud,
(2)   Telling of one's intentions,
(3)   Telling someone to do something.

Examples of these three ways in which one's intentions become public would be:

(1')   Jones simply overhearing Smith say, "Jones shall do A,"
(2')   Smith telling Jones, "I intend that you do A" (said in a merely autobiographical way),
(3')   Smith telling Jones, "Do A".

Of these three ways of "expressing" one's intentions, (3) seems to capture most closely, Sellars argues, what the thin interpretation of imperativism would place at the center of an analysis of ought-judgments. That is, with (3) we have a bare *telling-to* stripped of the performative trappings in which commanding is clothed.

Sellars claims, however, that even though tellings-to need not be as encumbered with performative overtones as commandings, they are, nevertheless, performances of a sort. For one thing, tellings-to require an audience, and he goes on to argue that this feature is all that is required to show that they *cannot* figure in inference either as premises or as conclusions.[11]

Sellars' argument that no telling-to can be the conclusion of a reasoning is summed up in the following passage:

> It makes sense to suppose that an expressed reasoning could have occurred without being expressed; and if so, there cannot be such things as expressed

reasonings the premises or conclusions of which are promisings, tellings to, or tellings that. In particular, there is no such thing as imperative inference. (IIO, 171.)

It may seem puzzling initially why Sellars should require that all reasonings, or inferrings, be capable of being rehearsed without an audience. This requirement may seem *ad hoc* and without support. Certainly Sellars spends little time defending it; but a little reflection shows, I think, that it really is as obvious as he takes it to be.

Consider what it might be about some linguistic episode that could make it necessary that it occur only in public, i.e., in interaction between two language users. The only reason sufficient to explain this would seem to be that the appropriateness of that linguistic episode must depend partly at least on the *situations* of the speaker and the audience. It is in virtue of my wants or intentions or my assessment of your submissiveness, perhaps, that renders it reasonable for me to tell you to do something. Tellings-to, to put it a different way, are actions that can be deliberate or hasty, justified or unjustified, successes or failures. And, of course, it makes sense to speak of these actions, i.e., tellings-to, as being supported by reasons. But for an action, even of the telling-to sort, to be supported by reasons is *not* for it to be the conclusion of a reasoning. Indeed, since a telling-to, insofar as it is an action, is something that can be done for reasons, it cannot itself be a conclusion of an inference. To think otherwise would be to confuse the decision or intention to tell someone something with the telling-to performance itself.

In the end, then, it is the fact that tellings-to, like commands, are actions that make the notion of imperative inference unacceptable to Sellars. But in disposing of Hare's prescriptivist account of the logic of moral judgment, Sellars may appear to have exhausted the ways in which contemporary ethical theory can account for the action-guidingness of moral judgments. He has rejected Prichard's view because of its essentially *ad hoc* character; he has rejected emotivist accounts on the grounds that they remove moral discourse from the conceptual order altogether; and now he rejects Hare's view on the ground that there can be no imperative inference. Where can he turn for an account that will do justice to the practical force of moral judgments but that will avoid the difficulties of the available views?

Sellars resolves this difficulty by claiming that the fundamental conceptual item out of which moral judgments are constructed is the expression of intention. By giving an account of expressions of intention that shows both how they play a role in inference and how they are connected necessarily to action (through their relation to volitions), Sellars accomplishes, he thinks, what Hare set out to do with imperatives. In the next section I will set out Sellars' account of practical reason and examine his notion of an expression of intention as it is defined by the role it plays within this structure.

IV

It is impossible to understand Sellars' account of the logic of moral judgments without setting out in some detail his general view of the nature and structure of practical reason.[12] In particular, his account of practical reason is partially determined by his goal of fitting such an account within his substantive views on the philosophy of mind, according to which mental acts are construed on the model of overt utterances for which they are seen as the causal antecedents. Also, he relies heavily here on certain views about the nature of implication that he has developed elsewhere, including the controversial view that causal laws are to be treated as material rules of inference. Having admitted the difficulties here, I will proceed nevertheless to set out briefly his account of practical reasoning.

The most important feature of Sellars' account of practical thought is his commitment to the view that there is such a thing as practical reasoning. Unlike many other philosophers who have been attracted to a broadly empiricist philosophy of mind, Sellars believes that the ordinary processes of deliberation and practical thinking do involve reasoning that is worthy of the name. Sellars' account of practical reasoning encompasses three main topics: (1) intentions; (2) volitions; and (3) the processes of practical inference. I will take up these topics in that order.

The central practical statement, according to Sellars, is the expression of intention (EI). Examples of EIs would be the following:

(1)   I will go to town in ten minutes.
(2)   Jones shall pay me the money.
(3)   You shall bring it to me.

Sellars has developed a technical use of 'shall' that, regardless of person, signals an expression of intention. The function of 'shall' as an operator that converts indicative sentences into EIs is brought out by the following translation of (1) through (3):

(1)   Shall (I will go to town in ten minutes)
(2)   Shall (Jones will pay me the money)
(3)   Shall (You will bring it to me)

Two further points will make the notion of expression of intention clearer. First, EIs are to be distinguished from biographical statements describing or reporting intentions (*SM*, 185). Such biographical statements are true just in case the appropriate person has the intention imputed to him. Expressions of intention on the other hand are neither true nor false (which is not to say, of course, that they cannot be criticized in various ways for being defective, e.g., on the grounds that they are less than candid). Second, expressions of intention always express the speaker's intentions; although I can report your intention, I cannot express it (*SM*, 184). When I intend that Jones go to town, I am intending to do whatever may be necessary (with standard qualifications) to bring about Jones' going to town. When I *report* that Jones intends to go to town, I am, of course, expressing no intention at all. This point suggests that we use subscripts on the shall-operator to indicate whose intentions are being expressed. Thus,

(4)   Shall (Jones will go to town) (said by Jones)
(5)   Shall (Jones will go to town) (said by Smith)

will become, respectively,

(4')   Shall $_{Jones}$ (Jones will go to town)
(5')   Shall $_{Smith}$ (Jones will go to town)

Intentions are practical in that they inevitably (changes of mind and so forth aside) turn into volitions. A volition, on Sellars' view, is an intention whose time has come. Whereas expressions of intention manifest my commitment to act at some future time (perhaps precisely datable, perhaps not), volitions are commitments on my part to act here and now. It is, Sellars argues, part of the conceptual framework of practice that intentions ripen into volitions and that volitions issue in actions. The ordinary sequence of events would proceed as follows:

(1)   Shall $_{Jones}$ (I will leave in three minutes)
      (said at 2:00)
(2)   Shall $_{Jones}$ (I will leave in two minutes)
      (said at 2:01)
(3)   Shall $_{Jones}$ (I will leave in one minute)
      (said at 2:02)
(4)   Shall $_{Jones}$ (I will leave now)
      (said at 2:03)
(5)   Jones leaves.

The volition "occurs" at (4) and issues in action at (5).

The details of the connections here need not detain us, but it is important to see that the connections (*ceteris paribus* clauses suitably understood) are necessary ones: to learn the language of intentional expressions is to learn the transitions represented in this sequence. The transitions involved in the moves from (1) to (4) are intralinguistic moves, licensed by rules for the proper use of the intentional 'shall'.[13] When we move from (4) to (5), however, we move within a language to an action. Sellars argues that there are linguistic rules that license not only moves within languages—intralinguistic moves—but also moves from extralinguistic items to linguistic items—what he calls language-entry transitions—and from linguistic items back to extralinguistic items—what he calls language-exit transitions. Thus, some concepts (e.g., 'or') may be completely defined by rules licensing intralinguistic moves; other concepts (e.g., 'red' and 'this') may be partially understood in terms of language-entry devices. A 'shall' thought that expresses a volition is a paradigm case of a language-exit device (cf. SRLG, 329-30).

Volitions are seen on Sellars' view then as being, on the one hand, here and now intentions and, on the other hand, as causal antecedents of actions. He is not unaware, of course, of the criticism that volitions have encountered in contemporary philosophy, and he spends considerable energy responding to these objections (cf. TA, 108). Again, we must pass over the detail of his response, but we can note that he thinks that many of these objections have been based on two misunderstandings of volitions: it has been thought by many critics, first, that volitions are themselves actions and, second, that they cause agents to act. Sellars, on the contrary, argues that volitions are not actions but rather mental acts in the classical sense; thus the infinite regress these critics see in the offing is avoided. Against the second claim, he argues that volitions can *cause actions* without *causing the agent to perform the action*. Thus, on his view, the deterministic implications of this view are avoided.[14]

If we can identify expressions of intention and volitions as the main ingredients in practical reasoning, the next step is to show how they are tied together in patterns of inference—or pieces of practical reasoning. That certain intentions imply other intentions seems initially plausible. If I intend some action A' and if some other action on my part, A'', is a necessary condition of my performance of A', then it would seem plausible to say that my intention to do A' implies an intention to do A''.[15] Or, put schematically:

(1)   Shall $_{Jones}$ (Jones will do A')
(2)   (Jones will do A') implies (Jones will do A'')
(3)   Therefore, shall $_{Jones}$ (Jones will do A'')

One difficulty with this argument immediately leaps to the eye, however. Many persons, through lack of willpower or ignorance, notoriously do *not* intend what is implied by their intentions, just as many persons do not believe what is implied by their beliefs. This objection counts against Sellars' views, however, only if he construes the implication relation as holding between *acts* of intending. But he need not, and in fact does not, hold this. Just as we can distinguish between some person's act of believing and the content of his belief, we can also distinguish between some person's act of intending and the content of his intention (cf. *SM,* 182-83). *That* a person intends a certain action does not imply, of course, that he will intend the implications of that intention. But even to say this presupposes that it makes sense to talk about the implications of *what* is intended by that person. As Sellars says, "An ideally rational being would intend the implications of his intentions just as he would believe the implications of his beliefs." (*SM,* 183.) If we recognize then that Sellars is claiming that implication relations hold between contents of intentions and not between acts of intending, the objection above does not tell against his account.

Sellars argues that there are only two rules that govern implications among EIs:[16]

(R1) No EI can be derived from anything other than another EI.
(R2) All implications among EIs are warranted by the following schema:
'A' implies 'B' iff shall (A) implies shall (B)

The first rule parallels Poincare's rule that no imperative sentence can be derived from an indicative; the second rule suggests that there is no "special" logic of intentions but rather that implication relations among intentions are parasitic upon implication relations among the statements that express the content that is intended in an intention.

In order to see how these rules apply in an actual case of practical inference, we can examine Sellars' treatment of the inferential character of what Hare took to be a case of imperative inference. As noted above, Hare suggested the following argument as an instance of imperative inference:

(1) Take all the boxes to the station.
(2) This is one of the boxes.
(3) Therefore, take this to the station.

As we have seen, since Sellars rejects imperative inference altogether, he must reject this argument as an instance of imperative inference. But one cannot escape the feeling that there is something like inference going on here. Sellars suggests that we can account for that feeling by seeing how this argument can be treated not as an inference from an imperative plus an indicative to another imperative but as an inference from one EI to another making use of certain "factual" beliefs. Thus, Jones might reason as follows:[17]

(1) Shall $_{Jones}$ (Jones will take all the boxes to the station)

(2) This is one of the boxes.

(3) (Jones will take all of the boxes to the station) implies (Jones will take this box to the station)

(4) Shall $_{Jones}$ (Jones will take all of the boxes to the station) implies Shall $_{Jones}$ (Jones will take this box to the station)

(5) Shall $_{Jones}$ (Jones will take this box to the station)

In this piece of practical reasoning, Jones comes to see that his original intention to take all of the boxes to the station (which from the point of view of this piece of reasoning is underived) implies the derivative intention to take this box to the station. The steps in the argument are justified as follows: (1) is the intention that starts the whole process going; (2) is a belief of Jones; (3) follows from (2); (4) follows from (3) in accord with Sellars' second rule for deriving intentions: (5) follows from (1) and (4) by *modus ponens*.

Sellars suggests that all practical reasoning can be reconstructed on this model. One notices immediately that one strength of this model is that there are no inferences from indicatives to intentions (or from "facts" to "values"). Thus, this model will not encounter the difficulties raised by the so-called is-ought problem. Also, this structure allows practical reasoning to be really practical in that the EIs that are the conclusions of such reasoning will grow (in the fullness of time and changes of mind, physical and psychological impediments aside) into volitions and thus action. But this practical force is not bought at the expense of reducing practical thoughts and expressions to nonconceptual ejaculations or interjections. Finally, since EIs do not require an audience and are not actions, this account of practical reasoning does not encounter the difficulties that we have seen that an imperativist account succumbs to.

We next have to show how Sellars can develop from this view of practical reasoning his claim that moral judgments are essentially practical. If all instances of practical reasoning issue in EIs and if moral reasoning is practical reasoning, then moral judgments must be construed as special forms of EIs; and this is Sellars' final conclusion. Indeed, Sellars' positive views on the logic of moral judgments consist in proposing complications in the structure of simple EIs in order to suit them as models for certain basic kinds of moral judgments.

In this regard there are two features of moral judgments that Sellars has to build into EIs if they are to capture what we mean when we use moral judgments. First, he has to account for the universal character of moral judgments. If moral judgments are EIs, that is, we must show how intentions can be universal in the way that we think of moral judgments as being universal. Second, Sellars must account for the intersubjectivity that we ordinarily take to characterize moral judgments. When I claim that Jones morally ought to do A and you claim that Jones morally ought to refrain from A, we ordinarily think that one of us must be wrong. That is, we think that moral judgments can clash in a way that would make it appropriate to say that the one contradicts the other. But EIs seem to lack this element of intersubjectivity. While EIs can certainly clash, their essential egocentricity (each person can express only his own intentions) would seem to insure that contradiction can occur among them only in a metaphorical sense. Thus, since Sellars fully agrees that ordinary moral discourse exhibits intersubjectivity, he must show how this feature can be accommodated within a view that construes moral judgments as EIs.

In the next section, we will take up Sellars' treatment of universalizability, and in the section following we will turn to his views on intersubjectivity.

V

Although Sellars thinks that moral judgments are to be understood on the model of EIs, it is clear that they are not *just* EIs. To judge the action of some person morally is not just a matter of expressing one's intentions with respect to that person's actions. For one thing, as virtually all moral philosophers have noticed, moral judgments are implicitly universal. The point is often made by saying that when one assents to a particular moral judgment—e.g., "Jones morally ought to join the resistance"— one must be prepared to support it with a universal principle—e.g., "Anyone who is in a situation relevantly similar to Jones ought to join the resistance." If the person in question is not prepared to make the principle truly universal (if, for example, he wants to remove himself from its scope), one would be justified in concluding that he is not expressing a moral judgment at all. We might capture the central point here in terms of moral approval or disapproval in the following principle: If P morally (dis)approves of q's doing A in S, P morally (dis)approves of anyone's doing an action of type A in a situation relevantly similar to S.

Needless to say, this formulation of the principle of universalizability is not unproblematic. Much remains to be said about how "relevantly similar circumstances" are to be defined, and the notion of an action-type has to be given a clear sense. Also, one has to avoid suggesting that the claim that particular moral judgments presuppose universal principles implies that anyone who makes a moral judgment must have a relevant moral principle already formulated and at hand. The point rather is that one must not bring forward a patently nonuniversal "principle" in support of one's moral judgment, and one must believe that there is a universal principle applying to the action in question even if one cannot, in the moment, formulate it (cf. IIO, 163).

Sellars agrees that moral judgments are universalizable, but he has approached this topic in a different way than have most recent ethical theorists. Instead of investigating universalizability as a logical property of moral judgments, Sellars focuses his attention on the notion of action on principle. That is, he is more interested in universalizability as it might be seen as characterizing the action and practical reasoning of a moral agent than as simply a logical feature of moral judgments.[18]

Sellars' account of action on principle is designed to handle two different sorts of difficulties that arise with it: first, he attempts to make explicit the manner in which the *universal performance* of some action is intended or desired in action on principle; second, he wants to account for the role that *principles* play in the reasoning that leads to action done on principle.[19] We will look first at Sellars' account of the difficulties in these two areas and then turn to his positive account.

To act on principle is to be committed in some sense to everyone's doing an action of a certain sort. But one can be committed to the universal performance of an action for quite different reasons; Sellars suggests four such reasons (cf. IIO, 182-83). Consider someone wishing that everyone keep promises. He might wish this because (1) he thinks that the consequences of the joint action of everyone's keeping his promises would be valuable; (2) he thinks that the consequences of each person's keeping a promise would be valuable; (3) he thinks that the universal keeping of promises would be valuable for its own sake; or (4) he thinks that each instance of promise keeping is valuable for its own sake. Each of these reasons might justify one in intending (or wishing for) universal conformity with the moral rule against promise breaking. And also, of course, each of these would justify some person in thinking that *he* should conform to the moral rule prohibiting promise breaking.

The question arises, however, as to whether the actions of a person who acted in accord with any of these reasons would constitute action on principle. Sellars thinks there is good reason to doubt it in each case. When we say that a person acts on principle we imply, among other things, that he does an action for its own sake, i.e., that his motivation is of a nonconsequentialist sort. But this suggests that neither (1) nor (2) will do. Neither do we think, however, that a person who acts on principle is aiming at a merely universal accord with some principle for its own sake as one would in (3). As Sellars says, "action on principle is not silly as it would be if it were a matter of wishing that I keep this promise as a logically necessary condition of a world-long and world-wide keeping of promises." (IIO, 184.)

This leaves the fourth reason above, but it too seems not to measure up. We think that in action on principle a decision to do some particular action follows, in some sense, from a commitment to the universal performance of the action. But in the fourth reason above this mode of reasoning seems inappropriate. The fourth reason suggests rather that my commitment to the universal performance of an action follows from my commitment to the particular actions in accord with the policy.

The first problem for Sellars' account of action on principle is set then by the fact that it is difficult to specify the grounds on which the universal performance of an action is intended in action on principle. The second problem is suggested by his remark that "approving on principle is not just the same as being disposed to 'just like' each item which one comes to think of as being of a certain kind." (IIO, 188-89.) The thought behind this remark is that action on principle is more than mere consistency in acting and approving of the actions of others. Consider for example the approvings of three quite different sorts of men—Jones, Smith, and Roberts.

Jones' approvings are purely random. He finds himself approving of one thing one day because it is F and another thing the next day because it is not-F. Needless to say, Jones will have great difficulty formulating policies or principles; and those of us who live with him will be incapable of predicting what he will approve of next or explaining why he approves of what he does turn out to approve of. Jones is a man with neither settled practical principles nor a firm character.

Smith, on the other hand, has approving with much more structure than Jones'. His approvings are regular and, like the darling of the precinct worker, he is a man whose vote can be counted on. We can, given sufficient familiarity with Smith's behavior and the ordinary canons of induction, formulate general principles with which his approvings conform and that we can in turn use both to predict and explain his approvings. Smith is a man who might seem to have both settled principles and firmness of character. Sellars invites us to consider, however, that a man like Smith might be the sort of person who, though regular in his approvings and his behavior in accord with those approvings, does not, in approving, act out of regard for any principles of action at all. Smith, that is, might be the sort of man who buys red cars whenever he buys cars, paints his house red whenever he paints his house, and buys strawberry ice cream whenever he buys ice cream, but who never has the thought that red cars, red houses, or red ice cream are good *because* they are red. Smith's approvings, while regular, predictable, and explainable, need not be *reasoned*.

We finally come to Roberts whose approvings are the furthest advanced on the road to self-consciousness. His approvings are regular, predictable, and explainable and in addition are accompanied by thoughts on his part of the "If anything is F, would that it be defended" type. To say that his approvings are reasoned, then, is to say that they are accompanied by thoughts of certain sorts that partly explain his approving. While Smith's approvings can be explained on merely associationist principles, Robert's approvings require some reference to the form of reasoning from which they issue in order to explain them.

It seems clear that only Roberts of the three men considered here has the kind of approvings that we associate with action on principle. Any account of acting on principle, then, must take account of not only the peculiar sense in which the universal performance of an action is intended (or wished for) in such action but also the *reasoned* character of the decision to act on that principle. To put the same point the other way around: not just any wish for the universal performance of an action nor just any kind of consistency in acting or approving on the part of some person will justify the claim that he is acting on principle.

With some understanding of the complexities that Sellars thinks any adequate account of action on principle must confront, let us turn to his own account. Sellars' basic view is that to act on principle is to be disposed to have certain underivative intentions. If, for example, Jones performs an action type A (because he is in circumstances C) *on principle,* then he must be disposed to reason about every other person when that person is likely to be in C.

  (1) X is (or will be) in C.
  (2) Shall Jones (X will do A, if he is in C)
  (3) Therefore, Shall Jones (X will do A)

Notice that in accounting for the universal character of Jones' intention, we do not characterize the practical reasoning involved as originating in an intention with a universal content. We do not suggest, that is, that the practical reasoning that issues in action on principle must begin with intentions of the following form:

  Shall Jones (x) (if X is in C, then X will do A)

To think of such universal intentions as occupying the place of premises in the practical thinking leading up to action on principle would be to confuse, Sellars argues, the premises of such reasoning with the rules that govern the reasoning (cf. IIO, 185). Sellars' basic insight here is that the universality implicit in action on principle is *not* to be explained with reference to the universal content of the intention involved but rather with reference to the disposition to reason in a certain way in *all* cases.[20]

If Sellars is right, then we can see how the first complexity in action on principle is to be handled. It is simply not true that in action on principle we directly intend or wish for the universal performance of an action; rather we are disposed to have underivative intentions of the form

Shall (If X is in C, then X will do A)

whenever we think of someone being in C. Sellars invokes the notion of an axiom schema to further develop this point.

> A more plausible approach, which has the advantage of interpreting the universality of moral principles in terms of each case rather than the totality of cases, draws on the concept of an *axiom schema*. According to it, instead of saying that
>
> Shall (X)(X doing A, if X is a person in C)
>
> is an axiom, we should rather say that every statement derived from the schema
>
> Shall (X doing A, if X is a person in C)
>
> by replacing X with the name of a person is an axiom or first principle of moral reasoning. (IIO, 192.)

We explain the universality of moral judgments, then, by characterizing their origin in practical thinking as being of a certain sort. Particular moral judgments are EIs that issue from practical thinking that would, in relevantly similar situations, produce relevantly similar EIs.

We can also see, I think, how this characterization of action on principle accommodates the reasoned character of such action. Action that issues from an EI that is in turn derived from an axiom schema of the form Sellars proposes *cannot* be explained on merely associationist principles. This possibility is excluded, since in these EIs the condition (the if-clause) is brought within the scope of the shall-operator. We are not saying, therefore, that the person in question is disposed to have certain intentions whenever he notices the relevant features of some person's situation. Rather, the underivative intentions he has are intentions that each person do the appropriate action *because* he is in a certain situation. Put another way, for Jones to have intentions that conform to Sellars' axiom schema is for Jones to intend that each person do A because that person is in C; it is not merely for Jones to be disposed to have the intention that a person do A whenever Jones notices that the appropriate person is in C.

There are many questions that could be raised about this account of action on principle. Indeed, Sellars has admitted that his most lengthy discussion of the topic merely "scratches the surface." (TA, 138.) Given the purposes in this essay, however, I must leave the topic here. It should at least be clear, nevertheless, that Sellars can give an account of the universalizability that characterizes moral judgments when these judgments are construed as having the force of EIs. It is especially important to see that Sellars does not account for this universalizability by interpreting moral principles as having the force of EIs with universal contents. This interpretation, which might have seemed the obvious one for him to take, is certainly implausible, and its implausibility has surely deterred others from modeling moral judgments on EIs.

It is also worth remarking that Sellars' general approach to the topic of universalizability would seem to be worth the attention of others who have wrestled with this topic. His general thought that universalizability should be investigated as having its roots in the forms of practical reasoning associated with moral judgments seems sound. When universalizability is treated, as it usually is, as "merely" a logical feature of moral judgments, one is inclined to overlook the complexities of it to which Sellars' approach calls our attention.

VI

In his *Ethics*, G. E. Moore developed an argument against subjectivistic accounts of moral judgments that has continued to be very influential.[21] Moore argued that any subjectivistic account of moral judgments is bound to be inadequate because it cannot account for the sense in which the moral judgments of two different persons can be real logical contradictories. His argument took the following form:

(1)   According to subjectivist ethical theories, if one person asserts that P ought to do A and another person asserts that it is not the case that P ought to do A, they are not contradicting each other, since what the first person is asserting is different from what the second person is denying.

(2)   But it is clear that in ordinary moral discourse we suppose that a conflict of this sort does involve contradiction in that both persons cannot be right.

(3)   Therefore, all subjectivist ethical theories must be mistaken as accounts of what we mean when we use moral judgments.

Some have argued that the second premise of this argument is question-begging in that it prematurely closes the question that is the whole point of subjectivist theories to open. Indeed subjectivists have frequently argued that all Moore's argument really does is force them to provide some account within their theories of *why we feel* that moral judgments can stand in a relation of contradiction.[22]

It is an important feature of Sellars' approach to ethical theory, however, that he takes Moore's argument very seriously indeed. Sellars claims, in fact, that the most formidable objection to his attempt to model moral judgments on EIs derives from our feeling that moral judgments are *intersubjective* in a way that EIs cannot hope to be. He takes it as a criterion of success for any account of moral judgments that the account be able to accommodate the intersubjectivity of such judgments. The two features of EIs that seem to render them inappropriate on this score are (1) the absence of an external negation in EIs and (2) the conceptual impossibility of two persons having the same intention. We will explore each of these features of EIs briefly and then turn to Sellars' attempt to resolve the difficulty.

That EIs lack an external negation becomes clear if we reflect on the possible ways in which negation can enter into the structure of first person ought-judgments and then EIs.[23] With ought-judgments we can distinguish the following four forms:

(1) P ought to A.
(2) P ought not to A.
(3) It is not the case that P ought to A.
(4) It is not the case that P ought not to A.

Each of these forms is basic in the sense that none can be reduced to any of the others. When we turn to EIs, however, we find that only two forms are legitimate:

(5) Shall (P will A)
(6) Shall (P will not A)

The forms that are lacking are those that would be represented by

(7*) Not-Shall (P will A)
(8*) Not-Shall (P will not A)

Sellars has a lengthy argument to show that these forms are inadmissible, but it seems to me that the point is obvious enough (cf. IIO, 198). The only danger is that someone might suppose that certain biographical statements capture these forms. Thus, we can perfectly well say all of the following:

(9) Jones intends to do A.
(10) Jones intends not to do A.
(11) Jones does not intend to do A.
(12) Jones does not intend not to do A.

But it should be clear that (11) and (12) do not correspond to intentions that Jones has and that he could express in EIs. They report, rather, the absence of intentions on Jones' part with respect to his either doing A or not doing A. The legitimacy of (11) and (12), then, should not lead us to suppose that a well-formed EI could have an external negation.

The paucity of legitimate forms for EIs leads to difficulties because in the absence of external negation it is not clear how EIs can stand in the relation of logical contradiction in the way that Moore and Sellars think ought-judgments clearly can. Jones and Smith can straightforwardly contradict each other if Jones claims that Roberts ought to do A and Smith claims that it is not the case that Roberts ought to do A. The two ought judgments,

> (13)   Roberts ought to do A, and
> (14)   it is not the case that Roberts ought to do A,

stand in a relation such that they cannot both be true. But we seem unable to reproduce this kind of clash with respect to EIs. The intentions of Jones and Smith clearly might *diverge* as represented by the following two statements:

> (15)   Shall $_{Jones}$ (Roberts will do A)
> (16)   Shall $_{Smith}$ (Roberts will not do A)

The difficulty here, however, is that while Smith and Jones are clearly involved in some sort of conflict, they do not seem to be contradicting each other. Sellars has suggested that the most we can say here is that a disagreement in attitude is involved (cf. *SM*, 189).

This point is tied to the second difficulty with EIs—the impossibility of two persons having the same intention (cf. *SM*, 188). When we introduced the notion of an EI in IV, we noted that EIs always express the intentions of the speaker—that they are in this sense abidingly egocentric. The intentions that I express are always my intentions, although, of course, I can report your intentions, describe them, raise questions about them, and so forth. But if intentions are in this strong sense egocentric, it would seem impossible for two persons ever to have the same intention. We must be careful here because the surface grammatical form of expressions of intentions suggests that we frequently *do* have the same intention. Thus, both Smith and Jones might intend that Roberts do A; indeed it might be true to say that all the members of some group intend that some action be done or some state of affairs be brought about, e.g., all of the citizens of a city might intend that the sewer system be repaired. But, although it appears in these cases that different persons have the same intention, it turns out that this cannot be true in the same strong sense in which two people, for example, can have the same belief.

This becomes clear if one recalls the way in which EIs sustain their connection with action. Though two persons might intend that some state of affairs be brought about, it is *really* the case that each of them intends that he do what he can to bring about that state of affairs. If Jones intends that the sewer system be repaired, the cash value of this intention is that he intends that he, Jones, take certain steps to bring it about that the sewer system be repaired, and likewise for Smith.

The same ought-judgments clearly can be expressed by different persons, however, and this is a partial explanation of why ought-judgments have an external negation. If both Jones and Smith believe that Roberts morally ought to do A, they are, in a strong sense, believing the same thing; and if Jones asserts that Roberts ought to do A while Smith asserts that it is not the case that Roberts ought to do A, they are, in a straightforward sense, contradicting each other.

These difficulties are important ones for Sellars because they would seem to suggest that any attempt to treat ought-judgments as special forms of EIs is bound to founder on the lack of intersubjectivity of the latter. His response is not, however, to abandon the claim that moral judgments are EIs but rather to suggest that they are EIs of a special kind. His problem is to construct an EI that will accommodate the intersubjectivity of moral judgments while retaining the features of "simple" EIs that attracted him to them in the first place.

The special kind of EI that Sellars introduces is what we might call the We-EI.[24] He suggests that there are EIs that express the intentions of a group but are asserted (or expressed) by members of a group. If there are such intentions, then we could express Smith's and Jones' agreement about what Roberts is to do by statements of the following form:

(17)   Jones: Shall $_{we}$ (Roberts will do A)
(18)   Smith: Shall $_{we}$ (Roberts will do A)

This formulation indicates how the intentions in question are the same and we can also see how, in virtue of this sameness, real contradiction between we-intentions can arise.

It is remarkable, I think, that Sellars spends so little time defending or explaining his notion of we-intentions, since they play a crucial role in his overall account of moral judgments. He does tell us some of the things that We-EIs are not, and he also makes a number of provocative remarks about how they are related to a special form of consciousness. It is important to consider his remarks here and develop some of the insights they contain as well as some of the difficulties with them. I am going to suppose that Sellars is right in claiming that we-intentions as he introduces them would handle the intersubjectivity characteristic of moral judgments; the questions I want to raise are rather questions about what we-intentions really are.

One way of approaching this topic is to consider one simple account of what we-intentions are. This account, as we shall see, will not do justice to Sellars' notion of we-intentions, but its failure is illustrative of some important points. This account would suggest that we-intentions are really compounds of a sort that involve as components both I-intentions and certain biographical statements about other members of one's group. Consider, for example, a group made up of three men—Jones, Smith, and Roberts. When Jones we-intends that P do A, we would characterize this intention in the following way:

Shall Jones (P will do A) and Smith and Roberts also intend that P do A.

The point of this, of course, is that while Jones cannot do the intending for Smith and Roberts, he can report their intentions. Given that this is so, we might think that we-intending is just ordinary I-intending that is accompanied by the belief that everyone else in one's group intends the same thing. To avoid certain obvious objections, this characterization could be fixed up by giving the biographical statements a suitably counterfactual character. So Jones, rather than asserting that Smith and Roberts in fact agree with him, might assert that they would agree with him *if* they had at their disposal the facts that he has at his disposal, were free of emotional disturbance, and so forth. We might further modify it so that Jones does not assert that *all* the members of the group would share his intention but that most would or that the normal ones would, and so forth. In this way, this view of we-intending would take on some of the formal features of so-called ideal-observer theories in ethics.

But however we alter this basic model for we-intending, it will fail to capture what Sellars has in mind. It fails for two reasons. First, Sellars simply says that I-intending and we-intending are different *forms of intending* (cf. IIO, 203). He could not accept a view that would make we-intending simply a matter of I-intending plus something extra. The *intendings* in the two cases must be different. This is also made clear in Sellars' discussion of moral weakness, where he construes weakness of will as a matter of the conflict between I-intending and we-intending (cf. KBDW, 17-19). But if we-intending fits the model we have suggested above, there simply could not be conflict between the I-intending of some person and his we-intending. This conflict would be impossible because we-intending would just be I-intending plus certain beliefs.

But a second reason why this view will not do is that Sellars claims that we-intending involves a radical move away from ordinary I-intending. In some places he says that we-intending involves a special "form of consciousness"; in others, that it involves a special "form of life." He also suggests that we-intending results from "internalizing the concept of a group." (Cf. IIO, 203-5.) These ways of characterizing we-intending should make it clear, if it were not already, that Sellars sees a radical difference between I-intending and we-intending.

But how are we to construe this talk about a new form of consciousness? One way of approaching the topic, is to reflect on what is involved in coming to see oneself as a member of a group. We might consider first an amateur theatrical group that is trying to put on its spring production. We can readily understand how the members of this group might come to have the *same* intentions with respect to the success of their production. But to put the point this way is to suggest that group participation is a matter of the coincidence of a number of I-intentions, and again this does not seem sufficient to capture what Sellars is after.

Consider instead a local seamstress who is approached by members of the group and requested to make certain costumes that they need for their production. And further suppose that in the beginning of her association with this group, the seamstress is not aware that she is making costumes for a dramatic production. She approaches her work as just one more job, and she is guided in it by the norms of money-making, craftsmanship, or whatever, which usually guide her. Now let us imagine that the seamstress becomes aware of the role that her work is playing in the larger goals of the dramatic group and even that she becomes, as we might say, *interested* in the success of the production. Her enthusiasm might be such that she is inducted into the group as a member and continues to do the same work without compensation. It seems obvious that if events transpired in this way, we could plausibly say that the seamstress comes to see her relationship to the members of the dramatic group in a new way. Indeed they would cease being "them" and become "us." More important, the seamstress could come to see the standards applicable to her particular work in a new way. Where before she was just "doing a job" where her work was subject to her self-criticism in the same way that any other "job" would be, she now sees her work as playing a role in the larger enterprise of the dramatic group. In particular, the success of the particular costumes she is making cannot be determined apart from some role they may play in the overall success of the production.

Is this change that the seamstress undergoes what Sellars is getting at when he talks about a new form of consciousness? I am inclined to think so. In coming to see her particular project—in this case, the making of costumes—as being constrained in certain ways by the overall aims of the group, I think she is at least coming close to having what Sellars calls we-intentions.

Though this example may help us to capture the flavor of Sellars'
we-intentions, some difficulties remain. One of these is the problem of
construing the relation between I-intentions and we-intentions. In terms
of our example, we might wonder how the we-intentions that the
seamstress acquires in becoming one of "us" are related to her
I-intentions. Sellars says that "there is a particularly close logical connection" between the two, but he denies that the relation is one of
entailment. In particular, he claims that "we intend that x do A" need
not entail that "each of us intends that x do A." (IIO, 203.) And it is for
this reason that he wants to say that we-intending is not merely the
logical sum of the I-intendings of those who make up the group. Sellars
also claims (being true to his nominalistic predilections) that we-
intendings are not the intendings of any sort of group mind. But what, we
are inclined to ask, are the existence conditions of a we-intention?
Under what conditions is it true of the members of a group that they
we-intend some action or state of affairs? The answer we are tempted to
give here is that a group we-intends some object just in case the group
has a shared intention for this object. But this answer will not do as
Sellars makes clear in the following passage:

> The group has shared intentions by virtue of the fact that its members intend in
> the mode "shall$_W$". But that the members intend in this mode does not
> guarantee that in point of fact there are shared intentions. Intending in the
> mode "shall$_W$" is a "form of life", a conceptual framework within which
> moral discourse exists and without which it is impossible. Yet the actual
> existence of shared universal intentions is no more an antecedent condition of
> participation in moral discourse than actual agreement on matters of fact is an
> antecedent condition of participating in factual discourse. In each case the
> forms of discourse set this agreement as a task. To abandon the idea that
> disagreement on moral matters is even in principle capable of resolution is not
> to retreat to a moral solipsism; it is to abandon the moral framework itself, and
> to retreat to the language or "form of life" of purely personal intention. (IIO,
> 205.)

In this passage Sellars is concerned to distinguish the following three
items: (1) the presence of shared intentions within a group, (2) the
presence of intending in the mode "shall$_W$" within a group, and (3) the
presence of moral discourse within a group. With respect to these items,
he further suggests that (2) and (3) always go together—indeed that they
are two aspects of one and the same phenomenon. To engage in moral
discourse *is* to intend in the mode "shall$_W$." But (1) is not a necessary
condition of either (2) or (3). Although Sellars says that "the group has
shared intentions *by virtue of the fact* that its members intend in the
mode shall$_W$," he goes on to add that "that the members intend in this
mode does not guarantee that in point of fact there are shared inten-

tions." The achievement of shared intentions by a group is rather a "task" that is set by intending in the mode shall$_w$; it is not an "antecedent condition" of such intentions.

The upshot of this passage then is that we cannot look to the presence of shared intentions as the existence conditions of we-intending. Indeed, we-intending seems just to consist in the presence of certain forms of discourse, in particular the presence of moral discourse. But this account of we-intending seems to cause difficulties for Sellars in that he introduced we-intentions to explain the intersubjectivity that is characteristic of moral judgments; but when we press for an account of we-intending, the response is that we-intending is what goes on when we engage in moral discourse or reflection. This same circle is involved when, in the passage above, Sellars characterizes we-intending as a form of life or a conceptual framework "within which moral discourse exists and without which it is impossible." If we ask what the form of life or conceptual framework here referred to *is*, the only possible answer would seem to be one which would characterize it in terms of moral thought and talk.

The point I am making, of course, is that if the notion of we-intending is to be of use in elucidating the logical force of moral judgments, this mode of intending has to be characterizable independently of any reference to our linguistic behavior in using moral judgments. If I understand him, however, Sellars has not shown how such an independent characterization is possible.

One more related question needs to be raised. You will recall that Sellars invoked intentions as the fundamental conceptual items on which moral judgments are to be modeled primarily in order to be able to account for the *practical force* of moral judgments. It is because EIs are logically tied to action, through the mediation of volitions, that they are suited to this role. But though I-intentions have been constructed in order to have this practical force, it is not at all clear that we-intentions will have this force or at least that they will have it in the same way. I-intentions, as we have seen, in the fullness of time become volitions, and volitions issue in action. But what about we-intentions? Do we-intentions stand in the same relation to volitions as do I-intentions? I know of no place in Sellars' writings where he explicitly takes up this question, but it is clearly crucial to his overall theory. Whatever may be the practical force which accompanies I-intentions, it is irrelevant to the practical force that moral judgments bear; moral judgments are, after all, not I-intentions but rather we-intentions. These questions would not arise were Sellars to characterize we-intentions in such a way that they entail I-intentions; but as we have seen above, he rejects this view. Indeed, as I have pointed out, it is at the heart of his treatment of the problem of moral weakness, that I-intentions and we-intentions must be able to conflict.

One wishes that Sellars had introduced the notion of we-intentions more precisely by locating it within his general account of practical reasoning. In doing this he could have said more about (1) how they arise, (2) how they are related to I-intentions, and (3) how they are related to volitions. Until these matters are settled, it will be difficult to make any final assessment of Sellars' account of the intersubjectivity of moral judgments; indeed, it will be difficult even to know how to understand this account.

VII

In our discussion of Sellars' account of moral judgments so far we have seen how he has attempted to flesh out Prichard's insights by showing that moral discourse is action-guiding, intersubjective, and unique. By construing moral judgments as intersubjective EIs, he thinks he has fulfilled the first two goals. And the uniqueness of moral discourse is a function of the uniqueness of the we-intentions on which Sellars models them. There is one rather large and troublesome question, however, left over for his account. This last difficulty is set by his agreement with Kant that moral judgments are implicitly "reasonable" in a way strongly analogous to the reasonableness of true beliefs.

Sellars raises this question in a number of different ways in different places. Thus, he talks in one place about whether normative ethics is a rational discipline, by which he means "a field of inquiry in which good reasons can be offered for answers to questions belonging to that field." (SE, 194.) The context of this discussion makes it clear that by "good reasons" he means reasons as good as those that are given in the sciences and mathematics. In another place, Sellars asks how we are to understand the difference between a merely inherited set of categories for evaluating actions and a fully reasoned and reflective morality. The suggestion here is that any account of morality that could not accommodate its reasoned character would be inadequate (cf. IIO, 205-6).

The question Sellars here raises is the classical question of the justification of moral judgments. One might suppose that he has already answered this question by tying moral discourse to intersubjective we-intentions; but this would be a mistake. If Sellars is successful in his identification of moral judgments with we-intentions, he will certainly have accounted for the intersubjectivity of moral discourse; but if his account were to end here, he would make the truth (or assertibility) of moral judgments relative to the we-intentions of a group. In raising the question of the reasonableness of moral judgments, however, he wants to raise questions of the adequacy of particular we-intentions. In the discussion below, it will simplify things if we set out Sellars' views on justification in ethics without for the most part bringing in his interpretation of moral judgments as intersubjective EIs. It should be clear from what has gone before how this discussion could be translated into the we-intention mode.

Sellars' general approach to the justification of moral judgments is an attempt to reconcile his basically Kantian or deontological view of moral motivation with a utilitarian or teleological view of moral justification. He maintains, that is, that particular moral judgments are ultimately justified by showing how they are involved in the pursuit of some overarching end or goal. He realizes of course that he must square this strategy with his insistence that moral action is action on principle where the action performed is performed for its own sake. While many moral philosophers have regarded such a compromise as impossible to achieve, Sellars proposes to bring these two features of moral judgments together by distinguishing two different levels at which intentions can operate in action.[25]

Suppose, for example, that someone has a basic intention to bring about some state of affairs S (e.g., a satisfying life for himself or a maximization of the general welfare). And further suppose that he discovers that a necessary condition of realizing S is that everyone act in certain specifiable ways in certain specifiable situations. He may discover, further, that the best way to insure that everyone acts in these ways is for everyone to acquire dispositions to act in these ways in these circumstances without regard to the consequences of particular actions. Thus, it would be reasonable for him to set about promoting the development of such dispositions in himself and others. What we would have in such a case, Sellars claims, is an entry of intentions into action at two different levels. At the first level is the intention to bring about S; but this intention can, in the way we have seen, "lead to" intentions of the "Shall (X will do A, if X is in C)" sort, which we have seen in section V are characteristic of action on principle (cf. IIO, 207).

This general framework for justification would seem to allow Sellars to reconcile the Kantian strain in his thought with a teleological justificatory base. Particular moral actions would be actions on principle in that they would spring from dispositions to act in certain ways in certain situations; the practical reasoning associated with such actions would be of the sort we explored in section V. But the decision to acquire and nurture in oneself and others these dispositions to act, and hence the actions themselves, would be ultimately justified with reference to one's goal in acquiring such dispositions. The motivational structure of moral action will then be true to Kant's strictures, while the ultimate justification for such action will have a teleological form.

In order to fill in this framework, Sellars must identify some goal or end that will support the superstructure of moral judgment and moral action as we know it. Such a goal will have to satisfy two conditions. First, it must be such that moral judgments with roughly the same content as those which most persons accept can be derived from it; it must, that is, give rise to particular judgments that are recognizably *moral*. But, secondly, and more importantly, it must be a goal that is intrinsically reasonable to pursue. Since the point of the enterprise of justification is to show that moral judgments are reasonable, it will not do simply to show that they are derivable in the manner suggested from *some* goal. This would show at most that they have a certain relative reasonableness; but Sellars is determined to show that moral judgments are reasonable in the stronger sense of Kant's categorical imperative. And in order to do this he must show that they are derivable from some goal that is intrinsically reasonable to pursue.

Before coming to Sellars' own account of the ultimate end of morality, it will be instructive to consider two alternative views that, though they ultimately prove defective, point the way to Sellars' view. The first account of the ultimate object of morality is one associated with what Sellars calls the "art of living" conception of morality (cf. *SM*, 200-204). Sellars connects this view to a central strand of ethical thought in classical Greek philosophy. On this view, moral judgments tell us what we must do if we are to achieve a satisfying life for ourselves; actions are morally required in the sense that they are required for a satisfying life. Hence the moral ought-judgment

(1)   Jones morally ought to A

is taken as (roughly) equivalent to

(2)   If Jones wants to lead a satisfying life, then he ought to A.

There are obvious objections, however, to this view. In the first place, it seems clear that the actions that such a view would enjoin would not be the same actions that would be required by morality. Although, as Sellars points out, Plato labored mightily to defend the coincidence of the demands of the art of living and of morality, almost everyone would agree that he failed. But even if he had succeeded in showing that the art of living was materially equivalent to morality, he would not have overcome our feeling that there is a conceptual distinction here (cf. *SM*, 204). The binding force we attribute to moral judgments seems different in kind from the binding force attributable to action guides derived from such an art of living. If nothing else, the tension we frequently feel between the demands of morality and the demands of prudence would support our feeling that we have two distinct things here.

One might suppose that the difficulties that the art-of-living conception of morality encounter could be avoided if we substitute for this Platonic notion the more all-encompassing model of benevolence. Thus, a moral judgment would tell me not what is required for me to lead a satisfying life but rather what is required for me to promote the general welfare. The moral ought-judgment

> (3)   Jones morally ought to A

is, on this view, taken as roughly equivalent to

> (4)   If Jones wants to promote the general welfare, he ought to do A.

This view certainly appears more plausible as an account of the moral 'ought' than does the art-of-living conception. In particular, the actions that would be enjoined by a commitment to benevolence seem to be materially equivalent to those required by morality. But again there are difficulties. For one thing, Sellars thinks that we should balk at a conception of morality that rests the binding force of moral judgments on what people *want* (cf. IIO, 206). Like Kant, he wants to keep separate the realms of the moral and the "merely pathological." A more serious objection, moreover, is that this view allows a certain amount of slippage between one's commitment to the general welfare and one's decision to perform particular actions that will promote the general welfare. To make this clear, we must look a bit more closely at the point of view of benevolence.

One who takes the point of view of benevolence constructs principles of action by determining which principles, if observed by everyone, would promote the general welfare. He would recognize certain empirical generalizations of the form

> (1)   If the general welfare is to be promoted, everyone must do actions of type A in situations of type S.

He would then strive to develop dispositions in himself and in others to act in accord with this principle. The difficulty here is that it would be silly to strive to promote absolute unanimity in the commitment of persons to these principles. We know that it is impossible, and probably unnecessary, to bring everybody's actions in line with such principles. What is important is that *most* people act in accord with these principles. But if we need not strive for universal conformity, does not each person have reason to slip through the net of morality in virtue of the fact that only *most* people need to conform to the relevant principles?[26]

This query is as old (at least) as Glaucon and Adeimantus, and Sellars thinks it is unanswerable. If benevolence is taken as the moral point of view, then no particular agent has a compelling reason for bringing his actions in line with moral principles. As Sellars says, "The bridge between benevolence and the life of principle requires a sense of 'benevolence' which logically precludes the above compromise." (IIO, 209-10.)

But if benevolence fails as a model for the moral point of view, Sellars thinks nevertheless that the general welfare is the end in terms of which moral judgments are ultimately justified. In order to make good the claim of the general welfare to play this role, however, we must first see how the two difficulties with the point of view of benevolence can be avoided. These two difficulties were: (1) benevolence is based on merely wanting the general welfare to be promoted, while the ultimate end of morality must be something that is *intrinsically reasonable* to pursue; and (2) one could avoid the requirement to act in accord with principles of action derived from this end, since all that is really required is that *most* people observe these principles.

Sellars thinks that these difficulties can be avoided if we bring in, one more time, the notion of we-consciousness.

> The sense of "benevolence" that is required is not the impartial love of everybody, which is, as Kant saw, the espousal of a principle of conduct (roughly that one ought to help other people realize their ends), but the simple recognition of people generally as we. (IIO, 210.)

Here again, as in his account of we-intentions, Sellars spends remarkably little time elucidating a notion that he introduces to play a crucial role in his overall argument. He does suggest, however, how this notion of we-consciousness will overcome the difficulties in treating the general welfare as the ultimate end of morality.

Sellars' explanation of how the commitment to promote the general welfare can be intrinsically reasonable is summed up in the following passage:

> It is a conceptual fact that people constitute a community, a *we*, by virtue of thinking of each other as *one of us*, and by willing the common good *not* under the species of benevolence—but by willing it as one of us, or from a moral point of view. (*SM*, 222.)

His thought here would seem to be that in the version of benevolence we have explained above the interests of others are something we can take an interest in only by *wanting* to promote these interests. And whether or not one has the appropriate want will depend on the contingent features of one's affective life. But when one comes to see others as "one of us," there is no longer a gap to be bridged by a want. Indeed, one's commitment to promote the interests of one's fellows would seem to be a necessary feature of seeing them as one's fellows. Insofar as one sees other persons as "one of us," therefore, one necessarily aims at promoting their welfare. And to say this, Sellars seems to think, is just to say that the intention to promote the general welfare is intrinsically reasonable.

Sellars responds to the second objection in this passage:

> If we replace "*most people* but not I" by "*we* but not I" in the formulation of the objection, we move from consistency to incoherence. There is no *logical* place for a compromise between benevolence and self-love, where "benevolence" is understood as the consciousness of oneself and one's fellow men as we. (IIO, 210.)

The objection alleged that any person could escape the requirements of the relevant principle of action, since at most it would be required that *most* people act in accord with these principles in order to promote the general welfare. Sellars suggests in this passage that when one sees the general welfare as the welfare of *us*, the logical gap that allowed one to promote conformity with moral principles on the part of most people while making an exception of myself would be closed. One would no longer have the logical space for discriminating between *our* welfare and *my* welfare, since one's conception of one's own welfare would be inextricably bound up with one's conception of the welfare of the group.

Sellars' invocation of the notion of we-consciousness in order to respond to these objections to making the general welfare the ultimate end of morality requires more examination than I can give it here. My own feeling is that his account is essentially incomplete in that he has not shown with sufficient clarity how his conception of we-consciousness is to be distinguished from "ordinary" benevolence. Nor does his identification of we-consciousness with "what Royce called Loyalty" and with "what Christians call love of Neighbor (caritas)" help much (cf. IIO, 212). In his treatment of the justification of moral judgments, as in his account of their intersubjectivity, Sellars shows a profound grasp of the difficulties to be met; in both cases, however, his final solutions call for further clarification on his part.

While I have pointed out a certain incompleteness in Sellars' account of the intersubjectivity and the reasonableness of moral judgments, I have done nothing to show that Sellars is not on the "right track" in both of these areas. One has the impression indeed that Sellars invokes the notions of we-intending and we-consciousness in order merely to gesture in the direction where he thinks the ultimate solutions are to be found. In pointing to the essential "groupiness" of moral discourse, he is, of course, picking up on a classical theme in moral philosophy, a theme that has been carried forward recently in an intriguing fashion by

Thomas Nagel.[27] One can only hope that Sellars will further develop these notions in his future work.

NOTES

[1] In order to work within this model, of course, one must believe that one has some grasp of the distinction between the "merely factual" and the moral. I, at least, do not have any such grasp, and it is a measure of the distance we have moved away from the problematic of CM in recent years that many other moral philosophers would share my skepticism.

[2] It would be difficult, however, to point to any "naturalist" who actually held this position. One of the recurrent themes of CM has been the search for and positive identification of living, breathing naturalists. Virtually every classical moral philosophers was at one time or another accused of being a naturalist, but the evidence was always inconclusive. Among recent philosophers, Ralph Barton Perry was the favorite candidate throughout the 1930s and 1940s, while Phillipa Foot has assumed this role in the 1950s and 1960s. Again there seems to me good reason for rejecting both of these characterizations, especially in the case of Mrs. Foot. In any event, whether there were ever any moral philosophers who espoused naturalism as defined within CM is irrelevant, since naturalism as so defined did play a significant role within CM in the minds of those who opposed it. Whether one thinks that what was being opposed was an "ideal type" or a straw man will depend on ones more general attitude toward the presuppositions of CM.

[3] The clearest (and crudest) example of this argument is found in Charles Stevenson, "The Emotive Meaning of Ethical Terms" *Mind* (1937), where he argues that a naturalistic account of the meaning of ethical terms cannot do justice to their "magnetism."

[4] See Prichard's "Does Moral Philosophy Rest on a Mistake?" and "Moral Obligations," both found in *Moral Obligation* (Oxford: Oxford University Press, 1949).

[5] See Sellars' characterization of Ross' view in IIO, 160.

[6] Sellars raises objections to emotivism in a number of places, but his most sustained attack is found in SE, 405-8.

[7] R. M. Hare, *The Language of Morals* (Oxford: Oxford University Press, 1952), p. 13.

[8] Ibid., p. 20.

[9] Ibid., p. 27.

[10] Sellars develops these arguments in IIO, 169-73.

[11] Although Sellars claims in IIO, 170, that 'tellings-to' require an audience, he does hold that I can tell myself to do something. He says in TA, 107, "While we *can* address imperatives to ourselves in inner speech—tell oneself to do something—the thought expressed by:

I shall drive this nail

should not be construed as though it would be more perspicuously expressed by:

Myself, drive this nail.''

In *SM*, 187, he says, "We can, and do on occasion, tell ourselves to do something, but deciding what to do is no more telling ourselves what to do than deciding what is the case is telling ourselves what is the case.''

[12] Sellars' clearest and most concise discussion of practical reason is found in TA. Important discussions are also found, however, in IIO and *SM*, chap. 6.

[13] As Sellars points out, to set out the details of these rules would be extremely complicated. We would have to include rules that allow us to locate ourselves temporally and spatially in a world in which temporal location at least never remains the same from moment to moment.

[14] For further discussion of these issues see Gary Gutting's paper in this volume on Sellar's treatment of the free-will problem.

[15] As we noted above, Sellars' account of practical reason depends heavily on his views about material rules of inference. A discussion of the central role these rules play in Sellars' account of scientific reasoning can be found in G. Gutting's paper on Sellar's philosophy of science in this volume. For our purposes, we need only note that when Sellars talks about one intention implying another he includes cases in which the action intended in the first intention is a causally necessary condition of the action intended in the second. See SRLG, 330ff.; "Particulars", 292ff.; *SM*, 180-81.

[16] Since (R1) would appear to be derivable from (R2), one might prefer to speak here of only one rule, and in some places (see *SM*, 179) Sellars seems to accept this view. In TA, 110-11, Sellars speaks of their being two rules, however, and we will follow his view as expressed there. It should be clear that nothing of importance hangs on the principle of counting we use here.

[17] For Sellars' more elaborate account of the correct construal of this argument, see IIO, 173ff.

[18] Hare's view, as I understand it, treats universalizability as simply a logical feature of moral judgments.

[19] Sellars' most extensive account of action-on-principle is found in IIO, 180ff.

[20] A more obvious objection to allowing universal intentions to play the role of premises in moral reasoning is that, as Sellars says, "it would be silly to espouse such resolutives knowing full well that in a great many cases people who are in C simply have not done, nor will they do A." IIO, 192.

[21] G. E. Moore, *Ethics* (New York: Oxford University Press, 1965), p. 33ff.

[22] For example, Charles Stevenson in "Moore's Argument Against Certain Forms of Ethical Naturalism," *Facts and Values* (New Haven: Yale University Press, 1963), pp. 117-37.

[23] Sellars' most extensive discussion of the absence of external negation in EIs is found in IIO, 196ff. Also, see *SM*, 185ff.

[24] For Sellars' discussion of we-intentions, see IIO, 200-205; *SM*, 215-18; SE, 41-11; PSIM, 38-40.

[25] One finds what might initially seem different accounts of moral justification in SE, IIO, and *SM*. In SE, Sellars emphasizes the distinction between vindication and validation, which also plays a large role in his treatment of the problem of induction (see G. Gutting's paper on Sellar's philosophy of science in this volume). In *SM*, the account of moral justification grows out of a lengthy and subtle analysis of the distinction between hypothetical and categorical imperatives. I have chosen here to follow the account in IIO. Though not as complete, nor as subtle, as the later *SM* account, it seems to me to contain the essentials of his view set out in the most straightforward manner. In doing this, I neglect

entirely Sellars' insightful discussion of hypothetical imperatives. My excuse for this neglect is twofold: (1) I think that Sellars' account of the hypothetical imperative, though interesting and important, is not as central to his general conception of moral justification as its prominence in *SM* would seem to suggest; and (2) my discussion of this topic would have made this essay, already too long, intolerably longer. Anyone interested in pursuing Sellars' views on this matter, however, will find it necessary to supplement my account here with careful attention to chap. 6 of *SM*.

[26]For Sellars' discussion of this difficulty, see IIO, 207-9.

[27]Thomas Nagel, *The Possibility of Altruism* (Oxford: Clarendon Press, 1970).

General Bibliography for Wilfrid Sellars (through 1975)

I. Books and Published Articles by Wilfrid Sellars

"Abstract Entities." *The Review of Metaphysics* 16 (1962-1963):627-671. Reprinted in *PP*.

"Acquaintance and Description Again." *The Journal of Philosophy* 46 (1949):496-505.

"Actions and Events." *Nous* 7 (1973):179-202. Reprinted in *EPH*.

"The Adverbial Theory of the Objects of Sensation." *Metaphilosophy* 6 (1975):144-160.

"Are There Non-deductive Logics?" In *Essays in Honor of C. G. Hempel,* edited by Nicholas Rescher et al., pp. 83-103. Dordrecht, Holland: D. Reidel, 1969. Reprinted in *EPH*.

"Aristotelian Philosophies of Mind." In *Philosophy for the Future,* edited by Roy Wood Sellars, V. J. McGill, and Marvin Farber, pp. 544-70. New York: The Macmillan Company, 1949.

"Aristotle's Metaphysics: An Interpretation." *PP*.

"Autobiographical Reflections." In *Action, Knowledge, and Reality: Studies in Honor of Wilfrid Sellars,* edited by Hector-Neri Castañeda, pp. 277-93. Indianapolis: The Bobbs-Merrill Company, Inc., 1975.

"Being and Being Known." *Proceedings of the American Catholic Philosophical Association* 35 (1960):28-49. Reprinted in *SPR*.

"Classes as Abstract Entities and the Russell Paradox." *The Review of Metaphysics* 17 (1963-1964):67-90. Reprinted in *PP* and in *EPH*.

"Comments on 'Matter as a Principle' by Ernan McMullin." In *The Concept of Matter in Greek and Medieval Philosophy,* edited by Ernan McMullin, pp. 213-17. Notre Dame: University of Notre Dame Press, 1963.

"Comments on Mr. Hempel's Theses." *The Review of Metaphysics* 5 (1951-1952):623-25.

"The Concept of Emergence" (with Paul Meehl), In *Minnesota Studies in the Philosophy of Science,* edited by Herbert Feigl and Michael Scriven, vol. 1, pp. 239-52. Minneapolis: University of Minnesota Press, 1956.

"Concepts as Involving Laws and Inconceivable without Them." *Philosophy of Science* 15 (1948):289-315.

"Conceptual Change." In *Conceptual Change,* edited by P. Maynard and G. Pearce, pp. 77-93. Dordrecht, Holland: D. Reidel, 1973. Reprinted in *EPH*.

"Counterfactuals, Dispositions, and the Causal Modalities." In *Minnesota Studies in the Philosophy of Science,* edited by Herbert Feigl, Michael Scriven, and Grover Maxwell, vol. 2, pp. 225-308. Minneapolis: University of Minneapolis Press, 1958.

"The Double-knowledge Approach to the Mind-body Problem." *The New Scholasticism* 45 (1971):269-89.

"Empiricism and Abstract Entities." In *The Philosophy of Rudolph Carnap,* edited by Paul Arthur Schilpp, pp. 431-68. La Salle, Illinois: Open Court, 1963. Reprinted in *EPH*.

"Empiricism and the Philosophy of Mind." *Minnesota Studies in the Philosophy of Science* edited by Herbert Feigl and Michael Scriven, vol. 1, pp. 253-329. Minneapolis: University of Minnesota Press, 1956. Reprinted in *SPR*.

"Epistemology and the New Way of Words." *The Journal of Philosophy* 44 (1947):645-60.

Essays in Philosophy and its History. Dordrecht, Holland: D. Reidel, 1975.

Form and Content in Ethical Theory. Lawrence, Kansas: University of Kansas, 1967. Reprinted as a substantial part of chapter 7 of *SM*.

"Fatalism and Determinism." In *Freedom and Determinism,* edited by Keith Lehrer, pp. 142-74. New York: Random House, 1966.

"Gestalt Qualities and the Paradox of Analysis." *Philosophical Studies* 1 (1950):92-94.

"Giveness and Explanatory Coherence." *The Journal of Philosophy* 70 (1973):612-24.

"Grammar and Existence: A Preface to Ontology." *Mind* 69 (1960):499-533. Reprinted in *SPR*.

"The Identity Approach to the Mind-body Problem." *The Review of Metaphysics* 18 (1964-1965):430-51. Reprinted in *PP*.

"The Identity of Linguistic Expressions and the Paradox of Analysis." *Philosophical Studies* 1 (1950):24-31.

"Imperatives, Intentions, and the Logic of 'Ought'." *Methodos,* 8 (1956):228-68.

"Inference and Meaning." *Mind* 62 (1953):313-38.

"Intentionality and the Mental" (a symposium by correspondence with Roderick Chisholm). *Minnesota Studies in the Philosophy of Science,* edited by Herbert Feigl, Michael Scriven, and Grover Maxwell, vol. 2, pp. 507-39. Minneapolis: University of Minnesota Press, 1958.

"The Intentional Realism of Evert Hall." *The Southern Journal of Philosophy* 4 (1966):103-15. Reprinted in *PP*.

"Is There a Synthetic *A Priori*?" *Philosophy of Science* 20 (1953):121-38. Reprinted in a revised form in *SPR*.

"Kant's Views on Sensibility and Understanding." *The Monist* 51 (1967):463-91. Reprinted as chapter 1 of *SM*.

"Language as Thought and as Communication." *Philosophy and Phenomenological Research* 29 (1968-1969):506-27. Reprinted in *EPH*.

"The Language of Theories." In *Current Issues in the Philosophy of Science*, edited by Herbert Feigl and Grover Maxwell, pp. 57-77. New York: Holt, Rinehart, and Winston, 1961. Reprinted in *SPR*.

"Languages, Rules, and Behavior." In *John Dewey: Philosopher of Science and Freedom*, edited by Sidney Hook, pp. 289-315. New York: The Dial Press, 1949.

"Logical Subjects and Physical Objects." *Philosophy and Phenomenological Research* 17 (1956-1957): 458-72.

"The Logic of Complex Particulars." *Mind* 58 (1949):306-38.

"Maxwell on Meaning Postulates." In *Current Issues in the Philosophy of Science*, edited by Grover Maxwell and Herbert Feigl, pp. 183-92. New York: Holt, Rinehart, and Winston, 1961.

"Meaning as Functional Classification." *Synthese* 27 (1974):417-37.

"Meditations Leibniziennes." *American Philosophical Quarterly* 2 (1965):105-18. Reprinted in *PP*.

"Metaphysics and the Concept of a Person." In *The Logical Way of Doing Things*, edited by Karel Lambert, pp. 219-52. New Haven: Yale University Press, 1969. Reprinted in *EPH*.

"Mind, Meaning, and Behavior." *Philosophical Studies* 3 (1952):83-95.

"Naming and Saying." *Philosophy of Science*, 29 (1962):7-26. Reprinted in *SPR*.

"A Note on Popper's Argument for Dualism." *Analysis* 15 (1954-1955):23-24.

"Notes on Intentionality." *The Journal of Philosophy* 61 (1964):655-65. Reprinted in *PP*.

"Obligation and Motivation." *Philosophical Studies* 2 (1951):21-25.

"Obligation and Motivation"(a revised and expanded version of the above). In *Readings in Ethical Theory*, edited by Wilfrid Sellars and John Hospers, pp. 511-17. New York: Appleton-Century-Crofts, 1952.

"On Knowing the Better and Doing the Worse." *International Philosophical Quarterly* 10 (1970):5-19. Reprinted in *EPH*.

"On the Introduction of Abstract Entities." *EPH*.

"Ontology and the Philosophy of Mind in Russell." In *Bertrand Russell's Philosophy*, edited by George Nakhnikian, pp. 57-100. New York: Barnes and Noble, Inc., 1964.

"The Paradox of Analysis: A Neo-Fregean Approach." *Analysis* 24 (1963-1964):84-98. Reprinted in *PP*.

"Particulars." *Philosophy and Phenomenological Research* 13 (1952-1953):184-99. Reprinted in *SPR*.

"Phenomenalism." In *Intentionality, Minds, and Perception*, edited by Hector-Neri Castañeda, pp. 215-274. Detroit: Wayne State University Press, 1967. Originally printed in *SPR*.

Philosophical Perspectives. Springfield, Illinois: Charles Thomas, Publishers, 1967.

"Philosophy and the Scientific Image of Man." In *Frontiers of Science and Philosophy*, edited by Robert Colodny, pp. 35-78. Pittsburgh: University of Pittsburgh Press, 1962. Reprinted in *SPR*.

"Physical Realism." *Philosophy and Phenomenological Research* 15 (1954-1955):13-32. Reprinted in *PP*.

"Presupposing." *The Philosophical Review*, 63 (1954):197-215.

"Pure Pragmatics and Epistemology." *Philosophy of Science* 12 (1947):181-202.

"Putnam on Synonymity and Belief." *Analysis* 15 (1954-1955):117-20.

"Quotation Marks, Sentences, and Propositions." *Philosophy and Phenomenological Research* 10 (1949-1950):515-25.

"Raw Materials, Subjects, and Substrata" (with Discussion). In *The Concept of Matter in Greek and Medieval Philosophy*, edited by Ernan McMullin, pp. 259-72, 276-80—see remarks by Sellars on pp. 55-57, 100-101, and 245-47. Notre Dame: University of Notre Dame Press, 1963. Article reprinted in *PP*.

"Realism and the New Way of Words." *Philosophy and Phenomenological Research* 8 (1947-1948):601-34. Reprinted in *Readings in Philosophical Analysis*, edited by Herbert Feigl and Wilfrid Sellars, pp. 424-56. New York: Appleton-Century-Crofts, 1949.

"Reason and the Art of Living in Plato." In *Phenomenology and Natural Existence: Essays in Honor of Marvin Farber*, edited by Dale Riepe, pp. 353-77. Albany: State University of New York Press, 1973. Reprinted in *EPH*.

"Reflections on Contrary to Duty Imperatives." *Nous* 1 (1967):303-44.

"Reply to Aune." In *Intentionality, Minds, and Perception*, edited by Hector-Neri Castañeda, pp. 286-300. Detroit: Wayne State University Press, 1967.

"Reply to Dennet and Putnam on 'Meaning as Functional Classification' " (together with a discussion of the same article by Sellars, Putnam, Quine, and Kripke). *Synthese* 27 (1974):457-70.

"Reply to Alan Donagan." *Philosophical Studies* 27 (1975):149-84.

"Reply to Marras." *Canadian Journal of Philosophy* 2 (1972-1973):485-93. Reprinted in *EPH*.

"Reply to Quine." *Synthese* 26 (1973):122-44. Reprinted in *EPH*.

Review of *Elements of Analytic Philosophy* by Arthur Pap *Philosophy and Phenomenological Research* 11 (1950-1951):104-9.

Review of *Methods of Inquiry: An Introduction to Philosophy and Scientific Method*, by C. West Churchman and Russell L. Ackoff *Philosophy and Phenomenological Research* 12 (1951-1952):149-50.

Review of *Language and Myth*, by Ernst Cassirer, *Philosophy and Phenomenological Research*, 9 (1948-1949):326-29.

"The Rosenthal-Sellars Correspondence on Intentionality" (with David Rosenthal). In *Intentionality, Mind, and Language*, edited by Ausonio Marras, pp. 461-503. Chicago: University of Illinois Press, 1972.

"Science and Ethics." *PP*.

Science and Metaphysics: Variations on Kantian Themes. London: Routledge and Kegan Paul, Ltd., 1967.

Science, Perception, and Reality. London: Routledge and Kegan Paul, Ltd., 1963.

"Scientific Realism or Irenic Instrumentalism: A Critique of Nagel and Feyerabend on Theoretical Explanation." In *Boston Studies in the Philosophy of Science*, edited by Robert Cohen and Marx Wartofsky, vol. 2, pp. 171-204. New York: The Humanities Press, 1965. Reprinted in *PP*.

"Seeing, Seeming, and Sensing." In *The Ontological Turn: Studies in the Philosophy of Gustav Bergmann*, edited by M. S. Gram and E. D. Klemke, pp. 195-215. Iowa City: University of Iowa Press, 1974.

"Seeing, Sense Impressions, and Sensa: A Reply to Cornman." *The Review of Metaphysics* 24 (1970-1971):391-447.

"A Semantic Solution of the Mind-body Problem." *Methodos* 5 (1953):45-82.

"Some Problems about Belief." In *Philosophical Logic*. Edited by J. W. Davis, D. J. Hockney, and W. K. Wilson, pp. 46-65. Dordrecht, Holland: D. Reidel, 1969. Reprinted in *EPH*.

"Some Reflections on Language Games." *Philosophy of Science* 21 (1954):204-28. Reprinted in a revised form in *SPR*.

"Some Reflections on Thoughts and Things." *Nous* 1 (1967):97-121. Reprinted as chapter 3 of *SM*.

"Some Remarks on Kant's Theory of Experience." *The Journal of Philosophy* 64 (1967):633-47. Reprinted in *EPH*.

"The Soul as Craftsman: An Interpretation of Plato on the Good." *PP*.

"The Structure of Knowledge: (1) Perception, (2) Minds, (3) Epistemic Principles." In *Action, Knowledge, and Reality: Essays in Honor of Wilfrid Sellars*, edited by Hector-Neri Castañeda, pp. 295-347. Indianapolis: The Bobbs-Merrill Company, Inc., 1975.

"Substance and Form in Aristotle." *The Journal of Philosophy*, 54 (1957):688-99. Reprinted in *PP*.

"Theoretical Explanation." In *Philosophy of Science: The Delaware Seminar,* edited by Bernard Baumrin, vol. 2, pp. 61-78. New York: John Wiley, 1963. Reprinted in *PP* and in *EPH*.

". . . this I or we or it (the thing) which thinks . . ." *Proceedings of the American Philosophical Association* 44 (1970-1971):5-31. Reprinted in *EPH*.

"Thought and Action." In *Freedom and Determinism,* edited by Keith Lehrer, pp. 105-39. New York: Random House, 1966.

"Time and the World Order: A Metaphysical and Epistemological Analysis of Becoming." In *Minnesota Studies in the Philosophy of Science,* edited by Herbert Feigl and Grover Maxwell, vol. 3, pp. 527-616. Minneapolis: University of Minnesota Press, 1962.

"Towards a Theory of the Categories." In *Experience and Theory,* edited by Lawrence Foster and J. W. Swanson, pp. 55-78. Amherst: University of Massachusetts Press, 1970. Reprinted in *EPH*.

"Truth and Correspondence." *The Journal of Philosophy,* 59 (1962):29-56. Reprinted in *SPR*.

"Vlastos and 'The Third Man'." *The Philosophical Review* 64 (1955):405-37. Reprinted in *PP*.

II.   Reviews of Sellars' Books

A.   Science, Perception, and Reality

Burrell, David B., C.S.C. *Philosophical Studies* (Ireland), 13 (1964):218-24.

Johnstone, Jr., H. W. *Philosophy and Phenomenological Research* 25 (1964-1965):421-23.

Lehrer, Keith. *The Journal of Philosophy* 63 (1966):266-67.

Louch, A. R. *Journal of the History of Philosophy* 4 (1966):277-78.

B.   Philosophical Perspectives

Collins, J. *The Modern Schoolman* 46 (1968-1969):70-71.

Harman, Gilbert. *The Journal of Philosophy* 66 (1969):133-44.

Harper, W. L. *Philosophy and Phenomenological Research* 30 (1969-1970):146-48.

Michalos, A. C. *Dialogue* 7 (1968-1969):514-17.

C.   Science and Metaphysics

Allaire, Edwin B. *Metaphilosophy* 2 (1971):352-58.

Aune, Bruce. *The Journal of Philosophy,* 67 (1970):251-56.

Bailey, John A. *Dialogue* 10 (1971):793-96.

Erickson, Stephen A. *Journal of the History of Philosophy* 10 (1972):111-14.

Gendron, Bernard. *International Philosophical Quarterly* 10 (1970):129-51.

Kopper, Joachim. *Kantstudien* 63 (1972):125-27.

Lenzen, V. F. *Philosophy and Phenomenological Research* 30 (1969-1970):464-65.

Mackinnon, Edward M. *The Philosophical Forum* (Boston), 1 (1969):509-45.

Mellor, D. H. *Ratio* 13 (1971):93-95.

Nyiri, F. C. *Inquiry* 13 (1970):321-31.

Pflaum, K. B. *Philosophical Studies* (Ireland), 18 (1969):233-35.

Rorty, Richard. *Philosophy* 45 (1970):66-70.

Stevenson, L. *Philosophical Quarterly* 20 (1970):86-87.

III. Articles about Sellars or Containing Discussions of Sellars

Ackermann, Robert. "Sellars and the Scientific Image." *Nous* 7 (1973):138-51.

Albritton, Rogers. "Form of Particular Substances in Aristotle's *Metaphysics*." *The Journal of Philosophy* 54 (1957):699-708.

Aquila, Richard E. "Perception and Perceptual Judgments." *Philosophical Studies* 28 (1975):17-31.

Aune, Bruce, "Comments on 'Phenomenalism'." In *Intentionality, Minds, and Perception*, edited by Hector-Neri Castañeda, pp. 275-85. Detroit: Wayne State University Press, 1967.

_____. "Prichard, Action, and Volition." *Philosophical Studies* 25 (1974):97-116.

_____. "Sellars on Practical Reason." In *Action, Knowledge and Reality*, edited by Hector-Neri Castañeda, pp. 1-26. Indianapolis: The Bobbs-Merrill Company, Inc. 1975.

Bayliss, Charles A. "Comments on Sellars' 'Logical Subjects and Physical Objects'." *Philosophy and Phenomenological Research*, 17 (1956-1957):483-87.

Bennet, Jonathon. "The Simplicity of the Soul." *The Journal of Philosophy* 64 (1967):648-60.

Bernstein, Richard. "The Challenge of Scientific Materialism." *International Philosophical Quarterly* 8 (1968):252-75.

_____. "Sellars' Vision of Man-in-the-Universe." *The Review of Metaphysics* 20 (1966-1967):113-43, 290-316.

Bonjour, Lawrence A. "Sellars on Truth and Picturing." *International Philosophical Quarterly* 13 (1973):243-65.

Carnap, Rudolph. "Replies and Systematic Expositions." In *The Philosophy of Rudolf Carnap*, edited by Paul Arthur Schilpp, cf. pp. 923-27. La Salle,

Illinois: Open Court Publishing Company, 1963. (A reply to "Empiricism and Abstract Entities.")

Castañeda, Hector-Neri. "Some Reflections on Wilfrid Sellars' Theory of Intentions." In *Action, Knowledge, and Reality,* pp. 27-54.

Clark, Romane. "The Sensuous Content of Perception." In *Action, Knowledge, and Reality,* pp. 109-28.

Coffa, J. Alberto. "Notas para un esquenna de la filosofia de la ciencia contemporanea." *Critica* 6 (1972):15-56.

Cornman, James W. "Materialism and Some Myths about the Givens." *The Monist* 56 (1972):215-33.

_____ . "Sellars, Scientific Realism, and Sensa." *The Review of Metaphysics* 23 (1969-1970):417-51.

_____ . "Speak Your Thoughts." *The Journal of Philosophy* 61 (1964):665-68.

_____ . "Theoretical Phenomenalism." *Nous* 7 (1973):120-38.

Delaney, Cornelius F. "Recent Work on American Philosophy." *The New Scholasticism* 45 (1971):457-77.

_____ . "Sellars and the Contemporary Mind-body Problem." *The New Scholasticism* 45 (1971):245-68.

_____ . "Sellars' Grain Argument." *The Australasian Journal of Philosophy* 50 (1972):14-16.

Dennet, Daniel. "Comments on Sellars' 'Meaning as Functional Classification'." *Synthese* 27 (1974):439-44.

Donagan, Alan. "Determinism and Freedom: Sellars and the Reconciliationist Thesis." In *Action, Knowledge, and Reality,* pp. 55-82.

Donnelly, John, and Lyons, L. S. "Recent Problems in Metaphysics." *The New Scholasticism* 45 (1971):290-323.

Duffrenne Mikel. "Comments on Language as Thought and as Communication'." *Philosophy and Phenomenological Research* 29 (1968-1969):528-35.

Eckelbarger, Charles. "Sellars on Thinking and the Myth of the Given." *Philosophical Studies* 25 (1974):231-46.

Feigl, Herbert. "The 'Mental' and the 'Physical'." In *Minnesota Studies in the Philosophy of Science,* edited by Herbert Feigl, Michael Scriven, and Grover Maxwell, vol. 2, pp. 370-497. Minneapolis: University of Minnesota Press, 1958.

Feyerabend, P. K. "Comments on 'The Language of Theories'." In *Current Issues in the Philosophy of Science,* edited by Herbert Feigl and Grover Maxwell, pp. 82-83. New York: Holt, Rinehart, and Winston, 1961.

_____ . "Reply to Criticisms: Comments on Smart, Sellars," edited by Robert Cohen and Marx Wartofsky, pp. 223-61. New York: The Humanities Press, 1965.

Fisk, Milton. "Comments on 'Raw Materials, Subjects, and Substrata'." In *The Concept of Matter on Greek and Medieval Philosophy*, edited by Ernan McMullin, pp. 273-75. Notre Dame: The University of Notre Dame Press, 1963.

Fraasen, Bas C. van "Critical Notice of H. Putnam, *Philosophy of Logic*." *Canadian Journal of Philosophy* 4 (1975):731-43.

———. "Theories and Counterfactuals." *Action, Knowledge, and Reality*, pp. 237-64.

———. "Wilfrid Sellars on Scientific Realism." *Dialogue* 14 (1975):606-16.

Gale, Richard M. "Strawson's Restricted Theory of Referring." *The Philosophical Quarterly* 20 (1970):162-65.

Gavin, Alexander H. "General Statements as Rules of Inference?" In *Minnesota Studies in the Philosophy of Science*, edited by Herbert Feigl, Grover Maxwell, and Michael Scriven, vol. 2, pp. 309-29. Minneapolis: University of Minnesota Press, 1958.

Grimm, Robert H. "A Note on 'Empiricism and Philosophy of Mind'." *Philosophical Studies* 10 (1959):45-48.

Grossmann, Reinhardt. "Perceptual Objects, Elementary Particles, and Emergent Properties." *Action, Knowledge, and Reality*, pp. 129-46.

Gunderson, Keith. "Asymmetries and Mind-body Perplexities." In *Minnesota Studies in the Philosophy of Science*, edited by Michael Radner and Stephen Winokur, vol. 4, pp. 273-309. Minneapolis: University of Minnesota Press, 1970.

Hall, Everett. "Comments on 'Logical Subjects and Physical Objects'." *Philosophy and Phenomenological Research* 17 (1956-1957):478-82.

Hanson, N. R. "Comments on 'The Language of Theories'." In *Current Issues in the Philosophy of Science*, edited by Herbert Feigl and Grover Maxwell, pp. 77-82. New York: Holt, Reinhart, and Winston, 1961.

Harman, Gilbert H. "Sellars' Semantics." *The Philosophical Review* 79 (1970):404-19.

———. "Three Levels of Meaning." *The Journal of Philosophy* 65 (1968):590-602.

———. "Wilfrid Sellars' Theory of Induction." *Action, Knowledge, and Reality*, pp. 265-76.

Hedman, Carl G. "On Correlating Brain States with Psychological States." *The Australasian Journal of Philosophy* 48 (1970):247-51.

Heelan, Patrick A. "The Logic of Framework Transpositions." In *Language, Truth, and Meaning*, edited by Philip McShane, pp. 93-114. Notre Dame: University of Notre Dame Press, 1972.

———. "Scientific Objectivity and Framework Transposition." *Philosophical Studies* (Ireland), 19 (1970):55-70.

Hesse, Mary. "An Indictive Logic of Theories." In *Minnesota Studies in the Philosophy of Science*, edited by Michael Radner and Stephen Winokur, vol. 4, cf. pp. 176-80. Minneapolis: University of Minnesota Press, 1970.

Jackson, Frank. "On the Adverbial Analysis of Visual Experience."
    Metaphilosophy 6 (1975):127-35.

Jaurez-Paz, Rigoberto. "Vlastos, Sellars, y el "tercer hombre' ex el Par-
    menides, notas sobre una polemica." *Revue Psicologia General y Ap-
    licada* 14 (1959):21-32.

Jensen, Uffe Juul. "Conceptual Epiphenomenalism." *The Monist* 56
    (1972):250-75.

Johnston, P. L. H. "A Hypothesis Concerning Singular Causal Laws."
    Philosophical Linguistics 4 (1972):60-69.

King-Farlow, John. "Myths of the Given and the *Cogito* Proof." *Philosophical
    Studies* 12 (1961):49-53.

Kitely, Murray. "Sellars' Ontology of Categories." *Nous,* 7 (1973):103-20.

Lehrer, Keith. "Reasonable Acceptance and Explanatory Coherence: Wilfrid
    Sellars on Induction." *Nous* 7 (1973):81-103.

Loux, Michael J. "Recent Work in Ontology." *American Philosophical Quar-
    terly* 9 (1972):119-38.

McGilvray, James. "The Function of Tenses." *Nous* 7 (1973):164-78.

Mackinnon, Edward M. "The New Materialism." *The Heythrop Journal* 8
    (1967):5-26.

_____ . "A Reinterpretation of Harre's Copernican Revolution." *Philosophy of
    Science* 42 (1975):67-79.

Margolis, Joseph. "On Picturing and Signifying." *Logique et Analyse* 10
    (1967):277-86.

_____ . "Scientific Realism, Ontology, and the Sensory Modes." *Philosophy of
    Science* 37 (1970):114-20.

_____ . "Some Ontological Policies." *The Monist* 53 (1969):231-45.

Marras, A. "On Sellars' Linguistic Theory of Conceptual Activity." *Canadian
    Journal of Philosophy* 2 (1972-1973):471-83.

_____ . "Reply to Sellars." *Canadian Journal of Philosophy* 2 (1972-1973):495-
    501.

_____ . "Sellars on Thought and Language." *Nous* 7 (1973):152-63.

Meehl, Paul E. "Nuisance Variables and the *Ex Post Facto* Design." In *Min-
    nesota Studies in the Philosophy of Science,* edited by Michael Radner
    and Stephen Winokur, vol. 4, pp. 373-402. Minneapolis: University of
    Minnesota Press, 1970.

_____ . "Psychological Determinism and Human Rationality: A Psychologist's
    Reactions to Professor Karl Popper's 'Of Clouds and Clocks'." In *Min-
    nesota Studies in the Philosophy of Science,* edited by Michael Radner
    and Stephen Winokur, vol. 4, pp. 310-72. Minneapolis: University of
    Minnesota Press, 1970.

Moore, Harold F. "Explanation and Understanding: Recent Models for Inter-
    preting Action." *International Philosophical Quarterly* 13 (1973):419-33.

Nelson, John O. "Can Systems of Imperceptible Particles Appear to Perceivers?" *Mind* 82 (1973):253-57.

Powers, Lawrence. "Some Deontic Logicians." *Nous* 1 (1967):381-400.

Putnam, Hilary. "Comments on Sellars' "Meaning as Functional Classification'." *Synthese* 27 (1974):445-55.

Quine, W. V. "Reply to Sellars' 'Some Problems about Belief'." In *Words and Objections: Essays on the Work of W. V. Quine*, edited by Donald Davidson and Jaako Hintikka, pp. 337-40. Dordrecht, Holland: D. Reidel Publishing Company, 1969.

Richards, Robert J. "Sellars' Kantian Perspective on the Compatibility of Freedom and Determinism," *The Southern Journal of Philosophy* 11 (1973):228-36.

Robinson, William S. "The Legend of the Given." *Action, Knowledge, and Reality*, pp. 83-108.

Rorty, Richard. "Incorrigibility as the Mark of the Mental." *The Journal of Philosophy* 67 (1970):399-424.

———. "The Subjectivist Principle and the Linguistic Turn." In *Alfred North Whitehead: Essays on his Philosophy*, edited by George I. Kline, pp. 134-57. Englewood Cliffs, New Jersey: Prentice-Hall, Inc., 1963.

Rosenberg, Jay F. "The Elusiveness of Categories, the Archimedean Dilemma, and the Nature of Man: A Study in Sellarsian Metaphysics." *Action, Knowledge, and Reality*, pp. 147-84.

———. "What's Happening in Philosophy of Language Today—A Metaphysician's-eye View." *American Philosophical Quarterly* 9 (1972):101-6.

Rudner, Richard. "Comments on Sellars' 'The Language of Theories'." In *Current Issues in the Philosophy of Science*, edited by Herbert Feigl and Grover Maxwell, pp. 84-89. New York: Holt, Rinehart, and Winston, 1961.

Schaffner, Kenneth F. "The Watson-Crick Model and Reductionism." *British Journal for the Philosophy of Science* 20 (1969):325-48.

Scheffler, Israel. "Comments on 'The Identity Approach to the Mind-body Problem'." In *Boston Studies in the Philosophy of Science*, edited by Robert S. Cohen and Marx W. Wartofsky, vol. 2, pp. 77-80. New York: The Humanities Press, 1965.

Smart, J. J. C. "Conflicting Views about Explanation." In *Boston Studies in the Philosophy of Science*, edited by Robert S. Cohen and Marx W. Wartofsky, vol. 2, pp. 157-69. New York: The Humanities Press, 1965.

Sosa, Ernest. "Quantifiers, Beliefs, and Sellars." In *Philosophical Logic*, edited by J. W. Davis, D. J. Hockney and W. K. Wilson, pp. 66-73. Dordrecht, Holland: D. Reidel, 1969.

Strawson, P. F. "A Reply to Mr. Sellars." *The Philosophical Review* 63 (1954):216-31.

____. "A Reply to Sellars' 'Logical Subjects and Physical Objects'." *Philosophy and Phenomenological Research* 17 (1956-1957):473-77.

Telok, Henry, and Louzecky, David James. "Plato's Third Man Argument." *Phronesis* 17 (1972):80-94.

Thomas, S. "Professor Sellars on Meaning and Aboutness." *Philosophical Studies* 13 (1962):68-74.

Turnbull, Robert G. "Things, Natures, and Properties." *Action, Knowledge, and Reality*, pp. 185-206.

Tye, Michael. "The Adverbial Theory: A Defence of Sellars Against Jackson." *Metaphilosophy* 6 (1975):136-43.

Vlastos, Gregory. "Addenda to the Third Man Argument: A Reply to Professor Sellars." *The Philosophical Review* 64 (1955):438-48.

____. "Plato's 'Third Man' Argument (*Parm*. 132A1-B2): Text and Logic." *The Philosphical Quarterly* 19 (1969):289-301.

Voelkel, Theodore S. "Sellars' Treatment of Sensation." *The Personalist* 54 (1973):130-48.

Wedeking, Gary A. "Are There Command Arguments?" *Analysis* 30 (1969-1970):161-66.

Wells, Rulon. "The Indispensable Word 'Now'." *Action, Knowledge, and Reality*, pp. 207-36.

Wilson, Fred F. "Marras on Sellars on Thought and Language." *Philosophical Studies* 28 (1975):91-102.

Wolterstorff, Nicholas. "On the Nature of Universals." In *Universals and Particulars*, edited by Michael J. Loux, pp. 158-85. Garden City, New York: Doubleday and Company, 1970.

Woolhouse, R. S. "Counterfactuals, Dispositions, and Capacities." *Mind* 82 (1973):557-65.

Young, Julian. "Intentionality." *The Review of Metaphysics* 26 (1972-1973):696-722.

Zaffron, Richard. "Identity, Subsumption, and Scientific Explanation." *The Journal of Philosophy* 68 (1971):849-60.

Zemach, Eddy M. "Reference and Belief." *Analysis* 30 (1969-1970):11-15.

____. "Sensations, Raw Feels, and Other Minds." *The Review of Metaphysics* 20 (1966-1967):317-40.

IV.   Books Containing Discussions of Sellars

Aune, Bruce. *Knowledge, Mind, and Nature: An Introduction to Theory of Knowledge and the Philosophy of Mind.* New York: Random House, 1967.

Bernstein, Richard J. *Praxis and Action.* Philadelphia: University of Pennsylvania Press, 1971.

Castañeda, Hector-Neri, ed. *Action, Knowledge, and Reality: Studies in Honor of Wilfrid Sellars.* Indianapolis: The Bobbs-Merrill Company, Inc., 1975.

Collins, James. *Interpreting Modern Philosophy.* Princeton: Princeton University Press, 1972. See pp. 335-40.

Cornman, James W. *Materialism and Sensations.* New Haven: Yale University Press, 1971.

Erickson, Stephen A. *Language and Being: An Analytic Phenomenology.* New Haven: Yale University Press, 1970.

Giegel, Hans Joachim. *Die Logik der seelischen Erignisse: Zu Theorien von L. Wittgenstein und W. Sellars.* Frankfurt am Main: Suhrkamp, 1969.

Graves, John C. *The Conceptual Foundations of Contemporary Relativity Theory.* Cambridge, Massachusetts: M.I.T. Press, 1971.

Lehrer, Keith. *Knowledge.* Oxford: Clarendon Press, 1974.

Mackinnon, Edward M. *Truth and Expression.* New York: The Newman Press, 1971.

Pollock, John L. *Knowledge and Justification.* Princeton: Princeton University Press, 1975.

Sicha, Jeffrey. *A Metaphysics of Elementary Mathematics.* Amherst: University of Massachusetts Press, 1974.

Wilkerson, T. R. *Minds, Brains, and People.* Oxford: Clarendon Press, 1974.

Will, Frederick L. *Induction and Justification: An Investigation of Cartesian Procedures in the Philosophy of Knowledge.* Ithaca, New York: Cornell University Press, 1974.

Witschell, Gunter. *Fragen, Untersuch auf d. Grundlage von "Philosophy and the Scientific Image of Man."* Akademische Vortrage und Abhandlungen no. 37. Bonn: Bouvier, 1972.

V.   Dissertations on Sellars or Discussing Sellars

Bonjour, Lawrence A. "Knowledge, Justification and Truth: A Sellarsian Approach to Epistemology." Princeton University, 1969.

Child, James W. "The Ontological Commitment of Physical Theories." Indiana University, 1967.

Doody, John A. "Scientific Realism and Instrumentalism: An Analysis of the Concepts of Description and Explanation." University of Notre Dame, 1974.

Eckelbarger, Charles G. "Wilfrid Sellars' Philosophy of Mind." The Ohio State University, 1969.

Evans, Robert H. "The Decline and Revival of Critical Realism." University of Pittsburgh Press, 1967.

Freddoso, Alfred. "A Defense of Conceptualism." University of Notre Dame, 1976.

Grontkowski, Christine R. "The Priority of the Scientific Image: An Investigation of Wilfrid Sellars' Ontological Commitment." Fordham University, 1969.

Hartjes, John F. "The Critique of the Given in Wilfrid Sellars and Edmund Husserl." The Catholic University of America, 1974.

Hopkins, Edwin E. "Wilfrid Sellars' Analysis of Physical Modality: In Search of an Argument." Duke University, 1971.

Klein, Peter D. "The Revolt Against Sense-data: A Defense of the Sense-data Framework." Yale University, 1966.

Lennon, Thomas M. "The Problem of Intentionality in Recent Analytic Philosophy." The Ohio State University, 1968.

McCaskill, David G. "Conceptual Schemes and the Revolt Against the Foundation Theory of Knowledge." Wayne State University, 1972.

McKim, Vaughn R. "Human Action and a Scientific Image of Man." Yale University, 1966.

Marquis, Donald B. "Scientific Realism and the Antinomy of External Objects." Indiana University, 1970.

Mason, Perry C. "Ontic Commitment and Abstract Entities in the Philosophy of Wilfrid Sellars." Yale University, 1969.

Moore, Harold. "Instrumentalism." Fordham University, 1970.

O'Connell, Richard A. "The Structure of Meaning and Knowledge." Wayne State University, 1974.

Pitt, Joseph C. "An Analysis of Wilfrid Sellars' Theory of Justification as Explanation." The University of Western Ontario, 1972.

Putz, Carl H. "The Nature of Scientific Laws." University of Pittsburgh, 1970.

Richards, Robert J. "Wilfrid Sellars: Towards a Scientific Explanation of Man." St. Louis University, 1971.

Rosenthal, David M. "Intentionality: A Study of the Views of Chisolm and Sellars." Princeton University, 1968.

Rottschaeffer, William A. "Ordinary Knowledge in the Scientific Realism of Wilfrid Sellars." Boston University Graduate School, 1973.

Wall, Thomas F. "Intentionality and the Analogy Theory of Thinking." Boston College, 1970.

Index